D1568489

DATE DUE

JUL 2 4 2014	

BRODART, CO.   Cat. No. 23-221

YOUNG AMERICAN MUSLIMS

YOUNG AMERICAN MUSLIMS

DYNAMICS OF IDENTITY

• • •

NAHID AFROSE KABIR

EDINBURGH
University Press

© Nahid Afrose Kabir, 2013

Edinburgh University Press Ltd
22 George Square, Edinburgh EH8 9LF
www.euppublishing.com

Typeset in 10/12.5 Sabon by
Servis Filmsetting Ltd, Stockport, Cheshire, and
printed and bound in Great Britain by
CPI Group (UK) Ltd, Croydon CR0 4YY

A CIP record for this book is available from the British Library

ISBN 978 0 7486 6993 6 (hardback)
ISBN 978 0 7486 6994 3 (webready PDF)
ISBN 978 0 7486 6996 7 (epub)
ISBN 978 0 7486 6995 0 (Amazon ebook)

The right of Nahid Afrose Kabir to be identified as author of this work
has been asserted in accordance with the Copyright, Designs and Patents
Act 1988.

CONTENTS

TABLES AND FIGURES

Tables

Figures

ABBREVIATIONS

610 WIOD	Radio station in South Florida
ABC	American Broadcasting Corporation; Australian Broadcasting Corporation
ACLU	American Civil Liberties Union
AQAP	Al-Qaeda in the Arabian Peninsula
BBC	British Broadcasting Corporation
CAIR	Council on American–Islamic Relations
CBS	Columbia Broadcasting System
CMES	Center for Middle Eastern Studies
CNBC	Consumer News and Business Channel
CNN	Cable News Network
FBI	Federal Bureau of Investigation
FIS	*Front Islamique du Salut*: Islamic Salvation Front
FL	Florida
GE	General Electric
IRS	Internal Revenue Service
MA	Massachusetts
MAPS	Muslims in American Public Square
MCT	McClatchy Tribune Information Services
MD	Maryland
MI	Michigan
MIT	Massachusetts Institute of Technology
MPAC	Muslim Public Affairs Council
MSNBC	Microsoft and the National Broadcasting Company
NBA	National Basketball Association
NOI	Nation of Islam
NPR	National Public Radio

NY	New York
PBS	Public Broadcasting Service
PBUH	Peace Be Upon Him
PETN	Pentaerythritol tetranitrate [explosive]
PhD	Doctor of Philosophy
SBS	Special Broadcasting Service (Australia)
THC	Tetrahydrocannabinol
UK	United Kingdom
UNESCO	United Nations Educational, Scientific and Cultural Organization
US	United States
USA	United States of America
VA	Virginia
YMCA	Young Men's Christian Association

GLOSSARY

Abaya	A loose black robe that covers the wearer from head to toe, traditionally worn by Muslim women
Alhamdulillah	Praise to Allah (God)
Allah	God
Azan	Call to prayer
Burqa	Loose outer garment worn by Muslim women
Dabke falasteeny	Palestinian folk dance
Desi	A person from the Indian subcontinent
Din	Faith
Eid-e-Milad-un Nabi	Birthday of Prophet Muhammad (PBUH)
Eid-ul-Adha	Muslim religious celebration
Eid-ul-Fitr	Muslim religious celebration
Fatwa	Religious ruling
Fiqh	Jurisprudence
Gurdwara	Sikh temple
Hadith	Teachings or tradition of Prophet Muhammad (PBUH)
Hajj	Pilgrimage to *Ka'bah* performed in the prescribed twelfth month of the Islamic calendar
Halal	Slaughter of animals in the Islamic way
Harram	Forbidden in Islam
Hawiyya	Arabic name for identity card
Hijab	Headscarf
Hookah	Water pipe for smoking
Hudud	Limits set by Allah
Insh'Allah	God willing
Izzat	Honour
Jambiya	Traditional dagger

Jihad	Religious struggle of Muslims
Jihadi	An individual who participates in a *jihad*
Jilbab	Long coat
Ka'bah	An important shrine of the Islamic world in Mecca
Kalima	First Islamic declaration of belief
Kar sevak	Hindu volunteer
Khalifah	Caliph
Khilafah	Caliphate
Kufi	Cap
Madrasah	Islamic school
Masjid	Mosque
Muharram	First month of Islamic calendar
Musalla	Prayer room
Mushaira	Urdu poetic symposium
Nasheed	Devotional Islamic song
Niqab	Face veil
Nowruz	Iranian New Year
Ramadan	Month of fasting
Ramadan kareem	'*Ramadan* is generous' (saying)
Rasul	Messenger or prophet sent by Allah with divine ordinance
Salaam	Muslim greeting
Salat	Muslim prayer
Sari	Indian women's clothing
Sawm	Fasting
Shahada	First Islamic declaration of belief. Another term for *kalima*
Sharam	Shame
Shariah	Islamic way
Shariah law	The code of law derived from the teachings of the Quran and the teachings and tradition of Prophet Muhammad (PBUH)
Sunnah	Teachings or tradition of Prophet Muhammad (PBUH)
Taliban	Students
Tasreeh	Permit
Thob	Full-length Arab traditional dress
Topi	Muslim men's cap
Ummah	Islamic community transcending all national boundaries
Umrah Hajj	Pilgrimage to *Ka'bah* performed any time of the year (other than the prescribed time of the *Hajj*)
Zakat	Alms giving

ACKNOWLEDGEMENTS

I express my sincere gratitude to Professor Jocelyne Cesari, director of the Islam and the West Program at the Center for Middle Eastern Studies, Harvard University, USA for inviting me to conduct this research.

For the information contained in this book I am indebted to the Muslims who most generously agreed to be interviewed. I sincerely thank the students and staff of the Islamic, public and charter schools who helped me to make this study a success. The various youth centres in Massachusetts, New York, Virginia, Maryland, Florida and Michigan have also been very supportive. Thanks to the Muslim leaders who participated in this survey. I am also grateful to the members and leaders of the Council of American–Islamic Relations who participated in this study.

In the USA, I express my grateful thanks to Imam Shamsi Ali, Imam Achmat Salie, Belal Kaleem, Dawud Walid, Muhammed Malik, Harun al Rasheed, Ahmed Hamid, Nasreen Rahman, Saiful Huq, Khojesta Huq, Shagir Ahmed, Rumana Ahmed, Razia Pothiawala, Quazi S. al-Tariq MD, Zarin Huq, Khadija Enayet, Humayun Khan, Rehana Khan, Mrs Rowshan Chowdhury, Samina Hossain, Zeenat Ara, Tasmina Rahman and Roohi Rahman. Many thanks to Barbara Puleau for appreciating the merit of this research. Gina Soos always maintained that this study was important. Thanks Gina, for your kind support. I am also thankful to cartoonist Khalil Bendib for allowing me to publish his cartoons in my book.

In the UK, I express my thanks to Edinburgh University Press, Ms Nicola Ramsay and Mr Eddie Clark for assisting me in the publication process.

In Australia, I express my sincere gratitude to Dr Mary Kooyman, who dedicated many hours to editing my drafts and making constructive comments. Many thanks to Professor Lelia Green for her kind support, and to Dr John Hall for his valuable advice. I am grateful to Ms Kate Leeson of the International Centre for Muslim and non-Muslim Understanding at the Hawke Research Institute, University of South Australia for copyediting the manuscript. I extend my warm appreciation for the constant support of my family, especially my husband, Dr Mohammad Ismat Kabir, and our three sons, Sakhawat, Naoshad and Mahtab Kabir, for allowing me to stay in the United States and carry out my research project while they looked after each other in my absence. Of course, the caring nature of my husband helped me concentrate on my research work and write this book.

In Bangladesh, special thanks to my brother, Faiz Matin, for providing me with contacts in the USA.

To my family

INTRODUCTION: MY JOURNEY AND THE 'MUSLIM QUESTION'

My acquaintance with American society has been developed on three occasions: first, as a spouse (and a student) when my husband was a doctoral student at the University of Texas at Austin, second, as a conference speaker/attendee, and finally, as a visiting fellow at Harvard University. I now provide a thumbnail sketch of my life journey from my childhood to my present circumstances.

I was born and raised in a Muslim family in the predominantly Muslim country of Bangladesh, but I spent several years of my childhood in Pakistan. I had a middle-class professional upbringing in Dhaka (the capital of Bangladesh, then known as East Pakistan) and Karachi (a city in the then West Pakistan). Both my parents were educated people. We moved back to Dhaka (in the then East Pakistan) in 1970. In 1971 East Pakistan gained independence from West Pakistan through a civil war and came to be known as Bangladesh. During the Pakistan period, my father was promoted to the position of an executive director in the State Bank of Pakistan. In the independent Bangladesh, he became the deputy governor of the Bangladesh Bank. My mother was a stay-at-home mum. I attended a private school and two missionary (private) schools and colleges in Dhaka and Karachi. In these educational institutions we had teaching staff from Europe and America. At home, I spoke Bengali (my mother tongue), and in schools and colleges the medium of instruction was English. I was also taught Urdu in Pakistan as it was a curriculum requirement. I was raised in a Muslim environment, where offering prayers five times a day, fasting in the month of *Ramadan* and reciting the Holy Quran were compulsory.

After completing BA Honours in History from the University of Dhaka in Bangladesh I got married and in 1981 I moved to the United States. While living in the US, I made some American friends, and studied history in the undergraduate school at the University of Texas. I appreciated the warm

[1]

friendship extended to me in the US, but experienced a degree of culture shock. I did not appreciate the pub life, alcohol consumption and what I perceived to be a lack of family bonding (children moving out of home at the age of eighteen, families only meeting occasionally on birthdays and at Christmas). Furthermore, I could not relate to the de facto relationships and acceptance of sex before marriage. I lived in the United States from 1981 to 1982, and then after my husband's completion of a PhD degree at the University of Texas at Austin we moved to the Middle East. We lived in Dhahran, Saudi Arabia for five years (1982–7). I was happy because we were living in the Muslim world, and our stay in Saudi Arabia also gave me the opportunity to perform the *Umrah Hajj*. We then migrated to Australia (1987–90), then moved back to the Middle East but this time to Muscat, in the Sultanate of Oman. We lived there for another five years (1990–5). During this period, I went back to Dhaka for one year and completed an MA in History. By this time I was a mother of three children and very happy as a stay-at-home mum. I wanted to stay in Oman for the rest of my life because it was a Muslim country. But neither Oman nor Saudi Arabia gave citizenship to expatriates, so we had no chance of living there as permanent residents.

Quite reluctantly I returned to Australia with my husband and children in 1995. Initially, I was unhappy and did not like life in the diaspora. Nevertheless when I started attending the postgraduate school at the University of Queensland, Australia, I began to feel settled. In 1998 I obtained an MA in historical studies in Indian history and in 2003 I was awarded a PhD based on the topic 'Muslims in Australia'. I then began making conference presentations on this research nationally and internationally. One thing worth noting is that between the time when I started my PhD project on the history of Muslims in Australia and the time I submitted and was awarded the degree, the world changed. After the 9/11 Twin Towers tragedy in New York, when about 3,000 people died (including 358 Muslims),[1] and the Bali bombings in 2002, when eighty-eight Australians died (including one Muslim), it had become a different place. Since then some Muslims residing in the West have been viewed as the new 'other'. I have discussed this phenomenon in my first book (based on my PhD thesis), *Muslims in Australia*.[2]

During my second visit to the United States, I made a presentation at a conference in Hawaii in 2003, and in 2004 I attended a conference on Islam in America in Detroit. I listened attentively to the relevant papers that discussed the placement of Muslims in American society since 9/11. In Detroit, I spoke both to Muslims of diverse backgrounds and to non-Muslims of Arab background and found that they were being treated as the 'other' because of their appearance. A few non-Muslim Arabs said that they had been targeted as the 'other' even before 9/11, through the media and video games.

From 2006 to 2008, as a postdoctoral and later research fellow at Edith Cowan University, Australia, I conducted studies on the identity of young Australian and British Muslims, and discussed my findings on young Australian Muslims in several refereed journal articles. My findings on young British Muslims were published in a book titled *Young British Muslims*.[3]

In 2009, my third visit to the United States was as a visiting fellow on the Islam in the West programme at the CMES, Harvard University. My fellowship at Harvard was for two years (2009–11), and during this period I conducted research on young American Muslims. I interviewed young Muslims (and a few Muslim adults) from six states: Massachusetts, New York, Virginia, Maryland, Florida and Michigan, in that order. I found that the participants described their identities variously, as I discuss later in this book. In this section I want to describe how I approached this study. In the first place I felt I could relate to the feelings of the participants because I am a fellow immigrant in a diaspora. I am also a parent trying to support my children in two cultural settings (ethnic/religious and host/wider society). And I am a researcher, trying to investigate in a fair and reasonable way the placement of the participants, who were mostly second-generation immigrants.

Many first-generation immigrants who live in a diaspora dream that one day they will return to their home countries, but second-generation immigrants rarely feel this way. A first-generation migrant may fear losing his/her culture in the new country but a second-generation person is less ambivalent about his new home. For example, Asaduzamman al-Nur (not his real name), of Yemeni background (male, 15, overseas born), who migrated with his parents as a one-year-old boy, spoke of his identity:

> I'm Arab American but now I'm probably 75 per cent more American . . . I mean people have families all around the world but they still live here. And America is a country which used to be of native Indians. But now it's a country of people who come here for their needs, like for work or religious reasons. It's kind of, what do you call it, like a beacon . . . Yeah, because I remember doing a song that was about the Statue of Liberty; it said it was a beacon.
>
> We came here because in our case my parents came here. In our place [Yemen] we don't have much to do. My dad's a butcher here but in Yemen butchers aren't exactly considered a high working people. It's kind of levelled in Yemen and we wouldn't get much work there, so we came here because we had to. (Asaduzamman, interview, Michigan, April 2010)[4]

For Asaduzamman, the difference between Yemen and America was highlighted by his father's employment. He thought that only in America were there opportunities and freedom – the liberty to fulfil the 'American dream'. In other words, regardless of social class, people in America can accomplish success according to their individual abilities. Asaduzamman felt connected to the United States, as reflected in his metaphor of the Statue of Liberty as a 'beacon for immigrants'.

Asaduzamman also praised his local area when I asked him to recommend the places I should visit in Michigan. Then he asked me, 'Do you think Michigan is a happy place or do you think it is a kind of okay place?' My response was, 'Yeah, I think it is an okay place.' Asaduzamman replied, 'Yeah. Because of the publicity and stuff and what happened to Mayor Kilpatrick . . . There was some scandal that broke out . . . Like he was using tax dollars for something.' Then he added:

> It's kind of, you know how they say in English, 'What comes to mind when you say a word?' When you say 'Detroit' I imagine it is kind of like a ghetto place. [However,] there's some good places in it. For example, Stony Creek, it's a great place. It has lots of beaches here and there. That has one of the clearest waters. Grand Rapids is one of our interesting places in Michigan. It kind of has beaches and colonial things, and peninsula, it's got its upper peninsula, we have islands around there I think. And it's just more natural.

Asaduzamman tried his best to make me feel impressed by Michigan, and particularly Detroit. He felt that Detroit's image may have been tarnished by Detroit Mayor Kilpatrick's $9 million scandal.[5] Asaduzamman contemplated that one day he might have to return to Yemen, so in his spare time, 'I read the Quran and try to understand it more. I am learning Arabic [in school].' He continued, 'I just deal with my responsibilities and when I, if I have completely nothing to do, I sometimes just watch some TV. That's the western side of me.' Talking about music he said, 'We listen to some Arabic music. But, like I said, I listen to more American music.' Then he said, 'And I'm trying to get back to my heritage 'cos I'm going to have [to] go back to Yemen soon. I can't just leave my home country.' On sport, Asaduzamman said, 'I like to play soccer because it's really a fun game. I like basketball but soccer is more, just feels more natural.' He then returned to his culture, 'Well, sometimes you play [soccer], it's kind of like a typical thing. Yemenis . . . their sport is soccer. And that's kind of the more culture side of me, I like to play soccer.'

This interview was conducted in one of the suburbs of Detroit where one can see many Arabs, Muslims, mosques and women wearing the *niqab*. While listening to Asaduzamman express his admiration for America and his local area, Detroit, and also his connection with his heritage (Yemen), I was impressed by the bicultural stance of his identity (though it tilted more towards his American identity). In my earlier studies on young Muslims in Australia and Britain I found that biculturalism was important for building their connection to the host country. By biculturalism I mean a blending of majority and minority ethnic/religious cultures. Biculturalism can work at two levels: first, as a national policy (a variant of multiculturalism or the 'melting pot') of acceptance/expectation that migrants will retain much of their culture/heritage but will adhere to (new) national laws and gradually adopt the national language/

culture; second, at the individual level, as a personal practice of blending the old and the new – retaining religion, ethnic culture and language and taking on new language and culture in order to have dual membership.

When ethnic minorities adopt parts of the majority culture, such as speaking English, reading English-language novels, listening to music or watching English-language television programmes, engaging in contemporary politics and participating in mainstream sports, while at the same time retaining their ethnic and religious practices, this enables them to participate as citizens of their host society, with a hyphenated/dual identity or diverse/multiple identities. I also found that retaining a single (ethnic, religious or national) identity may not be a cultural deficit as long as young people maintain a bicultural stance.

Earlier research on Muslims in America

Some scholars have already written about the growing Muslim community in America, and their issues and challenges. The first work on Muslims in America that came to my notice was Kathleen M. Moore's PhD thesis, '*Al-mughtaribun*', where she observed:

> Although Islam has been practiced in North America for more than one hundred years it has only recently received even nominal recognition as an American phenomenon. Islam is still widely perceived to be a foreign creed and is maligned by its association in the media with terrorist activity abroad and black separatism in the U.S. Because of the prevailing sense, however erroneous, that Islam is a threat to society it is a faith that is not easily accommodated.[6]

Other contributions, such as *Islamic Values in the United States, Muslim Communities in North America, Islam in the United States of America* and *Muslims on the Americanization Path?*, offer information on Muslim settlement in America, Muslim beliefs and values, diversity within the Islamic community and Muslims' encounters with the mainstream media.[7] As discussed earlier, much has changed in people's perception of Muslims since 9/11. After the Twin Towers attacks on 11 September 2001, the 'Muslim question' came to the fore: who are these people, what is their faith, is violence associated with their faith, why do some Muslims hate the West, is the American media going overboard with its representation of Muslims in America, how is Islamic visibility impacting on this group? Several publications have answered these questions; for example, in *Muslims in America: Seven Centuries of History 1312–2000, Islam in America* and *Muslims in America: A Short History* the authors reminded readers that Islam first came to America with the African explorers and again later with the slave trade.[8] Some books have offered comparative studies of Muslim settlement in the West, such as *Muslim Minorities in the West, Religion and Immigration, When Islam and Democracy Meet* and *Muslims in the West after 9/11.*[9]

The term 'Islamophobia' was coined in 1997 by the independent pro-diversity think tank the Runnymede Trust in the United Kingdom to describe xenophobia towards the Muslim 'other'.[1] In the case of Australia, anti-Muslim (and anti-Arab) sentiment has been prevalent during times of crisis, for example during the 1990–1 Gulf War.[11] In the United States, anti-Muslim (and anti-Arab) sentiment surfaced after Timothy McVeigh's act of terrorism in Oklahoma in 1996.[12] As various publications have reported, however, repercussions against some Muslims and Arabs intensified after the Twin Towers attacks. For example, the Council on American-Islamic Relations' report *American Muslims: One Year After 9-11* and the books *Muslims in the United States* and *Islamophobia and Anti-Americanism: Causes and Remedies* have all included discussions of the unprecedented wave of hate crimes against American Muslims since 9/11.[13] Hostility against some Muslims and Arabs increased with the enactment of the USA Patriot Act, as discussed in books such as *Policing American Muslim Communities, Race and Arab Americans before and after 9/11, Citizenship and Crisis, Homeland Insecurity, The Future of Islam* and *Islam in America.*[14]

Literature on young American Muslim identity is relatively limited. A few books, such as *Muslim Women in America, American Muslim Women, Educating the Muslims of America* and *Muslims in Motion* include brief discussions of the dynamics of young Muslims' identity. Only one book, *Muslim American Youth* by Selcuk Sirin and Michelle Fine, includes an elaborate discussion of the way young Muslims negotiate their hyphenated or dual identities with everyday cultural and global challenges.[15] In their study Sirin and Fine interviewed 204 young Muslims aged between twelve and twenty-five from New York, New Jersey, Florida and Michigan. They applied multiple research methods such as paper-pencil surveys (sketches), open-ended questions, focus groups and individual interviews to determine the participants' concept of hyphenated identity. Sirin and Fine found that, growing up in the midst of Islamophobia, Muslim American youth confronted developmental challenges because they were carrying the burden of international crises (as they are viewed with suspicion). For Muslim youth since 9/11, negotiating their identities has also become far more challenging because they are perceived as a potential threat to the wider society. Sirin and Fine's study overall found that young Muslim men and women did not differ in terms of their perceived discrimination, acculturation practices and anxieties. Nevertheless the way in which these young people negotiated their identities was quite different from that of their peers, as indeed was the way they dealt with everyday cultural and global challenges.

While appreciating the valuable work scholars have so far done on Muslims in America, I take the research one step further by incorporating a wide range of cohorts from diverse ethnicities and examining the dynamics of one's identity from single, hyphenated to multiple identities. I have introduced new arguments and debates in my work. I have shown under what context the participants developed their opinions, and I have done extensive research on diverse topics, for example, the media, politics and international relations. I hope this book will add to the existing scholarship on Muslims in America and particularly on young American Muslim identity.

Aim of the research

The primary objective of this study is to examine the life stories of Muslim youths and young adults with a special focus on their hopes and dreams. Key questions in this study are:

- How do cultural practices contribute to the development of being a worthy American citizen?
- How do Muslim youths and young adults define their identity, or their sense of belonging?
- To what extent have Muslim youths and young adults integrated into mainstream American culture? Where do they position themselves in the 'integration'/'assimilation' debate?
- What is the role of socioeconomic factors in the youths/young adults' identity construction?
- What is the role of the media in young Muslims' identity construction?
- Is political awareness a contributory factor for identity construction?
- What are the methods for 'a humanitarian way forward'?

Organisation of the book

This book contains a brief introduction and seven chapters (including the conclusion). Chapter 1 sets the scene. I briefly examine the history of Muslims in America and some of the contemporary issues facing American Muslims. I discuss social identity theory and explore how society can impact on the construction of one's identity. In Chapter 1, I also discuss my research methodology and my experience in collecting the data. In Chapter 2, I examine the cultural dimension of identity within the Muslim community. I discuss the different ideologies within the Islamic community and the placement of minorities within the Muslim majority. I also examine the place of women and the position of young men within the Muslim community. In Chapter 3, I consider the debate on identity or what it is to be an American. I discuss the identity of the respondents – their sense of belonging to America, to their country of origin and to their religion. I also discuss whether sports interests have any impact on the participants' identity. In Chapter 4, I examine how the American media is shaping young Muslims' identity. I examine some print media to test the validity of the participants' comments. Chapter 5 is concerned with identity politics. I examine only the views of Palestinian Americans because most of them spoke of their experience of differential treatment meted out by the Israeli authorities when they visited Palestine. In Chapter 6, I examine the interest of young Muslims in American politics. I evaluate the participants' political awareness and thereby discuss diverse topics such as domestic issues, education and unemployment, together with foreign affairs concerns. The final chapter, the conclusion, is a plea for further reconciliation. I point out the areas that need attention – the United States media's role, Muslim women, youth, Muslim leaders' role, the emphasis on biculturalism and sport – and suggest a humanitarian way forward.

Limitations

In this study, all of the interviews were in-depth and semi-structured, and all the 379 interviewees responded willingly to the topics of national identity, the media and President Obama. On the topic of culture (Chapter 2), only a few relevant voices were included. The topic of Palestine was raised by some participants of diverse backgrounds. Yet in the Palestine chapter (Chapter 6), I have only reported responses of the participants who had Palestinian inheritance. Qualitative research involves fieldwork, in this case organising and conducting face-to-face interviews, which in turn generates a lot of data to be analysed. Hence the work is very labour intensive and by necessity entails a smaller sample of subjects. Furthermore, this raises the question of whether the sample is representative in terms of sociocultural dimensions, geographic location and other factors. For example, some states in the Midwest, such as Arizona, could have been included but funding constraints prohibited me from extending this study any further. Similarly, the West Coast (and Los Angeles in particular) could not be incorporated in this study because of lack of funding.

In America Shi'ites form a minority within the broader Islamic community, although they constitute a higher proportion than in the general Muslim population: it is estimated that one-fifth of American Muslims are Shi'ites as against 13 per cent worldwide. However, there were only eighteen Shia participants in this study overall. Dearborn, a suburb of Detroit, has a large Shia population. I did conduct a few interviews in Dearborn. But my period of time there was much shorter than other places of my fieldwork. It is worth noting that in this study, I did not specifically look out for participants' religious affiliation, for example, who was a Sunni or who was a Shia. My focus was on how young Muslims in general fared in the wider American society.

Overall, there was a rich set of responses on all topics and this has enabled me to present themes that I believe are characteristic and informative. Ultimately, of course, the reader will judge the credibility of my work.

Notes

1. John L. Esposito, *The Future of Islam* (New York: Oxford University Press, 2010), p. 30.
2. Nahid Afrose Kabir, *Muslims in Australia: Immigration, Race Relations and Cultural History* (London: Routledge, 2005).
3. Nahid Afrose Kabir, *Young British Muslims: Identity, Culture, Politics and the Media* (Edinburgh: Edinburgh University Press 2010).
4. Names of the participants mentioned in this book are not real.
5. See '"Arrogant" Kilpatrick sent to jail', *Grand Rapids Press*, 29 October 2008, p. A3.
6. Kathleen M. Moore, 'Al-mughtaribun: Law and the Transformation of Muslim Life in North America', PhD thesis, University of Massachusetts, 1992, pp. 38–9.
7. Yvonne Yazbeck Haddad and Adair T. Lummis, *Islamic Values in the United States: A Comparative Study* (New York: Oxford University Press, 1987); Yvonne Yazbeck Haddad and Jane Idleman Smith (eds), *Muslim Communities in North America* (Albany: State University of New York Press, 1994); Sulayman S. Nyang, *Islam in the United States of America* (Chicago: ABC International Group, 1999); Yvonne Yazbeck Haddad and John L. Esposito (eds), *Muslims on the Americanization Path?* (New York: Oxford University Press, 2000).
8. Amir Nashid Ali Muhammad, *Muslims in America: Seven Centuries of History 1312–2000*, 3rd edn (Beltsville, MD: Amana, 2003); Jane I. Smith, *Islam in America*, 2nd edn (New York: Columbia University Press, 2010); Edward E. Curtis IV, *Muslims in America: A Short History* (New York: Oxford University Press, 2009).
9. Yvonne Yazbeck Haddad and Jane I. Smith (eds), *Muslim Minorities in the West: Visible and Invisible* (Lanham, MD: Altamira Press, 2002); Yvonne Yazbeck Haddad, Jane I. Smith and John L. Esposito (eds), *Religion and Immigration: Christian, Jewish, and Muslim Experiences in the United States* (Lanham, MD: Altamira Press, 2003); Jocelyne Cesari, *When Islam and Democracy Meet: Muslims in Europe and in the United States* (New York: Palgrave Macmillan, 2004); Jocelyne Cesari (ed.), *Muslims in the West after 9/11: Religion, Politics and Law* (London: Routledge, 2009).
10. Runnymede Trust Commission on British Muslims and Islamophobia, *Islamophobia: A Challenge to Us All* (London: Runnymede Trust, 1997).
11. Kabir, *Muslims in Australia*.
12. Jeremy Earp and Sut Jhally (dir.), *Reel Bad Arabs: How Hollywood Vilifies a People*, DVD (Northampton, MA: Media Education Foundation, 2006).
13. *American Muslims: One Year After 9-11* (Washington, DC: Council on American–Islamic Relations, 2002); Philippa Strum and Danielle Tarantolo (eds), *Muslims in the United States: Demography, Beliefs, Institutions* (Washington, DC: Woodrow Wilson International Center for Scholars, 2003); Mohamed Nimer (ed.), *Islamophobia and Anti-Americanism: Causes and Remedies* (Beltsville, MD: Amana, 2007).

14. Tony Gaskew, *Policing American Muslim Communities: A Compendium of Post 9/11 Interviews* (Lewiston, NY: Edwin Mellen Press, 2008); Amaney Jamal and Nadine Naber (eds), *Race and Arab Americans before and after 9/11: From Invisible Citizens to Visible Subjects* (Syracuse, NY: Syracuse University Press, 2008); Detroit Arab American Study Team, *Citizenship and Crisis: Arab Detroit after 9/11* (New York: Russell Sage Foundation, 2009); Louise Cainkar, *Homeland Insecurity: The Arab American and Muslim American Experience after 9/11* (New York: Russell Sage Foundation, 2011); Esposito, *The Future of Islam*; Smith, *Islam in America*.

15. Yvonne Yazbeck Haddad, Jane I. Smith and Kathleen M. Moore, *Muslim Women in America: The Challenges of Islamic Identity Today* (New York: Oxford University Press, 2006); Jamillah Karim, *American Muslim Women: Negotiating Race, Class, and Gender within the Ummah* (New York: New York University Press, 2009); Yvonne Y. Haddad, Farid Senzai and Jane I. Smith (eds), *Educating the Muslims of America* (Oxford: Oxford University Press, 2009); Nazli Kibria, *Muslims in Motion: Islam and National Identity in the Bangladeshi Diaspora* (New Brunswick, NJ: Rutgers University Press, 2011); Selcuk R. Sirin and Michelle Fine, *Muslim American Youth: Understanding Hyphenated Identities through Multiple Methods* (New York: New York University Press, 2008).

IDENTITY MATTERS

Defining Muslims

It is generally believed that all Muslims practise the same aspects of Islamic culture – names, dress codes and eating and drinking habits – and that they are a distinct non-Christian cultural group, separate from the main-stream American population. Yet Muslims in the United States (and else-where) are ethnically diverse and heterogeneous in language, skin colour and culture. The only element they have in common is their religion and even that has some variations. Nevertheless, most Muslims feel a strong affiliation with the broader Islamic community (*ummah*) and have a con-stant desire for greater Islamic political unity within the 'Abode of Islam' (*dar-al-Islam*). The centrepiece of unity among Muslims is the Quran – the very word of Allah (God). The Quran provides the same message for all Muslims, although interpretations of that message differ across the various Muslim groups and because of the different levels of textual meaning. Muslims' devotional practice rests on what are known as the five pillars of Islam:

1. *Kalima* (or *shahada*). *Kalima* is an open declaration of faith. It has to be said in Arabic, '*La ilaha il-lal-lahu, Muhammadur Rasu-lul-lah*', and means: 'I testify (confess) that there is no Allah but the one Allah and that Muhammad is the Messenger of Allah.'
2. *Salat*. This is the communal prayer that has to be performed five times each day – in the morning (before sunrise), at noon, in the afternoon, at sunset and at night, facing the *Ka'bah*, an important shrine of the Islamic world in Mecca. Before performing the *salat*, the believer must be in a state of purity, and therefore needs to carry out a series of ritual ablutions. The

salat may be performed wherever the Muslim happens to be, though some prefer to pray in mosques.

3. *Zakat*. This is almsgiving. Muslims are expected to give 2.5 per cent of their net income to other members of the same faith who are less well off or in need.

4. *Sawm*. This is fasting. During *Ramadan*, the ninth month of the Islamic calendar, Muslims must refrain from eating, smoking, drinking and sex between sunrise and sunset.

5. *Hajj*. The fifth pillar is the pilgrimage or visit to Mecca to pray around the *Ka'bah*, in *Zil Hajj*, the twelfth month of the Islamic calendar. Every Muslim should, if health, financial means and safety of the routes allow, undertake this pilgrimage at least once in his or her lifetime. Men who have performed the *hajj* are called *hajji* and women are *hajja*.[1]

In addition to the five pillars, Muslims must not eat certain foods, such as pork, or drink alcohol. Muslims slaughter animals according to teachings of the Quran called *halal*, and devout Muslims eat *halal* meat. Some women choose to wear the *hijab* and the *abaya* or *burqa* to pay due respect to the teachings and tradition of Prophet Muhammad (PBUH) – these teachings are known as the *Hadith* or *Sunnah*. In some Muslim countries, such as Saudi Arabia, the wearing of the *hijab* is mandatory, whereas in other countries, such as Bangladesh, it is a matter of personal choice. Muslims have two important festivals each year: *Eid-ul-Fitr*, which is celebrated immediately after *Ramadan*, and *Eid-ul-Adha*, the feast celebrated after the *hajj* on the tenth day of *Zil Hajj*. To mark the pilgrimage to Mecca, Muslims all over the world celebrate the Feast of Sacrifice in *Eid-ul-Adha*. Sheep are ritually slaughtered to commemorate Prophet Ibrahim's (PBUH) willingness to sacrifice his son. This meat is partly for one's own consumption and the rest is given to friends and distributed among the poor and needy.

Muslims are divided into two main sects, Sunni and Shia. About 87 per cent of all Muslims in the world are Sunnis and about 13 per cent are Shi'ite.[2] There are further divisions among the Sunnis and Shi'ites (see Chapter 2), though all believe in the five pillars of Islam.

In this chapter, I begin with a brief history of Muslims in America. Secondly, I examine some of the contemporary issues impacting on American Muslims. Thirdly, I introduce social identity theory and explain how it can help us to understand identity. Fourthly, I discuss my research methodology.

A brief history of Muslims in America

Muslim contact with America commenced during the 1700s when Muslim slaves were brought from Africa. Records show that a few Muslim slaves in the United States became famous. For example Kunta Kinte, who is depicted in

Alex Haley's book (and the television show) *Roots*, was brought from Gambia in 1767.[3] Kinte tried hard to hold onto his Islamic heritage and showed great courage by practising Islam in a very Christian environment. Some Muslims fought in the Revolutionary War; for example, Peter (Saleem) Salem, a former slave, fought in the Battle of Bunker Hill against British troops in 1775.[4] Muslim slaves were not allowed to develop institutional structures in the form of mosques or graveyards, so they could not establish an Islamic heritage for their descendants; nevertheless, some slaves such as Kinte and Salem retained their Islamic identity.[5]

Muslims from Syria and Lebanon began to migrate to the industrial cities of the Midwest in small numbers before World War I. More Muslims began to arrive in the inter-war period from Albania, Turkey, Yugoslavia, Syria, Lebanon and the Indian subcontinent. By the early 1920s, mosques had been established in Maine (1915), Connecticut (1919) and Highland Park, Michigan (1919), with others following in Michigan City, Indiana (1925), New York (1926), Pittsburgh (1930) and Sacramento (late 1930s).[6] The first purpose-built mosque, the Mother Mosque of America, was built in Cedar Rapids, Iowa, in 1934. As the Muslim community grew, the Federation of Islamic Associations of the United States and Canada was founded in 1953. The Muslim presence was gradually recognised by American authorities. In 1954, President Dwight Eisenhower inaugurated the Washington mosque by cutting its ribbon.[7]

After a change in federal immigration law in 1965, a wave of highly educated Arab/Muslim immigrants arrived in the US, to be joined from the 1970s by Muslims from south Asia. Gradually many Muslim organisations were established to address Muslim issues. Some notable ones are the Islamic Society of North America, the Islamic Circle of North America and the Muslim American Society.[8] The 1950s and 1960s also saw two prominent African Americans convert to Black Islam (Nation of Islam), later embracing Sunni Islam: Malcolm X (a radical leader of the Black Power movement) and the boxer Mohammad Ali (formerly Cassius Marcellus Clay Jr).

It is difficult to obtain a definite number for the total Muslim population in the United States at any stage because the US census has never asked citizens to declare their religious affiliation. However, based on its own survey together with its interpretation, the US census data (which provides the racial statistics and country of birth) in conjunction with the Pew Research Center estimated that in 2011 there were 2.75 million Muslims living in the United States,[9] which comprised 0.88 per cent of the total US population (312,119,000).[10] The Pew Research Center further determined the racial composition of the US Muslim population in this order: white 30 per cent, black 23 per cent, Asian 21 per cent, Hispanic 6 per cent, other or mixed race 19 per cent.[11] The breakdown of the Muslim population according to race is problematic; for example, the category 'white' includes mainstream Americans (Caucasians) and Arab Americans (who have lighter skin). Similarly, traditional African Americans (with an enslavement history), and immigrant Africans, such as Algerians, could be lumped together in the 'black' category. In another account, the Pew Research Center provided the US Muslim population according to their place of birth, in this order: US 37 per cent, Middle East (including Iran) and north Africa 29 per cent, Asia (Pakistan and other south Asia) 16 per cent, sub-Saharan Africa 7 per cent, Europe 5 per cent, other 6 per cent.[12]

There have been some eminent Muslims in American society, such as the boxer Muhammad Ali and the basketball player Kareem Abdul-Jabbar in sport, and in art and entertainment the rhythm and blues songwriter and producer Muhammad Luqman Abdul-Haqq (Kenny Gamble) had become famous.[13] In politics there have been some elected Muslim officials, for example Larry Shaw, a North Carolina senator; Yusuf Abdus-Salaam, a councillor in Selma, Alabama; Kazi Miah, a councillor in Hamtramck, Michigan; John Rhodes, a councillor in North Las Vegas; and Lateefah Muhammad, a councillor in Tuskegee, Alabama. Some have also held important positions: Hassan El-Amin was appointed as a district judge in Prince George County, Maryland; and two Muslims, Osman Siddique, of Bangladeshi origin, and Zalmay Mamozy Khalilzad, of Afghan background, have served as US ambassadors to other countries.[14] At the time of writing this chapter, there were two African American Muslim Congressmen: Keith Ellison, from Minnesota, and André D. Carson, from Indiana. In 2010, Rima Fakih was the first Muslim woman to become Miss USA.

In previous research in Australia and the UK, I was able to evaluate Muslims' labour market status (employment and unemployment level) by examining the official census data of the respective countries, but not for this study because, as stated above, in the United States there is no official census data by religion. So the total Muslim placement in the American labour market cannot be evaluated.

International events impacting on Muslim Americans

The Muslim world's news

From the 1970s to the 1990s, there was a gradual increase in the Muslim population, and during this period Americans were becoming more conscious of Muslims most often through sensational news reports on the Iranian Revolution (1979), the Iranian hostage crisis (1979–81), the Libyan terrorist bombing of Pan Am flight 103 over Lockerbie, Scotland, which killed all 259 passengers (1988), the Salman Rushdie affair (1989) and the Oklahoma bombing (1995). The Iranian hostage crisis was followed by a public backlash against Iranians in the United States characterised by frequent burning of

Iranian flags, shouts of 'Arab go home' (even though Iranians are not Arabs), and emotional bank tellers refusing to cash Iranian students' cheques.[15] In 1995, after the bombing of a US federal government complex in Oklahoma by the non-Muslim Timothy McVeigh, some Muslims in America, particularly the Arabs, were vilified by members of the wider community. It was initially speculated by the media that the perpetrator was a Muslim. Then, after the 11 September 2001 terrorist attacks, vilification against Muslims intensified. Paul Barrett observed:

A Gallup poll in 2006 found that four in ten Americans admitted feeling prejudice against Muslims. Nearly one-quarter said that they would not like to have a Muslim as a neighbor. Four in ten would require Muslims to carry special identification cards and undergo more intensive security checks at airports. Among American Muslims, 40 per cent told the Zogby International polling firm in 2004 that they had suffered discrimination since 9/11. Many Muslims in the United States have doubts about whether they are accepted as 'real' Americans.[16]

Since the 9/11 terrorist attacks some people believe that Islam is necessarily a violent creed. Passages of the Quran are sometimes taken out of context as evidence that Islam requires believers to kill or convert non-believers. Some Muslim countries, such as Afghanistan (under the Taliban), Iran, Saudi Arabia and Yemen, have established *shariah* law and enforced penalties under *hudud* (the criminal code of *shariah* law that commands stoning to death of adulterers and other horrific punishments), which has been interpreted by the public at large as evidence that Muslims are backward and violent.

When the Taliban ruled Afghanistan (from the mid-1990s until October 2001) the world witnessed several atrocities. The ultra-conservative Taliban espouse a very strict interpretation of Islam, which is unpopular among the majority of Afghans because it rejects Muslim moderation and the West. As Rashid Ahmed says, 'The Taliban have given Islamic fundamentalism a new face and a new identity for the next millennium – one that refuses to accept any compromise or political system except their own.'[17] The Taliban banned modern technology like the internet and television in Afghanistan during its harsh rule. Under Taliban rule, women were not allowed to work and girls were not allowed to attend school. Men were beaten for trimming their beards and associating with women other than family members. The Taliban executed homosexuals by lapidation, bulldozing walls to crush their bodies.[18] The Taliban's punishment for adultery made worldwide news. In 1996 an Afghan woman called Nurbibi, aged forty, and her stepson and lover Turyalai, aged thirty-eight, were stoned to death under the provisions for punishing adulterers in *shariah* law.[19] In 2001, the Taliban destroyed some 2,000-year-old Buddhist statues in Afghanistan because they regarded them as an insult to Islam.

In 2000 Nigeria's northern states adopted a harsh *shariah* code. The code's first victim who made worldwide news was a woman convicted of adultery, Amina Lawal. In 2002, Lawal was sentenced to death by stoning, and her pregnancy was taken as proof of the adultery. Worldwide condemnation of the case, and a campaign mounted by human rights organisations, eventually led to Lawal's acquittal. If the sentence had been carried out, she would have been buried up to her neck in sand then pelted with rocks.[20] Many other women convicted of adultery, however, may not be fortunate enough to receive such international attention.

In 2010, an Iranian woman, Sakineh Mohammadi Ashtiani, who was also convicted of adultery, made worldwide news. Ashtiani was found to have had 'illicit relationships' with two men after the death of her husband, and was initially sentenced to ninety-nine lashings. But, after she was flogged in front of her teenage son, the case was reopened and the judge ultimately ordered the death penalty, sentencing her to a violent end. Ashtiani had already spent five years in prison, and her children were horrified by her sentence. An international human rights group worked for her acquittal and it was reported that Tehran had provisionally suspended the death sentence.[21] Despite these well-publicised reprieves, the news of the application of the *hudud* in some Muslim countries, such as stoning to death for adultery, or public hanging for armed robbery, rape or other offences,[22] reinforces public opinion that all Muslims are brutal.

Such ongoing news from the Muslim world has no doubt added to mainstream Americans' negative perception of Muslims. For example, when the Israeli–Palestinian peace talks commenced in Washington, DC in 2010, the hardline Iranian president, Mahmoud Ahmadinejad, told a pro-Palestinian rally of thousands of Iranians that revived Middle East peace talks were 'doomed' to fail. Ever since the 1979 revolution, Iran has organised annual Palestinian solidarity marches across the country on al-Quds Day, the last Friday of *Ramadan*. Tens of thousands of Iranians rally in streets around the country shouting 'Death to America! Death to Israel!'[23] After 9/11, US president George W. Bush branded Iran (along with North Korea and Iraq) the 'axis of evil', so in protest millions of Iranians rallied and chanted 'Death to America' as they celebrated the twenty-third anniversary of the Islamic Revolution and burned the US flag.[24] In 2002, during the *hajj*, in spite of the Saudi ban on political demonstrations, the Iranians in the Iranian complex chanted 'Death to Israel, Death to America'.[25]

In addition to these instances of negative information, whenever there is news of home-grown terrorists people worldwide tend to get more concerned. Academic Muqtadar Khan observed that two images govern Muslims' minds: 'America the democracy' and 'America the colonial power'. The Muslims whose framework is 'America the democracy' form the majority, who are typically peaceful. But adherents to 'America the colonial power' are 'Muslim isolationists' (otherwise referred to as extremists), who argue that Muslims must strive to revive the institution of the *Khilafah* (caliphate), which will take care of all Muslim problems.[26]

Home-grown extremists

It is not generally known that Muslim extremists are in the minority world-wide; the exploits of a few extremists have been widely publicised in a climate of extreme fear. For example, in 2004–5 Masaoud Ahmed Khan, Seifullah Chapman, Hamad Abdur Raheem and others of the Virginia Jihad Network were convicted for, among other things, conspiring to provide assistance to Lashkar-e-Taiba (a *jihad*ist group based in Pakistan) in the aftermath of the 9/11 attacks. In 2009, US citizens Ehsanul Islam Sadequee and Syed Haris Ahmed were charged with plotting attacks, and both were jailed on terrorism-related charges. In October 2009 two men from the Chicago area, David Coleman Headley and Tahawwur Hussain Rana, confessed to plotting an attack on a Danish newspaper. Headley also confessed to helping Lashkar-e-Taiba plan its 2008 Mumbai attacks.[27] In December 2009 five Virginian youths, Waqir Hussein Khan, Ramy Zamzam, Umar Farooq, Ahmed Abdul Mini and Aman Hasan Yamer, aged 18–24, were arrested in Pakistan for allegedly seeking *jihad* training. The men, who denied the charges, were tried in Pakistan for planning terrorist attacks in the region,[28] and in June 2010 were sentenced to ten years imprisonment.[29] In November 2009, Major Nidal Hasan, a gunman from Fort Hood, Texas of Palestinian background, allegedly killed thirteen people. And on 25 December 2009, the 23-year-old Nigerian Abdulmutallab allegedly attempted to blow up a Detroit-bound Northwest Airlines flight with explosives tucked in his underwear. These incidents show that a small minority of Muslims are a threat to all communities – both Muslim and non-Muslim. In May 2010, Connecticut resident Faisal Shahzad confessed to an attempted Times Square car bombing.[30] In January that year, a 61-page report, *Anti-Terror Lessons of Muslim-Americans*, by scholars at Duke University and the University of North Carolina at Chapel Hill, found that since the 11 September 2001 attacks, 139 American Muslims had been accused of planning or carrying out violent attacks motivated by extremism. However, the scholars thought, with a total American Muslim population of 2.5 million, the number of Islamic radicals was very low.[31] Arguably, though, if their plots had been carried out successfully the scale of disaster would have been horrendous.

The USA Patriot Act

There is no doubt that many of the foregoing news items concerning the Islamic world have been disturbing. So it is not surprising that soon after the 9/11 terrorist attacks the USA Patriot Act was signed into law. It allows law enforcement agencies to use surveillance, and to search and deport people suspected of terrorism-related acts. Research has found that the lives of Muslims (and Arabs) in America have become exceedingly difficult because of the Patriot Act.[32] As Jane Smith said:

> The USA Patriot Act (Providing Appropriate Tools Required to Intercept and Obstruct Terrorism) Act of October 2001 effectively took away all legal protection of the liberty of American Muslims and Arabs. Numerous civil rights agencies have protested this act and worked to have it lifted, as yet to no avail.
>
> The US government has been vigilant in monitoring NGOs, civic, charitable and religious organizations that might be suspected in some way of harboring terrorism. The assets of some have been frozen. This has served to deprive US Muslims of one of the most important ways in which they can fulfill the obligation of paying *zakat*, through support of charities that give to the poor, widows and orphans.[33]

John Esposito observed that in the five years after 9/11 the Bush administration held 6,472 persons under 'terrorist' or 'anti-terrorist' programmes. Some of those alleged to be terrorists were not charged but were found to be involved in other minor offences such as violation of disability insurance law, failure to file a tax return, or for providing false statements. By 2006 the vast majority had been released without receiving any prison term, though the zeal (which some would claim to be excessive) of the Bush government had certainly generated fear in the wider society.[34] Smith observed that, since former US President George W. Bush won the first (and only) Muslim bloc vote because of his promise to protect Muslim civil rights, he should have been the one to preside over the abandonment of the laws that infringed the rights of Muslims and Arabs. Instead, some Arabs and Muslims were subjected to humiliation, deportation and in some cases illegal forms of torture during his presidency.[35]

Islamophobia

As discussed in the introduction, many Muslims faced repercussions after the 9/11 Twin Towers attacks. According to the Arab American Anti-Discrimination Committee, there were more than 7,000 violent incidents targeting Arab Americans or Muslims in the first nine weeks following the attacks. For example, businesses were vandalised and children were the targets of hate slurs in school.[36] Yasser Ahmed, manager of an Arab-owned candy and grocery store on Broadway in upper Manhattan, New York, said about ten people came to his store and shouted, 'You guys did it!' In Dearborn, Michigan, where nearly one out of every three residents is Arab American, Osama Siblani, the publisher of the *Arab American News*, said he and his colleagues received several hostile phone calls, including a death threat.[37] In other states, such as California, Illinois, Louisiana, Massachusetts, Texas and Virginia, there were reports of arson attacks at Islamic institutions, personal attacks, pig's blood thrown in mosques and the police profiling men in Middle Eastern-style head coverings, including non-Muslims such as Sikhs.[38] Privately, an informant told me that his brother was killed in the Twin Towers attacks, and soon after 9/11 his sister's house in New York was vandalised. In Boston, a Pakistani American family said that people stopped going to their restaurant after 9/11. Eventually, their business failed, and they closed their restaurant.

Not only Muslims were persecuted after 9/11: many Sikhs were vilified by members of the wider society because of their visibility (their beard and turban). For example, soon after the September 11th terrorist attacks a man beat a Sikh motel owner in SeaTac, Washington with a cane and told him to 'go to Allah'. Another man punched a Sikh cab driver and pulled out part of his beard. In Arizona, a man shot and killed a Sikh gas station owner and later shouted, 'I stand for America all the way.'[39] In suburban Cleveland, bottles filled with petrol were thrown through the windows of a Sikh temple and flames poured out. There were also incidents where Sikhs were yelled at as 'terrorists'. Many Sikhs (and Arabs and Muslims) were stopped and searched in public places by law enforcement agents.[40]

On a brighter note, since the 9/11 tragedy, many Muslims and non-Muslims have engaged in inter-faith dialogues and attempted to establish social cohesion in American society. Yet widespread discomfort about the presence of Muslims in America remains. In the conventional American media representation of Muslims, many prominent American Christian evangelical leaders have portrayed both Prophet Muhammad (PBUH) and Islam generally in a derogatory manner; for example, one described 'Muhammad as a wild-eyed fanatic and a killer, a terrorist and a demon-possessed pedophile, and Islam as an evil religion'.[41] As Smith observed, the

> Prophet of Islam serves as a model for Muslim belief and behavior, and for Muslims such images are deeply humiliating, as have been many of the cartoons and other depictions of Arabs and Muslims throughout the twentieth and early twenty-first centuries.[42]

Smith comments that before 9/11 Arabs and Muslims were portrayed as 'fools and knaves to oil-rich sheikhs with beards and huge bellies (with harem girls in the background)', and now (after 9/11) these images are converted to 'machine-gun-toting terrorists and suicide bombers'.[43] A participant of this study, Ismat (female, 16, overseas born of Bangladeshi background, identity: Muslim) observed:

> I feel like just in cartoons or [TV] shows every time you watch, you see a Middle Eastern person, you automatically think, 'Okay, terrorist'. That's how [the media

have] shaped cartoons to turn out to be, it's just your whole idea changes. (Ismat, interview, New York, November 2009)

In December 2002, a cartoon by the cartoonist Doug Marlette was briefly posted on the *Tallahassee Democrat*'s website showing a caricature of Prophet Muhammad (PBUH) driving a nuclear bomb-laden truck similar to that used by Timothy McVeigh in the 1995 Oklahoma City bombing. Its caption ran 'What would Mohammed drive?'. It offended many Muslims and the Florida office of the CAIR called for an apology from the newspaper. The *Democrat* declined to apologise because the cartoon was not published in its print edition.[44]

Notwithstanding this potential stigma, many Muslims (like other immigrants) are choosing to migrate to America in the hope of a better life and more opportunities. Arguably, the United States is benefiting from this influx but there are sections of the wider society that resist accepting Muslims. For example, in 2010 there was a resurgence of anti-Muslim attitudes when Muslims planned to build a community centre in lower Manhattan near the former site of the World Trade Center.

Park51 Islamic Center

In 2010 Imam Feisal Abdul Rauf proposed the building of a multi-storey Muslim cultural centre, the Park51 Islamic Center, two blocks away from Ground Zero in New York. It was to include a mosque, sport facilities, a theatre and restaurant and would be open to the public to show that Muslims are full community members. Muslim leaders said that it would be modelled on the YMCA and Jewish Community Center in Manhattan. The centre also planned to include a memorial to victims of the attack on the Twin Towers.[45] The construction of the centre, a $100 million project to be built on private property, was approved by city officials.[46] On 3 August 2010, New York City's Landmarks Preservation Commission unanimously approved the plans, and President Obama welcomed it because it also aimed to promote religious tolerance. 'This is America', Obama said, 'and our commitment to religious freedom must be unshakeable. The principle that people of all faiths are welcome in this country, and will not be treated differently by their government, is essential to who we are.'[47] Later, at a Friday *iftar* dinner at the White House to mark *Ramadan*, Obama said Muslims 'have the same right to practise their religion as anyone else in this country', including by building a mosque in lower Manhattan.[48] The New York mayor, Michael Bloomberg, a Jewish Republican turned independent, also defended the constitutional right of all religious groups who own private property to build a religious institution.[49] And the CAIR welcomed Obama's 'strong support for Muslim religious rights'.[50]

However, conservative politicians (mostly Republicans but also some Democrats) and some families affected by the 9/11 attacks were against this plan. They believed that it would be a painful reminder of the victims who died in the 9/11 terrorist attacks. Also a CNN/Opinion Research poll in August 2010 showed that 68 per cent of Americans opposed the Islamic centre plans, while only 29 per cent favoured them.[51] In another poll, conducted by the *New York Times*, two-thirds of New York City residents wanted the project to be relocated to a less controversial site farther away from Ground Zero, including those who said they favoured it being built.[52]

Apparently, the opponents of Park51 failed to realise that many Muslims had worked in the Twin Towers, with the presence of a *musalla* in the Twin Tower buildings being clear evidence of this. Nearly 3,000 people were killed when al-Qaeda hijackers crashed commercial airlines into the Twin Towers, the Pentagon outside Washington, and a Pennsylvania field. The number of Muslim casualties at the World Trade Center was about 358.[53] One of these was Salman Hamdani, of Pakistani heritage, aged twenty-three. Hamdani was a research assistant at the Rockefeller University in Manhattan. He was also a trained paramedic and a member of the New York Police Department's cadet program; so when he saw the Twin Towers in flames, he headed downtown to help in the rescue effort. He died in the rescue mission.[54]

As discussed, the opponents of Park51 still believed that only non-Muslim (mainstream) Americans were casualties of the 9/11 tragedy. For example, Sarah Palin, the 2008 Republican vice-presidential nominee, has urged 'peace-seeking Muslims' to reject the centre, branding it an 'unnecessary provocation'.[55] US Senator John Cornyn, a Texas Republican, commented, 'But I do think it's unwise . . . to build a mosque at the site where 3,000 Americans lost their lives as a result of a terrorist attack.'[56] New York Republican Congressman Peter King said the Muslim community was 'abusing' its rights and 'needlessly offending' many people. 'It is insensitive and uncaring for the Muslim community to build a mosque in the shadow of Ground Zero . . . Unfortunately, the president caved in to political correctness.'[57] And Mark Williams, chairman and spokesman for the Tea Party, said, 'The mosque would be for the worship of the terrorists' monkey god.'[58] Another fierce opponent of the Park51 mosque was the Florida evangelical pastor Bill Keller. Keller hosted a popular televangelism programme in Florida until 2007, when CBS forced him off the air for declaring, 'Islam is a 1,400-year-old lie from hell, and that history clearly shows Muhammad was a murdering paedophile.'[59] On 5 September 2010 Keller preached a sermon attended by about forty people at the New York Marriott Downtown, overlooking Ground Zero, and said, 'Islam is not and has never been a religion of peace . . . How could you build bridges with people who ask their Muslim brothers to fly a plane into the twin towers and kill thousands of innocent people?' He also said that all the people who were behind the proposed mosque will 'burn in hell'.[60]

The Quran-burning incident

Opposition to the plan to build the Park51 Islamic Center has continued. In 2010 Terry Jones, pastor of a small Florida church, vowed to mark the 9/11 anniversary and honour the deaths of the people killed in the al-Qaeda attack by burning a copy of the Quran. The day was also set to coincide with the festivities for *Eid-ul-Fitr*. Pastor Jones said the Quran burning was intended 'to remember those who were brutally murdered on September 11', and to send a warning 'to the radical element of Islam'. This made worldwide news and Anders Fogh Rasmussen, the NATO secretary general, warned that it would be a security risk for the troops present in Afghanistan.[61] Pastor Jones temporarily suspended the idea, but on 20 March 2011 he presided over the burning of a copy of the Quran at his Dove World Outreach Center in Gainesville, Florida.

The burning of the Quran sparked deadly attacks in Afghanistan. On Friday 1 April 2011 in Mazar-e-Sharif, northern Afghanistan's largest city, thousands of protesters came out of the large Blue Mosque and marched toward the United Nations mission a mile away. The angry mob entered the compound chanting 'Death to America', burned the US flag and killed seven UN workers. Demonstrations also spread throughout the country.[62]

Other related incidents

During the period when Park51 was being debated, a few other incidents of religious intolerance occurred. For example, in August 2010 in New York City, a Muslim cab driver of Bangladeshi heritage, Ahmed H. Sharif, aged forty-three, was carrying a young American passenger, Michael Enright, aged twenty-one. Enright had a casual conversation with the cab driver, asking him if he was a Muslim and greeting him by saying '*Assalamu alaikum*' (peace be upon you), and asking Sharif how his celebration of *Ramadan* was going. Then Enright suddenly attacked Sharif with a knife and slashed him in his face, arm and hands, which later required twenty-eight stitches. Sharif said the attack had shattered his American dream. 'I feel very bad. I have been here more than twenty-five years. I have been driving a taxi more than fifteen years. All my four kids were born here. I never felt this hopeless and insecure before.' A taxi drivers' association blamed the attack on prejudice towards plans for the Islamic centre.[63] Nevertheless, in August 2010, reporting on the Park51 issue, the *Time* reporter Bobby Ghosh remarked:

> Islamophobia in the US doesn't approach levels seen in other countries where Muslims are a minority: there's no American equivalent of France's ban on the burqa or Switzerland's new law against building minarets. Polls have shown that most Muslims feel safer and freer in the US than anywhere else in the Western world.[64]

Ghosh informed readers that the first wave of anti-Muslim rhetoric after 9/11 came from leading Christian figures such as Pat Robertson, Jerry Falwell, Saxby Chambliss and Franklin Graham. For example, Robertson and Falwell doubted whether Islam was a religion and branded Prophet Muhammad (PBUH) 'a robber, brigand and terrorist'.[65] As I read the *Time* report, I wondered whether Ghosh's observation that Islamophobia in America was more subdued than in France and Switzerland[66] was correct. It is true that Switzerland has outlawed the building of minarets, and France has banned the wearing of the *niqab* in public places, but in 2009 the Muslim population in Switzerland was about 5 per cent of the total,[67] and in April 2011 the Muslim population in France was estimated at about 10 per cent of the total.[68] The fact that in 2011 the Muslim population in America was only 0.88 per cent[69] suggests that either Europe has been a more favoured settlement destination of Muslim migrants or European immigration policies have been more accepting of Muslim migration. In any event, it seems fair to say that the vociferous resistance to the Park51 Islamic Center in America is unhelpful for the social cohesion of Muslims and non-Muslims in American society. Figure 1.1 shows the intensity of anti-Muslim rage in America and Europe.

With this backdrop of events impacting on Muslims in the United States, I turn to examine the identity of young American Muslims. In the next section, I explore the concept of identity and provide some anecdotes to illustrate how various factors can shape identity.

Examining the concept of 'identity'

Identity is the condition of being oneself (and not another). Arguably it is a process that is fluid and is shaped according to circumstances and opportunities. Identity may depend on the family one is born into, the culture and religion one belongs to, one's community and one's life experiences. In 2001 a team of sociologists identified ten 'identity markers' that people use to claim or attribute identity: place of birth, ancestry, place of residence, length of residence, upbringing and education, name, accent, physical appearance, dress and commitment to place.[70] Elsewhere, Fiona Douglas found identity to be a complex and fascinating phenomenon. 'At a basic level, identity is about who we are, and who and what we identify with. However, identity is also about who we want to be, and how we wish to be seen by others.'[71] In other words, Douglas suggested that identity can go beyond nationality and place of birth. It can be 'a state of mind'.[72] Identity is both individual and group oriented. Richard Jenkins stated:

- 'Identity' denotes the ways in which individuals and collectivities are distinguished in their relations with other individuals and collectivities.
- 'Identification' is the systematic establishment and signification, between

Figure 1.1 Five times a day, the call to anger.
From Muslim Observer, *2 September 2010*

individuals, between collectivities, and between individuals and collectivities, of relationships of similarity and difference.

- Taken – as they can only be – together, similarity and difference are the dynamic principles of identification, and are at the heart of the human world.[73]

Jenkins observed that group identification involves the 'centrality of power, and therefore politics, in identity maintenance and change. Asserting, defending, imposing and resisting collective identification are all definitely political.' Jenkins also suggested that external factors play a significant role in group or collective identity.[74] Identity recognises similarity, or shared belonging, and the differences that form the rhetoric of 'us' and 'them'. In other words it creates an 'ingroup' against an 'outgroup'. Paul Gilroy commented:

Identity is always particular, as much about difference as about shared belonging ... Identity can help us to comprehend the formation of the fateful pronoun 'we' and to reckon with the patterns of inclusion and exclusion that it cannot help but to create.

This may be one of the most troubling aspects of all: the fact that the formation of every 'we' must leave out or exclude a 'they,' that identities depend on the marking of difference.[75]

Gilroy finds the term 'identity' problematic because it creates division. Peter Burke and Jan Stets believe that social identity is based on membership in a group or category that gives one a shared feeling with others in the group. When one receives recognition, approval and acceptance from a group then one is more likely to feel a part of that group. Thus, 'one is verified as a member by being like the other members. Being verified in terms of social identity reinforces group–nongroup distinctions, thus maintaining boundaries and supporting the continued differentiations and cleavages in the social structure.'[76]

For example, when a Muslim woman looks Muslim by virtue of her Islamic attire, regardless of her ethnic background, she is identifying with the broader Muslim *ummah* and inadvertently distancing herself from non-Muslims. One of the participants in this study, Shahnaz (female, 29, overseas born, Bangladeshi background), identified herself as 'Muslim only'. By profession, Shahnaz is a scientist. She also spends her after-work time as a social worker. Shahnaz tells the story of how she endorsed her Islamic identity by wearing the *hijab*:

> *Hijab* is a long story of mine. I was so anti-*hijab* you cannot imagine. There was a girl in our office who converted to Islam and she called me one day and she said, 'I want to talk to you about this Islam, I am having difficulty and I know you don't do it too, but I want to talk to you.' So we were looking through the Quran and she said, 'Look, this is where it is saying to pull up your veils over your clothes.' And I said, 'Well, it doesn't say that you cover your head . . . the Quran said to pull it over your bosom.'[77]
>
> Later, I met this Egyptian woman and so we were sitting and I was reading the Quran in English and I was explaining to her and the *hijab* question came [up] and she was saying, you know, 'When I started *hijab*, I lost so many of my Muslim friends.' She lost Muslim friends when she started wearing *hijab* in Egypt. So, one day I thought, 'Should I take that risk?' If I wore the *hijab* then I might also lose some friends. It changed the whole profile of me. (Shahnaz, interview, Maryland, 2010)

Shahnaz observed that at work before she wore the *hijab* she was widely accepted by her colleagues. After she started wearing it she noticed the difference:

> It did, it changed so much. I guess one of the guys at work said, 'I miss your hair.' And I said, 'That is the purpose, you know that I wear it.' But anyway, it has made a big difference. Before *hijab* I was one of them, but now with the *hijab*, I am an outsider.

Everything, everything, everything, the whole attitude, it's just like you are different, you know. It's hard, it's very difficult, it's very frustrating, you know. They don't
take the value of you. I just tell Allah, 'I place you in front of them and me, I can't
hide my battle because I am just human and so you may fight my battle.'

This case hardly suggests discrimination because Shahnaz was still continuing
to do her job. Apparently Shahnaz's colleagues thought she chose to separate
herself from them with her religious visibility.

Stuart Hall observed that identity is constructed through internal homoge-
neity, and thereby it forms a closure.[78] Identity constructs internal unity and
thus it brings to the fore power and exclusion, and power play and exclusion
are only possible through the overdetermined process of 'closure'.[79] Hall also
noted the transitional nature of identity: 'Identity is actually formed through
unconscious processes over time, rather than being innate in consciousness
at birth. There is always something "imaginary" or fantasized about its
unity. It always remains incomplete, is always "in process", always "being
formed".[80]

Academics such as Peter Burke, Jan Stets and Sheldon Stryker have observed
that emotion can play an important role in the formation of one's identity.
Emotions have an influence on the formation of social networks; people with
'shared affective meanings' are more likely to enter into and maintain a social
relationship. And people with intense positive emotions towards a network or
group are likely to identify with it.[81] For example, a Muslim may identify with
another Muslim or an Islamic organisation. But with intense negative emotions, they will distance themselves from that network or group. For example,
if a Muslim turns out to be radical, his moderate Muslim friend may maintain
a social distance from him. Similarly, when individuals are highly committed
to a role identity, such as the parent identity, a failure to meet the role expectations may result in a greater negative emotional response.[82] For example, if
a Muslim father, without prior consultation with his daughter, pulls her out
from a public school and enrols her in an Islamic school, and if he is adamant
that his daughter should assume an Islamic identity and insists that she should
wear the *hijab*, then the daughter who previously felt positively about her identity may feel quite the contrary and reject her Islamic identity. (I discuss this
further in Chapter 3, in the 'Americanness' section.)

Henri Tajfel pointed out that individuals can more readily assert their
belonging to or membership of a certain group when they feel accepted in that
group. Social identity theory also suggests that individuals are more likely to
identify with a certain group if that identification is associated with enhanced
self-esteem.[83] My study on young British Muslim identity found that people's
self-esteem is enhanced if they get enough support from their respective communities, the way they are brought up in their respective homes, the values
and norms they learn from their educational and religious institutions, their

interaction and communication with wider society and recognition from that wider society.[84] Therefore, two factors – acceptance and recognition – play important roles in the formation of one's identity. Richard Jenkins provided this thumbnail sketch of the complexities of social identity:

> Society is structured categorically, and organised by inequalities of power and resources. It is in the translation of social categories into meaningful reference groups that 'social structure' influences or produces individual behaviour. Social identity theory focuses on how categories become groups, with the emphasis on inter-group processes.
>
> Individuals, in using stereotypical categories to define themselves, thus bring into being human collective life. Individuals will self-categorise themselves differently and the contingencies with which they are faced.[85]

Steph Lawler observed that identities are socially produced, and are uniting as well as oppositional, such as man–woman, black–white. Identities can also involve tension such as a person having two roles, for example a woman being a mother and a worker.[86] Dual or multiple identities can often compete with each other, so that 'the approval and disapproval of certain kinds of identity draws lines between "us" and "them"'.[87] For example, a visibly bearded Muslim, Rasheed (male, 19, US born, Pakistani background), said, 'Two years ago, I used to say "I'm Muslim", but now first and foremost of course I'm Muslim, but citizenship-wise I'm an American. I just have too strong ties to America.' Rasheed is visibly Muslim and is involved with Muslim organisations, but he appreciates American democracy, putting it like this:

> I mean it's freedom of speech, freedom of religion. The fact is that, you know, the people are the rulers. Government is representative of the people's ideas, right? I'm one of the subscribers to that, that the government should be afraid of the people, that is more along with my philosophies and it fits very well with America. And the people who have come here, on average, tend to be very accepting of others. (Rasheed, interview, Massachusetts, November 2009)

Rasheed connected his American spirit with his childhood memories when he said:

> Those of us who grew up in the '90s, we inherited the American spirit through all the cartoons that we watched, the media we got . . . there was a strong push for the pride in the America that we have.

Rasheed did not connect himself with his Pakistani ethnicity because he had been to Pakistan only once so far, and said, 'I have a very limited vocabulary in Urdu'. When I asked him about *mushairas* (Urdu poetic symposiums), Rasheed replied, 'Unfortunately that's a culture inaccessible to me because I can't really appreciate the language too well . . . Yeah, most of the high Urdu is beyond me.' Like any other young American, Rasheed liked music: 'I used to be into heavy rock. I've now mellowed out a little bit, I'm now into some softer rock. And I've started enjoying some indie music.' When I asked him whether in his childhood he celebrated Halloween and Thanksgiving, Rasheed replied:

> Not really Halloween. Halloween my parents were very strict on, and for Thanksgiving my family was more of a hub of our friends in the area. We would have a big celebration around Thanksgiving time and had *halal* turkey, *halal* rabbit, *halal* duck, *halal* quail.

Rasheed was a practising Muslim, but culturally he was more American. But when I asked him, 'What would be "un-American"?', he promptly replied, 'The Patriot Act restricts your freedom, it allows people to have more power over you, so it is morally or ethically reprehensible. And so that is in many ways "un-American".' Rasheed was also critical of some events at his university campus (perhaps his Islamic identity prompted him to share this view):

> Two years ago there was a national campaign by somebody to have Islamo-fascism Awareness Week, essentially as a response to Islam Awareness Week, which takes places once a year all over the nation. And so this [Islamo-fascism Awareness Week] is essentially, in our perspective, an attempt to slander in a way and incite anger against Islam and Muslims across the globe, and this is an event banned at many campuses. It was organised by some anti-Islam group trying to provoke anger.

'Islamo-fascism Awareness Week' was observed on 114 college and university campuses in the week of 22–6 October 2007. The organisers aimed to protest against the violent oppression of women in Islam and advertised in campus newspapers and circulated pamphlets on that issue. They also showed documentaries, such as *Obsession* and *Suicide Killers*, and organised panel discussions and talks by controversial speakers such as former senator and Republican presidential nomination candidate Rick Santorum, Ann Coulter, Robert Spencer, Nonie Darwish, Wafa Sultan, Michael Medved, Dennis Prager and Daniel Pipes.[88] Islamo-fascism Week was also mentioned by other participants of this study, who were distressed by the Islamophobic attitude of this group. I was told by a student in San Francisco (when I attended a conference there in 2009) that during Islamo-fascism Week some students on their campus held up the Hamas flag and threw shoes at it. The Hamas flag is green in colour and has the *shahada* (first pillar of Islam) written on it. As Rasheed said, it was done to provoke a reaction from Muslims.

rtant to engage young Muslims. Evidence from the UK and USA suggests his age group is susceptible to more radical versions of political Islam.[96]

Qualitative method

e employed the grounded theory method.[97] Grounded theory is a type alitative method. It is a non-statistical methodological approach that is 'letting the data speak' and not imposing pre-formed hypotheses. The of this research was to gain a better understanding of the participants gh their life stories, hopes and aspirations. Most importantly, it was ed to allow respondents to speak about issues important to them. In action with this, I have employed the constructivist method of interpreta- Constructivism emphasises the researcher's unique ability to make their neaning out of information (interviews) rather than measure causal rela- according to preconceived variables. The main data gathering method ce to face via semi-structured interview questions and a form of narra- alysis, whereby interview responses were regarded as a story about each ewee's life. Of course each narrative contains unique elements, but some as could be detected in the participants' lives that enabled the identifica- themes and low-order generalisations. I realise that my interpretation data could be biased. But by reporting on patterns and frequencies and laying my analysis of samples of interview responses, I endeavour to strate to the reader that I have dealt with the data in a fair and reason- anner.

recruit people for my sample I used snowballing and representative ng techniques. The snowballing technique involves referrals from initial pants to generate additional participants. Whereas this technique can tive in building up the number of willing participants, it comes at the producing an unrepresentative sample. To counteract this, I used the ntative sample technique of commencing with a diverse set of groups of ants from an entire population of possible participants. For example, I tely selected different schools, colleges and youth centres from a wide f educational institutions in different states. Similarly, I chose Muslim and community workers from different states because they had differ- onalities and regional views.

data gathered was framed by the interview questions, which were d to the Harvard ethics committee. All interviews were tape recorded. e participants wished that their views be written down. interviews, I asked the younger participants (aged fifteen to seventeen) eir lives, including early school memories, number of family members, work status, their own part-time work, identity/national identity, activities, music, entertainment and cultural interests, together with es, ambitions and dreams. There were specific questions on

The point is that identity involves emotions and tensions, particularly when the 'self' confronts a crisis, which may polarise identities. In this case Rasheed's Islamic identity prompted him to speak on the issue. With regard to the flexible nature of identity, sociologist Avtar Brah, in the British context, observed:

> Identity is not an already given thing but rather it is a process. It is not something fixed that we carry around with ourselves like a piece of luggage. Rather, it is constituted and changes with changing contexts. It is articulated and expressed through identifications within and across different discourses. To have a sense of being, say, Muslim is therefore different when confronted with non-Muslims than with friends and family. This sense of self will vary depending on whether the non-Muslims are friendly or hostile.[89]

Brah acknowledged that there could be cultural conflict within the Muslim community, and that that conflict might not have an impact on one's identity in the same manner when the (majority) non-Muslims are antagonistic to (minority) Muslims. That is, a Muslim's identity will shape up according to the friendly or hostile attitude of non-Muslims towards him or her. Regarding 'identity' as 'a work in progress', Brah observed that, when non-Muslims or mainstream westerners treat Muslims with hostility or difference (as 'the other'), Muslims can become anti-western, or choose to identify themselves with the broader *ummah*.[90] Brah said that the discourses and practices of Islamophobia can lead to the construction of one's Islamic identifications and prompt Muslims to connect to conflicts affecting Muslims globally, such as in Iraq, Chechnya and Kashmir. Thus Islamophobia increases a sense of grievance on behalf of all Muslims. It has also been observed that young Muslims (residing as a minority in the non-Muslim majority countries) can construct their exclusive 'Muslim' identity based on foreign policy, social exclusion and Islamophobia.[91]

In my previous work on Australian and British Muslim identity, I pointed out that most of the participants with an exclusive Muslim identity, or a 'Muslim first' identity, were peaceful and law-abiding citizens. Similarly, in my study of 379 American Muslims, thirty-six (eighteen male and eighteen female) participants said that they were 'only Muslim', fourteen (seven male and seven female) said that they were 'Muslim American', with the emphasis on 'Muslim first', and eleven (six male and five female) said that they were American Muslims, with the emphasis on Muslim being secondary. (The remaining 318 participants' identities are discussed in Chapter 3.) In its survey of 1,033 American Muslims in 2011, the Pew Research Center found 49 per cent of its participants identified themselves first as a Muslim, compared with 26 per cent who thought of themselves first as American.[92] I have argued consistently that having an exclusive Islamic identity is not harmful as long as the person is peaceful. I have also emphasised that Muslims' peaceful discussions, rallies or demonstrations in the western world should be encouraged – as long as their allegiances lie also with the host country.[93] In the face of current geo-political events, nevertheless, I have proposed biculturalism (discussed in the Introduction and Chapters 2 and 3) so that young Muslims can be given room to express their identities.

The research methodology

Rationale for choosing six states

The rationale for choosing Massachusetts, New York, Virginia, Maryland, Florida and Michigan consecutively for my study was as follows: I conducted research in Massachusetts because I was based in Boston as a visiting fellow at Harvard University, and I thought it was important to include the voices of young Muslims in the state in which I was residing. The Twin Towers terrorist attacks took place in New York, so I thought it was essential to examine the views of Muslims who had lived through this ordeal. Virginia and Maryland are bordered by Washington, DC, so I thought I should hear from the young Muslims of these two states to see if they felt more connected than other Muslims to America. People living in close proximity to the White House might feel special. My research interest in Florida was based on a request from some local Muslims in that state. I called an Islamic organisation in Florida and they were very impressed with my research topic and requested that I incorporate their state in my study. Finally, Michigan has the largest and the oldest Muslim and Arab population in the United States.[94] I visited Detroit in 2004 and was impressed by the Arab setting of Dearborn. For example, the names of some shops and medical centres were written in Arabic, which reminded me of my stay in the Middle East. So I was keen to obtain the views of young Muslims of this state and find out how they defined their identity or sense of belonging.

Recruitment techniques

I applied various techniques to gather participants for this study. First, I addressed large Muslim audiences at events such as *Ramadan*/fasting (*iftar*) in different venues, and explained to them the nature of my project. I told them that I was looking for participants for this study. Secondly, I contacted various principals of Islamic and public and charter schools, colleges and university coordinators, directors of youth centres, imams, and leaders of Muslim organi-sations through telephone calls and emails. I explained to them the nature of my study. If they showed interest in participating in the survey, I emailed them the relevant documents (recruitment/request letter, questionnaires, parents' and students' information sheets, and consent forms). Finally, at some insti-tutions I made PowerPoint presentations about my previous study, *Muslims in Australia*, hoping that the potential participants would respect me as a

researcher and want to support my study of the identi[ty of] Muslims. Many audience members later told me tha[t they] know about the presence and contribution of Muslims [...] said that they had not known that there were any Mus[lims ...]

Approach

Participation in this study was voluntary. All the you[ng ...] fifteen to seventeen) submitted their parents' signed co[nsent and] their own consent forms. In most cases, they wanted t[o ...] study and how the information would be used. Whe[n ...] to write a book (but that they would remain anony[mous ...] became more interested in being interviewed. I also t[old them] be my third book, the previous two books having bee[n about] Australia and Britain. Participants who were eighteen [...] signed consent forms and voluntarily participated in [...] pants commented, 'You are doing it for a good caus[e ...] minors) desired that their names be mentioned in m[y book ...] them that for ethical reasons I had to maintain conf[identiality and use] fictitious names.

As an insider (which I have discussed in the In[troduction ...] I felt privileged to be conducting this research an[d ...] various Muslim communities. My affiliation with Ha[rvard was] respected by the participants of this study. As an out[sider ...] to overlook my bias and be objective about the issu[es ...] In this study (and my previous research) I was min[dful of] integration, following Ali Kettani's observation in a[...] entail immigrants abandoning their identities. I beli[eve ...] retain their ethnic and religious identity while ad[opting the host] society's culture.[95] To sum up, my role as researc[her ...] one hand, as a Muslim studying Muslims I was an [insider ...] my theoretical and critical interest as a researcher p[...]

Why target young particip[ants]

I decided to study the identity of young Muslims (f[or ...] three reasons. First, this age group is growing up [...] ferent from that of previous generations. Secondly, [...] generation Muslims whose identity is wavering. T[hey ...] diaspora and the host country setting. The first-[generation ...] have desired that one day they would return 'hom[e' ...] I thought it would be fascinating to examine the vi[ews ...] about their 'identity and belonging'. Finally, from [...]

- how they felt as an American and as an American Muslim
- what it meant to be 'American' and 'un-American'
- whether all Americans should exercise their right to vote
- whether they would be interested in exercising their voting rights when they turned eighteen
- their opinion of President Barack Hussein Obama
- whether his rise as the first black American president inspired them
- what they thought of the American media
- whether the 9/11 tragedy had impacted on them
- what Muslims should do to achieve social cohesion.

For the participants aged eighteen and over, there were additional questions on voting, Islamic parties, views on *shariah* law, Muslim dress code in workplaces, Muslims' reaction to the cartoon of Prophet Muhammad (PBUH) cartoon first printed in Denmark, and their views on anti-terrorism laws, the US justice system, the economic system, American banks, US presidents, the US Congress, the US police and the US military. And for the Muslim leaders and other Muslim Americans (aged thirty and over), there were further specific questions on the overall Muslim settlement in America, their own migration story, whether they had noticed any changes in the Muslim community and the wider society, whether young Muslims' issues were being addressed in education, sport and employment, and whether there was enough dialogue between young people and Muslim leaders. I did not have any specific question on Palestine. During the discussions on identity and belonging, the media and President Obama, the 'Palestinian question' was brought up by some participants, of both Palestinian and non-Palestinian background.

Total number of participants

The number of interviews conducted in Massachusetts, New York, Virginia, Maryland, Florida and Michigan totalled 379. The numbers of institutions that participated in this study are as follows: schools: twelve, youth organisations: four, Muslim organisations: six; mosques: six. Details of the participants are shown in the four tables below.

Table 1.1 shows that participants aged fifteen to thirty constituted 89 per cent of the total: 76 per cent students and 13 per cent non-students. Participants over thirty made up the remaining 11 per cent. Table 1.2 shows a further subdivision of Table 1.1. The 'young adults – students' category comprises participants attending high school, college and university. The non-student category covers those who are not studying: leaders of Muslim organisations, imams, social workers, youth workers, other working people (employed and self-employed), homemakers and those looking for a job.

The religious affiliations of the interviewees were as follows: Sunni: 358,

Table 1.1 Participants by state and gender

State	Male (15–30)	Female (15–30)	Male (over 30)	Female (over 30)	Total
Massachusetts	13	11	8	4	36
New York	28	46	2	4	80
Virginia	7	16	0	3	26
Maryland	15	15	0	5	35
Florida	45	44	6	1	96
Michigan	38	60	5	3	106
Total	146	192	21	20	379

Table 1.2 Participants by age and gender

	Youths[a]	Young adults[b] – students	Young adults[b] – non-students	Adults[c] – students	Adults[c] – non-students	Total
Male	74	52	20	0	21	167
Female	114	50	28	1	19	212
Total	188	102	48	1	40	379

[a] 15–17 years old
[b] 18–30 years old
[c] Over 30 years old

Shia: 18, NOI: 3. These groups are defined in Chapter 2. The ethnic composition of the interviewees is shown in Table 1.3.

It should be noted that a few participants had hyphenated backgrounds, such as Palestinian-Russian, Pakistani-Indian, Lebanese-Italian, Lebanese-Ecuadorian, Turkish-Cuban, Egyptian-Filipino and French-Moroccan.

All 379 interviewees participated voluntarily, knowing that the study was about Muslim identity. I respected their identity as 'Muslims' and did not delve into their degree of religious practice. Many respondents were visibly Muslim, particularly those women who wore the *hijab* (even in state schools and colleges).

Fieldwork challenges

In order to obtain a representative sampling I had to persist at networking and establishing trust. Sometimes it was frustrating. For example, in Virginia I found an unusual calm in one of the youth centres. The timing of my visit in that state was not the best: it coincided with the arrest of the alleged terrorists the Virginia Five, five Muslim men from Virginia arrested in Pakistan on 9 December 2009.[99] People may have had doubts about the aim of my research. The sample numbers in Virginia (Table 1.1) reveal that I had less success in recruiting participants in that state. In another state, I was asked by a school

Table 1.3 List of ethnic backgrounds by state

Massachusetts (36 participants)	New York (80)	Virginia (26)	Maryland (35)	Florida (96)	Michigan (106)
Afghan	African American	Afghan	Afghan	Afghan	African American
African American	American (convert)	African American	African American	African American	Algerian
Algerian	Bangladeshi	Algerian	American (convert)	Albanian	Bangladeshi
American (convert)	Cuban	Bangladeshi	Bangladeshi	Algerian	Colombian
Bangladeshi	Egyptian	Indian	Egyptian	American (convert)	Egyptian
Egyptian	Fijian	Pakistani	Ethiopian	Bangladeshi	Iraqi
Indian	Guyanese	Puerto Rican	Indian	Burmese	Ivorian
Iranian	Indian		Kashmiri (Indian)	Cuban	Jordanian
Jordanian	Indonesian		Pakistani	Ecuadorean	Kurdish
Lebanese	Jamaican		Somali	Egyptian	Lebanese
Moroccan	Moroccan		Sri Lankan	Filipino	Libyan
Pakistani	Pakistani		Sudanese	Guatemalan	Pakistani
Palestinian	Palestinian		Syrian	Guyanese	Palestinian
Somali	Sudanese			Haitian	Somali
Sudanese	Tanzanian			Indian	South African
Uzbek	Turkish			Iranian	Sri Lankan
	Ugandan			Iraqi	Syrian
	West African (Guinea)			Jordanian	Tunisian
	Yemeni			Kashmiri (Indian)	West African
				Kurdish	Yemeni
				Lebanese	
				Mexican	
				Pakistani	
				Palestinian	
				Sierra Leonean	
				Somali	
				Syrian	
				Trinidadian	
				Tunisian	
				Turkish	

Table 1.4 Participants by ethnic background

Ethnic background	Number of participants
Pakistani	58
Palestinian	53
Bangladeshi	52
Egyptian	38
Yemeni	20
African American	19
Indian	12
Somali	12
Afghan	10
Guyanese	10
Lebanese	8
Syrian	7
Trinidadian	7
Other	73

superintendent what benefit the school board would receive from my research. I told the superintendent that if she wished I would give her a summary of my findings which would help them to evaluate the diversity in their schools. The superintendent declined my request, saying that they did not have any issues because Muslims and Arabs have been living in that region for a long time. Finally, in a different state, the Department of Education declined my application/request by saying that their public schools do not engage with any research based on religion. Their letter read: 'The . . . district has decided not to participate in your research proposal . . . 'An Understanding of the Identity of Muslim Youths and Young Adults in the United States of America'. The district does not collect information on student religious beliefs.[100]

However, most of the educational institutions that participated in this study acknowledged that this was an important inquiry, and such research would enhance the participants' self-esteem because they were acquiring skills in speaking to a person outside their comfort zone (educational institutions).

Notes

1. See also Jane I. Smith, *Islam in America*, 2nd edn (New York: Columbia University Press, 2010), pp. 8–22.
2. Seyyed Hossein Nasr, *The Heart of Islam: Enduring Values for Humanity* (San Francisco: HarperSanFrancisco, 2002), p. 65.
3. Amir Nashid Ali Muhammad, *Muslims in America: Seven Centuries of History 1312–2000*, 2nd edn (Beltsville, MD: Amana, 2001) pp. 9, 15.
4. Ibid., p. 17.

5. Gulam M. Haniff, 'The Muslim Community in America: A Brief Profile', *Journal of Muslim Minority Affairs* 23:2 (2003), pp. 303–11, see pp. 303–4.

6. *Arab Americans: An Integral Part of American Society* (Dearborn, MI: Arab American National Museum, 2009), p. 16; Abdus Sattar Ghazali, 'The number of mosque attendants increasing rapidly in America', American Muslim Perspective website, 4 August 2001, http://www.amp.ghazali.net/html/mosques_in_us.html, accessed 14 May 2012.

7. Haniff, 'The Muslim Community in America', pp. 303–4.

8. Ibid., pp. 307, 310.

9 *Muslim Americans: No Signs of Growth in Alienation or Support for Extremism* (Washington, DC: Pew Research Center, 2011), p. 20, http://www.people-press.org/files/legacy-pdf/Muslim-American-Report.pdf, accessed 15 May 2012.

10. According to the US Census Bureau, the total resident population of the United States on 2 September 2011 was 312,119,344: http://www.census.gov/population/www/popclockus.html, accessed 2 September 2011.

11. *Muslim Americans*, p. 16.

12. Ibid., p. 13.

13. Muhammad, *Muslims in America*, pp. 75–81.

14. Ibid., pp. 75–81.

15. See Nahid Afrose Kabir, *Muslims in Australia: Immigration, Race Relations and Cultural History* (London: Routledge, 2005), p. 157.

16. Paul M. Barrett, *American Islam: The Struggle for the Soul of a Religion* (New York: Farrar, Straus and Giroux, 2007), p. 6.

17. Rashid Ahmed, *Taliban: The Story of the Afghan Warlords* (London: Pan, 2001), p. 94.

18. M. Ruthven, *Fundamentalism: The Search for Meaning* (Oxford and New York: Oxford University Press), pp. 110–11, 121.

19. 'They, who are with sin, are stoned . . . Two adulterers die under Taliban law,' *Houston Chronicle*, 3 November 1996, p. 28. See also Nahid Afrose Kabir, *Young British Muslims: Identity, Culture, Politics and the Media* (Edinburgh: Edinburgh University Press, 2010), pp. 180–3.

20. Yvonne Kinsella, 'Outrage at Amina's plight', *Daily Mirror*, 6 August 2004, p. 5.

21. 'Iran "stoning woman" to get 99 lashes', SBS World News Australia website, http://www.sbs.com.au/news/article/1345357/Iran-stoning-woman-to-get-99-lashes, accessed 14 May 2012.

22. 'Nine executed in Iran under Sharia law', *Irish Times*, 2 August 2007, p. 11.

23. 'Ahmadinejad says Israel–Palestinian peace talks "doomed"', *World News Australia*, SBS One, 4 September 2010, 6.30 p.m.

24. Neil Macfarquhar, 'Iranians chant "Death to America"', *The Spectator* (Hamilton, ON), 12 February 2002, p. D05.

25. Reuters, 'Haj pilgrims denounce Israel and U.S.', 22 February 2002.

26. M. A. Muqtedar Khan, 'Constructing the American Muslim Community', in Yvonne Haddad, Jane Smith and John L. Esposito (eds), *Religion and*

Immigration: Christian, Jewish, and Muslim experiences in the United States (Walnut Creek, CA: Altamira Press, 2003), pp. 175–98.

27. Christopher Dickey, 'A thousand points of hate', *Newsweek*, 1 January 2010, pp. 34–6; see also 'From Pakistan to the world,' *Time*, 17 May 2010, pp. 18–19.

28. 'From Pakistan to the world'.

29. Waqar Gillani and Sabrina Tavernise, 'Pakistan sentences five Americans in terror case', *New York Times* website, 24 June 2010, http://www.nytimes.com/2010/06/25/world/asia/25pstan.html, accessed 14 May 2012.

30. 'From Pakistan to the world'.

31. David Schanzer, Charles Kurzman and Ebrahim Moosa, *Anti-Terror Lessons of Muslim-Americans* (Durham, NC: Duke University/University of North Carolina at Chapel Hill, 2010), http://fds.duke.edu/db/attachment/1255, accessed 14 May 2012.

32. Tony Gaskew, *Policing American Muslim Communities: A Compendium of Post 9/11 Interviews* (Lewiston, NY: Edwin Mellen Press, 2008), pp. 151–72. See also Detroit Arab American Study Team, *Citizenship and Crisis: Arab Detroit after 9/11* (New York: Russell Sage Foundation, 2009).

33. Smith, *Islam in America*, pp. 187–8.

34. John L. Esposito, *The Future of Islam* (New York: Oxford University Press, 2010), p. 163; see also Louise Cainkar, *Homeland Insecurity: The Arab American and Muslim American Experience after 9/11* (New York: Russell Sage Foundation, 2011), p. 128.

35. Smith, *Islam in America*, p. 186.

36. Talat Hamdani and Adele Welty, 'The case for a mosque a near Ground Zero', *New York Daily News*, 13 May 2010, p. 22.

37. Laurie Goodstein, 'In US, echoes of rift of Muslims and Jews', *New York Times*, 12 September 2001, p. 12.

38. Laurie Goodstein and Gustav Niebuhr, 'Attacks and harassment of Arab Americans increase', *New York Times*, 14 September 2001, p. 14; Matthew Purdy, 'For Arab-Americans, flag-flying and fear', *New York Times*, 14 September 2001, p. 14.

39. 'In their words: proud Sikh can't forget the backlash', *Seattle Post-Intelligencer*, 11 September 2002, p. A13.

40. Goodstein and Niebuhr, 'Attacks and harassment of Arab Americans increase'.

41. Smith, *Islam in America*, pp. 188–9.

42. Ibid.

43. Ibid.

44. Howard Kurtz, 'Clonaid, generating at least one kind of copy', *Washington Post*, 6 January 2003, p. C01.

45. Mark Steel, 'Tea Party jihad against Muslims', *Muslim Observer* website, 2 September 2010, http://muslimmedianetwork.com/mmn/?p=6789, accessed 14 May 2012.

46. 'Obama under fire over Ground Zero mosque', SBS World News website, 16

August 2010, http://www.sbs.com.au/news/article/1328302/Obama-under-fire-over-Ground-Zero-mosque, accessed 14 May 2012.

47. 'Obama defends Ground Zero mosque', *SBS World News Australia* website, 15 August 2010, http://www.sbs.com.au/news/article/1327712/Obama-defends-Ground-Zero-mosque, accessed 14 May 2012.

48. 'Obama under fire over Ground Zero mosque'.

49. Malik Miah, 'United States: behind anti-Muslim hysteria', *Green Left*, 5 September 2010.

50. 'Obama defends Ground Zero mosque'.

51. Ibid.

52 'Muslim community center in Lower Manhattan (Park51)', *New York Times* website, 30 March 2011, http://topics.nytimes.com/top/reference/timestopics/organizations/p/park51/index.html, accessed 14 May 2012.

53. See Esposito, *The Future of Islam*, p. 30.

54 Mehdi Hasan, 'Fear and loathing in Manhattan', *New Statesman*, 1 November 2010, p. 22.

55. 'Muslim community center in Lower Manhattan (Park51)'.

56. 'Obama under fire over Ground Zero mosque'.

57. 'Obama defends Ground Zero mosque'.

58. Steel, 'Tea Party jihad against Muslims'.

59. 'Pastor's rant vs. mosque. plans "9-11 Christian center"', *New York Daily News*, 3 September 2010, p. 12.

60. Lukas I. Alpert, 'Bill Keller, Muslim-hating pastor, wants to build Christian center to rival "Ground Zero mosque"', *New York Daily News* website, 5 September 2010, http://articles.nydailynews.com/2010-09-05/local/27074615_1_mosque-christian-center-ground-zero, accessed 14 May 2012.

61. 'US church vows Koran burning will go on', *West Australian*, 8 September 2010.

62. Jeffrey T. Kuhner, 'Ban Koran-burning? If Islam becomes a protected faith, free expression will be no more', *Washington Times*, 8 April 2011, p. B01.

63. James Bone, 'American dream is shattered, says Muslim attacked by a knifeman', *The Times*, 27 August 2010, p. 1.

64. Bobby Ghosh, 'Islam in America', *Time*, 30 August 2010, pp. 16–22, see p. 17.

65. Ibid., p. 19.

66. Ibid.

67. *Islam and Switzerland: The Return of the Nativists*, Economist Intelligence Unit, 11 December 2009, p. 11.

68. Steven Erlanger and Maïa de la Baume, 'French panel debates secularism and Islam', *New York Times*, 6 April 2011, p. 9.

69. 'Report: few U.S. Muslims radical', *Herald Sun* (Melbourne), 7 January 2010.

70. Richard Kiely, Frank Bechhofer, Robert Stewart and David McCrone, 'The markers and rules of Scottish identity', *Sociological Review* 49:1 (2001), pp. 33–55, at p. 36.

71. Fiona M. Douglas, *Scottish Newspapers, Language and Identity* (Edinburgh: Edinburgh University Press, 2009), p. 11.
72. Ibid., p. 19.
73. Richard Jenkins, *Social Identity*, 3rd edn (London: Routledge, 2008), p. 18.
74. Ibid. p. 41.
75. Paul Gilroy, 'Diaspora and the Detours of Identity', in Kathryn Woodward (ed.), *Identity and Difference* (London: Sage, 1997), pp. 299–343, see pp. 301–2; see also Jenkins, *Social Identity*, p. 21.
76. Peter J. Burke and Jan E. Stets, *Identity Theory* (Oxford: Oxford University Press, 2009), p. 127.
77. Shahnaz's view came from a purely religious perspective and she interpreted the Quranic verses on covering the head. However, whether Muslim women's *hijab* is a religious requirement or a cultural identity has been a debatable issue. Some scholars observe that it is more cultural than religious. They argue that the Quran emphasises modesty. They say that veiling was prevalent in pre-Islamic times during the Byzantine era; later it was viewed as an appropriate expression of the Quran. In the colonial period, the Muslim women's veil became a symbol of resistance, particularly in Egypt, and over the years the veil has become a symbol of Islamic self-assertion and a rejection of western cultural hegemony. See for example, Leila Ahmed, *Women and Gender in Islam: Historical Roots of a Modern Debate* (New Haven, CT: Yale University Press, 1992); Jonathan Bloom and Sheila Blair, *Islam: A Thousand Years of Faith and Power* (New Haven, CT: Yale University Press, 2001); John L. Esposito (ed.), *The Oxford Dictionary of Islam* (New York: Oxford University Press, 2003); Randa Abdel-Fattah, *Does My Head Look Big in This?* (Sydney: Pan Macmillan Australia, 2005); Karen Armstrong, 'My years in a habit taught me the paradox of veiling', *Guardian* website, 26 October 2006, http://www.guardian.co.uk/commentisfree/2006/oct/26/comment.politics1, accessed 15 May 2012.
78. Stuart Hall, 'Introduction: Who Needs "Identity"?', in Stuart Hall and Paul du Gay (eds), *Questions of Cultural Identity* (London: Sage, 1996), pp. 4–5.
79. Ibid. See also Steph Lawler, *Identity: Sociological Perspectives* (Cambridge: Polity Press, 2008), p. 3.
80. Stuart Hall, 'The Question of Cultural Identity', in *The Polity Reader in Cultural Theory* (Cambridge: Polity Press, 1994), p. 122.
81. Burke and Stets, *Identity Theory*, pp. 160–1.
82. Ibid. See also Sheldon Stryker, 'Integrating Emotion into Identity Theory', *Advances in Group Processes* 21 (2004), pp. 1–23.
83. Henri Tajfel (ed.), *Human Groups and Social Categories: Studies in Social Psychology* (Cambridge: Cambridge University Press, 1981); Henri Tajfel and John C. Turner, 'The Social Identity Theory of Intergroup Behaviour', in Stephen Worchel and William G. Austin (eds), *Psychology of Intergroup Relations*, 2nd edn (Chicago: Nelson-Hall 1986), pp. 7–24.
84. Kabir, *Young British Muslims*.

85. Jenkins, *Social Identity*, pp. 112–13.
86. Lawler, *Identity*, p. 3.
87. Ibid. pp. 143–4.
88. 'Islamo-fascism Awareness Week', Terrorism Awareness Project website, http://www.terrorismawareness.org/islamo-fascism-awareness-week/, accessed 15 May 2012.
89. Avtar Brah, 'Non-binarized Identities of Similarity and Difference', in Margaret Wetherell, Michelynn Laflèche and Robert Berkeley (eds), *Identity, Ethnic Diversity and Community Cohesion* (London: Sage, 2007), pp. 136–45, at pp. 143–4.
90. Ibid., p. 144.
91. See Dilwar Hussain, 'Identity Formation and Change in British Muslim Communities', in Margaret Wetherell, Michelynn Laflèche and Robert Berkeley (eds), *Identity, Ethnic Diversity and Community Cohesion* (London: Sage, 2007), pp. 34–9; Tariq Modood, *Multiculturalism: A Civic Idea* (Cambridge: Polity Press, 2007); S. Sayyid and AbdoolKarim Vakil (eds), *Thinking through Islamophobia: Global Perspectives* (London: Hurst, 2010).
92. *Muslim Americans*, pp. 11, 34.
93. Nahid A. Kabir, 'Why I Call Australia "Home"? A Transmigrant's Perspective', *M/C Journal* 10:4 (2007); Kabir, *Young British Muslims*.
94. Sally Howell and Amaney Jamal, 'The Aftermath of the 9/11 Attacks', in Detroit Arab American Study Team, *Citizenship and Crisis: Arab Detroit after 9/11* (New York: Russell Sage Foundation, 2009), pp. 69–100; see p. 72.
95. Ali M. Kettani, *Muslim Minorities in the World Today* (London: Mansell, 1986).
96. 'From Pakistan to the world', pp. 19–21.
97. Barney G. Glaser and Anselm L. Strauss, *The Discovery of Grounded Theory: Strategies for Qualitative Research* (Chicago: Aldine, 1967).
98. Kathy Charmaz, *Constructing Grounded Theory: A Practical Guide through Qualitative Analysis* (London: Sage, 2006).
99. Brigid Schulte, '5 Virginia men facing terrorism charges in Pakistan write of "noble" motivation', *Washington Post*, 16 May 2010, p. 12.
100. Letter dated 4 January 2010.

CHAPTER

2

THE CULTURE DEBATE

Identity is always 'in process', always 'being formed'. It is 'dynamic and fluid as individuals continuously relate to institutions, communities and other individuals'.[1] David Matsumoto and Linda Juang argued that cultural and personal identity are shaped to a large extent by our culture and the environment in which we live.[2] As we grow up our cultural setting tends to mould our sense of self in ways that 'make sense' within that cultural setting. It follows that different cultures produce different self-concepts in their members, and in turn these different concepts influence all other aspects of individual behaviour. Even what people actually mean and understand as the 'self' differs dramatically from one culture to another. Sometimes, while living within one's cultural environment (family and ethnic and religious community settings), people can be influenced by another culture (the wider society's schools, workplaces and institutions) depending on their geographical location and circumstances.

In a diaspora setting, the children of first-generation Muslims (like many other immigrants) go through enculturation and acculturation processes. Enculturation generally refers to the process by which individuals learn and adopt the ways and manners of their respective cultures.[3] Matsumoto and Juang stated that enculturation is related to ethnic identity development, whereas acculturation entails adopting a second culture.[4] In other words, enculturation is first-culture learning and acculturation is subsequent-culture learning. In this context, first-culture learning involves acquiring one's mother tongue, and adopting traditional dress, food, music and dance, and religion. The religion of Muslim youths is denoted by their names, eating and drinking habits, and adherence to religious rituals. Matsumoto and Juang observed that enculturation (into one's ethnic culture) occurs through parenting styles, child-rearing practices, peer groups, day care, the education system and religious institutions. Acculturation occurs through involvement in the external environment.[5] For example, youths acquire education, English-language skills, and knowledge of music and sport from their participation in the wider society.

Some scholars have noted that in the processes of enculturation and acculturation two fundamentally different senses of self can impact on one's identity. For example, on the one hand, there may be a non-western understanding of self that is 'collectivistic', and on the other hand, there could be a western understanding of self that is 'individualistic'.[6] In the non-western 'collectivistic' context, the individual is viewed as inherently connected to and interdependent on others; for example, individuals will respect their family's decision rather than be adamant about their own choices. This 'collectivistic self' of young Muslims is revealed later in the chapter in the discussion of women and Muslim youth. In the 'individualistic' context, a person is the sole maker of his or her destiny. That said, it is important to recognise that these cultural models are only tendencies, and it is entirely possible for an individual to embrace both an individualistic and a collectivistic stance as precursors to acquiring bicultural skills.

Studies by Alberto Melucci and Gary Gregg demonstrate that bicultural individuals can shift identities between the cultural frames of both ingroups and outgroups with relative ease.[7] That is, a bicultural identity caters for emotional tensions and creates a sense of adaptability.[8] Melucci observed that a (bicultural) identity of self becomes a dynamic system defined by recognisable opportunities and constraints.[9] Identity is both a system and a process, because the field is defined by recognisable opportunities and is simultaneously able to intervene to act upon and restructure itself. Two crucial and perplexing questions arise here: the continuity of the self and the boundaries of the self. The question is one of deciding where the subject of action begins and where it ends and how a person is likely to adapt to a new culture. For example, a Muslim may socialise with his non-Muslim colleagues at his workplace, drink tea with them but refrain from drinking alcohol (which is forbidden in Islam). Melucci noted that an individual's (bicultural) identity floats within the primary bonds of belonging, like kinship or local and geographical ties (family, community, country of origin and place of residence).[10] In other words, bicultural identity is flexible and may move through both independent and interdependent collective stances, which is again possible when an individual has a firm grip in both cultures through education, sport, and dialogue and communication.

In this chapter I briefly examine the religious, economic and social settings of young Muslims in America. Firstly, I discuss the different ideologies within the Islamic community, including the placement of minorities within the Muslim majority group such as Shi'ite and Sunni relations in America. Secondly, I examine the economic placement of the participants of this study. Thirdly, I examine women's place within the Muslim community. Fourthly, I evaluate the male youths'/young adults' social issues within the broader

Islamic community. Finally, I discuss the implications of homeschooling in the youths' upbringing.

Islam in America

The religious affiliations of the 379 interviewees were: Sunni: 358, Shia: 18, Nation of Islam (NOI): 3. The two branches of Islam, Sunni and Shi'ism, are explained below. Some Sunni and Shia Muslims consider the NOI to be an offshoot of Islam, but I will attempt to explain the NOI's place in the broader Islamic community.

The word *Sunni* in Arabic comes from the term *ahl al-sunnah wa'l-jama'ah*, 'people who followed the teachings of Prophet Muhammad (PBUH)' and worldwide they are in the majority. Shi'ism comes from the Arabic term *shi'at 'Ali*, meaning 'partisans of Prophet Ali', ibn Abi Talib, son-in-law and cousin of Prophet Muhammad (PBUH). The major point of contention between Sunnism and Shi'ism is who succeeded the Prophet Muhammad (PBUH) as the 'rightly guided' caliph of Islam.[11] After the death of Prophet Muhammad (PBUH), while Ali and other family members were burying him, the rest of the Muslim community gathered in Medina and chose Abu Bakr as the Prophet's successor, not in his prophetic function but as ruler of the newly established Islamic community. He was thereby given the title of *khalifah rasul Allah*, or the vice-regent or the Messenger of God, from which comes the title 'caliph'. A number of people thought that Ali should have become Prophet Muhammad's successor and rallied around him, forming the first nucleus of Shi'ism (or Shi'ites). Ali himself refused to oppose Abu Bakr and in fact worked closely with him and his two successors, Umar and Uthman, until he himself became the fourth of the 'rightly guided' caliphs of Sunni Islam.[12]

The followers of Sunnism are divided into four schools of law (*fiqh*, or jurisprudence): Hanafi, Maliki, Shafi'i and Hanbali. Today the Hanafi school has the largest number of followers in the Sunni world. Malikism is based mostly on the practice of Medina and is very conservative in its approach to the *fiqh*. The Shafi'i school is followed by some Arabs, particularly the Egyptians. The Hanbali School adheres to a very strict interpretation of the *shariah* code. Wahhabism and Salafism, which are dominant in Saudi Arabia, are really offshoots of Hanbalism. Both Wahhabism and Salafism are very much opposed by the vast majority of Sunnis and also by Shi'ites.[13]

In contrast to the traditionalist branches of Islam, the Wahhabis and Salafis reject the importance of juridical schools and advocate a direct relation to the revealed text of the Quran. The puritanical Salafi line of thought prevails in the Arabian peninsula and also in Syria, Jordan and Egypt. The main difference between Salafi and Wahhabi ideology is the difference in audience. That is, some Muslims prefer the term 'Salafi' while some prefer 'Wahhabi', but in reality their adherents follow the same puritanical ideology.[14] Also the Salafis hold certain opinions on the issue of visiting graves. They believe that Prophet Muhammad (PBUH) encouraged his companions to visit graveyards, because it is something that can remind Muslims of death and make them think about preparing for it by doing good deeds. The Salafis believe that Prophet Muhammad (PBUH) gave stern warnings about not falling into excess in this regard, because the end result is to associate dead persons with Allah and that negates one's Islam.[15] The Wahhabis and Salafis denounce the celebration of *Eid-e-Milad-un Nabi* (the birthday of Prophet Muhammad (PBUH)) and Sufism.

Sufism is a mystical movement that preaches tolerance and recognition of the commonality between all religions through poetry, lyrics, music, songs and chanting of different kinds and in many dialects. The Sufi sect allows an individual to join or leave a group at will, sometimes even without the requirement to be a Muslim.[16] Most Sufis belong to the Hanafi school of law and, of course, Sufism differs from the conservative Wahhabi and Salafi ideologies. Sufi Muslims believe that by nature Islam is a religion open to people of every race. The Sufi saint Bayazid al-Bistami said, 'Sufis, in general, seek God's mercy for everyone, not solely Muslims.'[17]

The other major branch of Islam, Shi'ism, follows all the four Sunni schools of law, together with one additional school called the Ja'fari.[18] The difference between the Sunni School of Law and the Ja'fari is minor, especially when it comes to the practice of rites (the five pillars of Islam). In certain fields, such as the laws of inheritance or the legality of temporary marriage, there are, however, notable differences.[19] The Shi'ites believe that the Wahhabi, Salafi and Tablighi movements emerged from the Sunni school.[20] The Tablighi Jamaat, initiated in the Indian subcontinent, claims to be a peaceful and apolitical revivalist movement that promotes Islamic consciousness among Muslims.[21]

In America Shi'ites form a minority within the broader Islamic community; however, they constitute a higher proportion than the 13 per cent they represent worldwide: it is estimated that 20 per cent of American Muslims are Shi'ites.[22] In this study, out of 379 participants, only eighteen (about 5 per cent) were Shi'ites. Some Shi'ites feel that they are discriminated against by Sunnis. For example, in 1999 Frankie Cancel, a Hispanic convert to Shi'ism, complained that the Sunni chaplain at Fishkill correctional centre in New York insulted Shi'ites on a regular basis, and that the Islamic services provided within the facility were only affiliated to Sunnism.[23]

After the US invasion of Iraq in 2003, the sectarian clashes in Iraq had repercussions in America. In 2006 during the *Muharram* procession through the streets of Manhattan, Shi'ites were confronted by some Sunni protestors who denounced the ritual and distributed fliers condemning the Shi'ites as heretics and unbelievers. For several years, Shi'ites had marched through the streets of Manhattan in the month of *Muharram* using self-flagellation and chest beating as part of their ritual, so it was not something new on the streets.

Also, in 2006, after the execution of the former Iraqi Sunni ruler Saddam Hussein, three mosques and some Shi'ite businesses in Dearborn were vandalised. Sunni Muslims in Dearborn were alleged to have carried out the attacks, though no one was arrested.[24] In my study in 2010 a Shi'a leader in Florida expressed his concerns that their institutions were vulnerable to Wahhabi attacks (interview, May 2010).[25]

In this study three interviewees affiliated their beliefs with the NOI. The NOI has been controversial since its inception. Its initial leaders (for example Elijah Muhammad) placed emphasis on black superiority and separatism. They believed that mainstream (white) Americans were responsible for the destitute conditions of the black people.[26] But mainstream Muslims (Sunnis and Shi'as alike) believe that all people are equal before Allah. The NOI teaching that 'whites' have descended from the 'devil'[27] contradicts the Muslim concept of egalitarianism. The late NOI leader Malcolm X was opposed to integration with 'white' Americans until he performed his *hajj* in 1964. At the *hajj*, Malcolm X realised that people of all races can perform the pilgrimage without any racial bias, departed from his separatist ideology and thereafter preached equality. His son Wallace Muhammad also encouraged the belief that 'whites' should be considered fully human and even encouraged them to become members of the NOI.[28]

When I was writing this book, Louis Farrakhan was the leader of NOI. Farrakhan generally followed the black separatist ideology of Elijah Muhammad. During my fieldwork, I visited a NOI mosque and found that it was not open to 'white' people. The minister of the mosque, Brother Ahmet, explained that their mosque served as a healing clinic for black youth who had been persecuted by 'whites', so they wanted to avoid the painful reminder of oppression (interview, New York, January 2010). Brother Ahmet shared his life story and involvement with the NOI:

> My childhood as a young black man growing up in America was very similar to what we see today. Born to a young mother, and no father around, and born into poverty.
>
> Yes, I was surrounded by crimes, drugs, you name it. The same scenario that many of our young men live today. I was labelled a problem child in school. But many of the problems I had in school came because of the problems I had at home. By the time I was twelve years of age, I was kicked out of the school . . .
>
> Sports were definitely a great part of my life. I also found out that I had speaking skills and began to get involved in drama and other things of that nature. But it wasn't until [then] I had an opportunity to discover gifts, skills, talents and abilities. But the Nation [of Islam] really pulled the complete cover off of gifts, skills, talents and abilities for me.

Brother Ahmet said that with the help of the NOI he later managed to complete his education. Jane Smith observed that Louis Farrakhan's NOI was controversial but it has provided important social and community services to the marginalised community, particularly to black and Hispanic youths. The US government also supports its drugs and AIDs programs.[29]

The economic position of Muslims

In my previous studies on Muslims in Australia and the UK, I was able to evaluate their labour market status from official census data. But in the United States official census data on the basis of religion is not available. So for this section I had to seek other sources to gauge the economic position of Muslims in America. Later, I evaluate the economic status of the participants of this study.

Jamillah Karim discussed the class disparities among different ethnic and racial groups in the USA. She observed that of all the ethnic and racial groups, African Americans have been the most disadvantaged. For example, in 2003, African Americans had the lowest median household income: $33,500, compared to Hispanics ($37,600), whites ($52,000) and Asians ($64,000).[30] Anna Bowers observed that the majority of Muslim converts in America, both in the United States overall and in its prisons, are African Americans. Nationally, 49 per cent of prison inmates are African American, compared to 13 per cent of the overall population.[31] The high percentage of African Americans in prison can be attributed to poverty, lack of education and the institutional racism associated with the war on drugs.[32]

In 2009, a Gallup poll found that the economic disparity among Muslims reflected racial income differences in the country. For example, while 44 per cent of Muslim Asian Americans had a monthly household income of $5,000 or more, only 17 per cent of Muslim African Americans reported such an income.[33] The poll also found that young adult Muslims (aged 18–29) make up a far larger percentage (36 per cent) of their religious group than their counterparts in the general population (18 per cent), but Muslim Americans in that age group were particularly discontented with both their jobs and their communities.

In 2011, the Pew Research Center's survey found that about 26 per cent of American Muslims were college graduates compared to 28 per cent of the total population, and about 14 per cent of American Muslims were school dropouts compared to 13 per cent of the total population. However, Muslims born in America were more likely than the total population to have graduated from high schools. About 26 per cent of American Muslims were still enrolled in colleges or universities compared to 13 per cent of the total population.[34]

In the labour market, the Pew Research Center's survey found that in 2011 about 41 per cent of American Muslims had full-time employment compared to 45 per cent of the total population. In addition to this about 18 per cent of US Muslims had part-time employment and about 20 per cent were self-employed or small business owners. Underemployment was, however, more common among Muslims compared to the total population. About 29 per cent were either unemployed or working part-time but preferring to have full-time employment, compared with 20 per cent of adults nationwide. Underemployment was particularly widespread among Muslim adults aged under thirty.[35]

In 2011, the annual household income of 14 per cent of American Muslims was $100,000 or more compared to 16 per cent of the total population; 40 per cent of American Muslims had annual household incomes of between $30,000 and $100,000 compared with 48 per cent of the total population; and 45 per cent of American Muslims had annual household incomes of less than $30,000 compared to 36 per cent of the total population.[36] The Pew Research Center observed that the average annual income of Muslim Americans had declined since its last survey in 2007, when the proportion of Muslim Americans (35 per cent) and the total population (33 per cent) earning under $30,000 was similar. This decline indicated that Muslims were intensely affected by the 'bursting of the housing market bubble in 2006 and the recession that followed from late 2007 to mid-2009'.[37] In the next section I examine the economic placement of the participants of this study (see Table 2.1 and Table 2.2).

The employment statuses can be defined as follows:

- 'Employed, category 1' includes skilled/tertiary-educated people such as university academics, educators, physicians, pharmacists, engineers, teachers, researchers, lawyers and consultants.
- 'Employed, category 2' (mostly non-professionals)[38] includes religious leaders, community workers, imams, religious teachers in Sunday schools, clerical workers, administrative staff, child care workers, nurses, physical

Table 2.1 Employment status of students' parents (student age group: 15–30)

Employment status	Father	Mother
Employed, category 1	85	22
Employed, category 2	90	53
Self-employed	77	7
Unemployed	17	1
Incapacitated	5	0
Retired	1	1
Student	2	4
Homemakers/'stay-at-home mums'	0	200
Other	13	2
Total	290	290

Table 2.2 Employment status of 'non-student' participants (age group: 21 and over)

Employment status	Male	Female
Employed, category 1	23	26
Employed, category 2	10	13
Self-employed	7	2
Unemployed	0	0
Incapacitated	0	0
Retired	1	0
Student	0	1
Homemakers/'stay-at-home mums'	0	5
Other	0	1
Total	41	48

therapists, dental assistants, security officers, mechanics, salespeople, chefs, waiters, cab drivers, construction workers, factory workers, carpenters and handypeople. Some people in category 2 have overseas university degrees but these may not have been recognised in the USA.

- 'Self-employed' includes people engaged in small businesses, shopkeepers, petrol station owners, contractors, estate agents, and owners of big businesses such as construction companies.
- 'Unemployed' includes members of the labour force (15–64 years) not at work. In this category some people have been laid off from their previous jobs, or are looking for a job.
- 'Incapacitated' includes people who cannot work for health reasons.
- 'Retired' includes people over sixty-five.
- 'Student' includes mature students (aged over 30) studying in colleges or universities.
- 'Homemakers' is for housewives or, as the participants said their mothers were, 'stay-at-home mums'.
- 'Other' includes overseas students, single parents, step-parents, divorced people, the deceased and fathers working overseas.

Analysis

Table 2.1 shows the economic situation of the parents of 290 students. Out of 290 fathers, 252 (about 87 per cent, including 29 per cent professionals) were employed. Out of 290 mothers, eighty-two (28 per cent, including 8 per cent professionals) were employed. Seventeen fathers (6 per cent) were unemployed/looking for work, while only one mother was looking for work. Five fathers (2 per cent) could not work because of health issues. The number of stay-at-home mums was 200, which was about 70 per cent.

Table 2.2 shows the adult 'non-student' participant (over 21) workforce status. Out of forty-one adult male participants, forty (about 98 per cent, including 56 per cent professionals) were employed, and out of forty-eight female participants, forty-one (about 85 per cent) were employed. None of the participants in Table 2.2 were unemployed or looking for jobs. Only five women (about 10 per cent) were 'stay-at-home mums'. In 'employed, category 1', out of forty-nine participants only eighteen (twelve male, six female) held professional positions in the wider society, for example, in public schools, state government and the private sector. The majority (thirty-one participants, mostly educators) held positions in Islamic institutions. A few of them said that although they had higher university degrees (for example, PhDs) they had not been successful in securing relevant positions in mainstream American institutions. And all participants (with the exception of two administrative officers) in 'employed, category 2' held positions in Islamic institutions. Some participants in this category said that they had not been successful in secur-ing positions in mainstream American institutions (the women thought that perhaps this was because they wore the *hijab*).

However, both tables show a large number of stay-at-home mums (205 mostly first-generation women), which reveals that either educated mothers preferred to stay at home and look after their children, or mothers have insuf-ficient education or desire to pursue a career. In some cases, Muslim women are discouraged from taking an outside role by their husband or members of their extended family. I did not ask the participants about the qualifications of their parents, but one second-generation female participant, Aysegül (15, US born, of Turkish background), said that she wanted to pursue a career and pointed out that in her family women's higher education was not a priority:

> And I want, *insh'Allah*, I'm praying to God, I want to be a lawyer. I want to be the
> first educated girl in my family. 'Cos my cousins and everybody, they dropped out
> of high school, they all got married. There's not really anybody, you know, from my
> mom's side well educated. (Interview, New York, February 2010)

In this study, some second-generation young Muslims who were educated in America and looking for jobs said that they had difficulties finding work. Some anecdotes follow.

Difficulties in the job market

A female participant, Bushra (21, US-born student of Bangladeshi origin, national identity: Bangladeshi Muslim American), believed that her Islamic identity, revealed by her *hijab*, deprived her of employment:

Basically, I've been applying to a lot of jobs, especially after my father lost his job last fall. So I've been applying to a lot of fast food places so I could help with payments and bills with my parents. And a fast food shop called me back for an interview, and told me to go in to speak with one of the managers.

The manager just asked me general questions about myself . . . Then she asked me about my *hijab*, 'Do you have to wear that thing on your head?' I replied, 'My *hijab*, I do, I have to wear my *hijab* all the time.' And she said, 'Oh,' and she had a little weird look on her face. I asked her, 'Is that a problem?' And she said, 'You can't wear that on the job.' I said, 'Why?' She said, 'Our fast food shop has certain terms and policies that may prohibit that.' I asked her, 'What are these terms and policies?' She said, 'All employees are required to wear a uniform cap while they work.' I said, 'I have no problem with that. I can wear a cap on top of my *hijab*, that's perfectly fine.' (Interview, Michigan, May 2010)

Bushra said that she was told the manager would make her decision in the next couple of days. But Bushra heard nothing from the manager so she called a week later to find out about the job. Bushra found that the manager had decided to hire someone else, so she asked the manager, 'Was there something wrong with my interviewing, or social skills?' Then she asked, 'Did my head-scarf have anything to do with it?' The manager replied, 'No, it didn't.' Bushra then told the manager that she felt discriminated against and the manager apparently became very defensive. Bushra said:

Muslim women may be questioned for wearing a *hijab*, and that is not fair. That is not fair, because she may be an American citizen, born here. So that is invading her civil liberties and the First Amendment to her rights.

Another female participant, Zohra (30, Palestinian background, national iden-tity: Muslim American), who was born and raised in the United States, also believed that she was discriminated against for wearing a *hijab*. Zohra had a teaching degree from an American university but was not able to get a job. Zohra shared her viewpoint:

It's very prejudiced . . . I fight for jobs. I want a part-time job and it's very difficult to find a job with the *hijab*, to be honest. They say it's not the *hijab*, it's the qualifica-tions, but when you know somebody else was hired and they have only a high school degree when, well, you have three degrees, you say, 'Hey, you know, something's wrong here.' So there is a lot of prejudice. Even though people don't like to admit it, there is a lot of prejudice around. (Interview, New York, February 2010)

In Maryland I met a Muslim woman who said she wears a *hijab* at her work-place and this works positively in her work environment because her company has endorsed diversity. But this was an exception.

It is difficult to pin down why, in some cases, the *hijab* is still a marker of the 'other'. Sometimes, customer-related jobs do not approve any kind of dress other than their specified (western) dress code. Then when a Muslim employee decides to wear a *hijab* in the workplace, her male colleagues may perceive that she wants to remain different, so they are hesitant to interact with her. Differential treatment of the 'other' – based on dress – could be discrimination,[39] but it is just as likely to be a matter of social awkwardness.

It appears that some young Muslim men also face resistance in the US labour market. In 2010 a couple of final year engineering students, Ulfat and Dawood, expressed their concerns that there were no jobs for them in the United States. As Ulfat (US born of Guyanese background, national identity: 'Muslim only') said, 'Every year a lot of engineers are graduating but there are no jobs' (interview, Florida, March 2010). Dawood (26, overseas born of Lebanese origin, national identity: Lebanese) was also frustrated because of his unemployment: 'When I came to this country in 2006, there was a recession, so I didn't find a good job, a full-time job from the beginning till now' (interview, Michigan, May 2010). So he commenced postgraduate studies. Zainab (30, US born of Palestinian background) said that her brother was experiencing discrimination in his job because he was an Arab:

> My brother tried so many times to get a promotion but he was denied many times to go into a different unit . . . Why is he being pushed back? Why is he just being thrown in the dumps just to translate, okay, when the occasional Arab comes in? (Interview, New York, January 2010)

During the recession in America (since 2007), it has been difficult even for those participants born, raised and educated in the US. For those overseas born, with overseas degrees, finding an appropriate job has been especially difficult because in some cases their overseas degrees are not recognised, and their poor English skills are a factor. But, as Zainab observed, there could be a subtle barrier in the way of promotion for Arabs actually in the workforce even though they were born and educated in the United States.[40]

Muslim women

Over the last few years a few Muslim women in America have defied Muslim men's traditional norms. In 2003, for example, the Indian-born journalist Asra Nomani went into a mosque in West Virginia using the men's rather than the women's entrance. She sat down in the men's section and, when asked to leave, she refused. Her story generated a great deal of media coverage over a short period. Later, Nomani wrote a book, *Standing Alone at Mecca*.[41] In 2004, the African American scholar-activist Amina Wadud became the first woman to lead a mixed-gender congregation and give the sermon at a Friday prayer service. Several mosques refused her request to host their services, and finally she held an Islamic service at the Synod House of the Cathedral of St John the Divine in New York. The event generated an international debate on whether Wadud's actions were Islamically acceptable.[42] There have been other occasions when women have expressed dissatisfaction with the way they were treated at a mosque. In 2008, when a Muslim woman and her non-Muslim mother wanted to enter a mosque in Colorado, they were told they would not be allowed to pray there because there were no other women in the mosque.[43]

Upon reflecting on the Asra Nomani, Amina Wadud and Colorado mosque issues, I believe that dialogue is needed between Muslim men and women on mosque-related and other matters. As discussed earlier (see Introduction), I lived in Muslim countries for many years. I have found that most of them are steeped in the patriarchal model where gender segregation and differentiation is emphasised. Women are expected to exhibit subservient behaviour, such as to be modest and kind, obey their husbands, and bring up the children. Men are expected to exhibit masculinity by being strong and tough and bearing primary financial responsibility for their families.[44] Many women in those countries have become used to and are accepting of such norms. Thus, even in America – where women in general enjoy near-equal status with men in most matters – Nomani's and Wadud's actions to break with traditional practices in the mosques brought objections from many first-generation Muslim women.

Nomani was born in India and migrated to the USA at an early age. Being raised in the USA, she probably acculturated into the 'American way of life'. Anyway, Nomani was not willing to comply with the traditional practice in the mosque of women having a separate space for prayers. Likewise, as an African American convert, Amina Wadud was not happy with traditional practice in the mosques. Incidentally, in many Muslim countries women do not attend mosques; they pray at home. But when such women immigrate to a western country they may want to attend mosques for social and cultural reasons, and may wish that their children should also attend mosques. Yet it is reasonable to predict that most of these Muslim women would prefer to have a separate space for themselves in the mosques for their privacy and to comply with their religious beliefs about maintaining distance from men (other than their spouses).[45] As for the Colorado mosque issue, sometimes men discourage women from attending mosque on their own (without any male relatives) for security reasons and because of fear of rape or assault.

In this study, a young girl (16) complained that men in mosques can be very rude to women (interview, New York, November 2009). Of course, some Muslim men still display patriarchal, masculine attitudes in mosques, and this behaviour is objectionable because it gives younger people who are being raised in the western world a negative perception of their religion. In the next section I discuss the cultural complexities that young Muslim women face as they are raised in America.

Cultural restrictions

Yvonne Haddad and Nazli Kibria observed that in the United States some girls face cultural restrictions from their parents, who are mostly first-generation Muslims.[46] These restrictions may come from the mother as well as the father. For example, a Bangladeshi mother would expect her daughter to live the life-style she had in Bangladesh, which would restrict the daughter from integrating with mainstream Americans. Thus the daughter would not be allowed to go to parties or socialise with non-Muslim friends.

Of course, cultural restrictions are not confined to immigrant families. For example, an African American woman, Mehnaz, aged twenty-two, who identified herself as 'only Muslim', said, 'My Dad converted [to Islam] when he was eighteen and my Mom when she was thirteen, she took her *shahada* [converted to Islam].' Mehnaz had a bicultural upbringing:

> I played basketball, soccer, softball; my favourite sport was swimming, though. I was on the swim team in my high school and I was fast. I absolutely love swimming, so yeah, I'm interested in playing sports, but as far as watching sports, no, I change the channel. (Interview, Maryland, April 2010)

Mehnaz also liked music. She said, 'I have Michael Jackson all over my iPod and absolutely love it and I miss him and I wish he would have got some more music out.' Her 'Muslim self' made her realise that she should read Islamic books:

> I used to read novels, but I realised that I was spending too much time reading those and not enough time reading Islamic books, so right now I'm reading a book called *The Pillars of Islam and Imam* and it's just basics of Islam. Because sometimes, even born and raised Muslim, I had to go back to the basics to remind myself.

Mehnaz was a single parent who worked in an Islamic institution. It is normally expected that cultural restrictions are imposed in a patriarchal family where the father is the figurehead. But in this case, Mehnaz, as a mother, was protective of her daughter and she feared that outside influences would impact on her child. Mehnaz said, 'I can't stand the TV now because everything is sex, violence, women half naked, it's too open now with everything.' She expressed further concerns:

> It's almost like there's no sense of censorship any more. Even children's channels show all kind of things that they shouldn't be seeing. Like I said, it's scary to think my daughter is growing up in this country with all these things being promoted as acceptable. How can you feel comfortable wearing *hijab* when everybody around you is wearing nothing and they're confident with it and look good and everybody's

notes

telling them 'Your body looks good, you want to shake this way, your body looks good when it does that, get this surgery to make you look better', you know?

Sometimes immigrant parents who have similar cultural fears to Mehnaz send their children to their country of origin for a few years to keep them within their cultural boundaries. Mehnaz, being an African American parent, did not have such a choice.

Cultural contrasts

In this study many of the second-generation participants spoke of the cultural contrast between their host country and their country of origin. For example, US-born Sadiqah, of Palestinian-Jordanian background (23, national identity: Arab Muslim), spoke of her cultural experience in Jordan:

Actually for four years my father took us back to Jordan to learn Arabic, so my elementary education was in Jordan and then we moved here and he was really afraid of putting us into public school, so he put us into the Islamic school for a couple of years and then high school was in public school. (Interview, Florida, March 2010)

After her college degree, Sadiqah was again sent to Jordan for further studies, and she was expected to marry an Arab while she was there. At the time of interview, Sadiqah was struggling with cultural issues:

Well, in the beginning, I used to say I was more Arab or more Muslim, but once I moved overseas I realised how American I really was. I don't have the traditional Arab mentality . . . I'm very open minded. I'm very understanding. I feel they have cultural niches over there where they have to just be a religious group, a liberal group, there is no moderation at all and over here I think it's just so open to accepting anything and everything.

Though Sadiqah identified herself as an Arab Muslim, she was at the same time distancing herself from that identity. She took pride in her western/American values, saying 'we the Americans' are 'open minded', 'very understanding', and she believed that 'they, the Arabs' are 'liberal but at the same time they're very close minded'. Sadiqah explained this by saying, 'Liberal in the sense where they adopt western dress, but not the etiquette of the West and not the understanding of other groups.' She continued with her observations:

I've found here in the West, people are not as selfish when it comes to public domain. Over there they'll throw something on the street; they don't care. If they hit you while they're walking, they don't look back and say 'Excuse me', they just keep going. Over here there's a lot of social etiquette where they'll be 'Oh, please excuse me' or 'I'm sorry'. Over there it's very hard to find that.

Sadiqah's depiction is not exclusive to the Arab world; it is a typical characterisation of any developing country such as Bangladesh or Pakistan.

New immigrants to the western world, however, are also bothered by cross-cultural issues. For example, a recent immigrant to America, Muneera (16, Yemeni background, national identity: Yemeni American), was shocked at the way American Muslim Arabs dressed, and the way they spoke and interacted with the opposite gender (interview, Michigan, May 2010). Muneera had been used to seeing Yemeni men wearing *jambiyas* (traditional daggers), and women in the *abaya* and the *niqab*, so she commented, 'But here they wear pants and their scarves.' Regarding language, Muneera said, 'Here they mix it up, English Arabic, I get confused . . . I talk fast [fluent] Arabic, but here they are slow and stop [not fluent].' Muneera was critical of 'too much freedom' in America, and compared her 'home' (Yemeni) culture to American culture:

> Over here too much freedom like boyfriend, girlfriend and stuff . . . they go out and they haven't married and a lot of girls, they get kids. In our country we marry when we are small, from fifteen years and up, and we don't go outside dating them [before marriage].

Muneera spoke further of her 'home' culture:

> For us, 'cos in Yemen, when we [the girls] walk I had to look down and walk . . . We cannot talk to boys, but talk to them about important things, for the homework, but there can be no eye contact . . . Like if your grandmother saw you talking with a man there would be trouble . . . If the girls did something wrong, it will bring shame to their family.

Muneera also spoke of the extreme side of her 'home' culture:

> If you love someone, you should go tell your Mom, then your Mom focuses. Asking you for the boy, sometimes if they catch them, they get killed too and they brought shame to their Dad . . . The boy because he take the girl and there are two that are dead. They say that he stole that girl and he took her [*sic*].

Muneera was indicating that lovers might become victims of honour killings if their relationship was not approved by their parents. When I asked if young lovers got any protection from the police or government, Muneera replied, 'They don't care. It's like family matter.' In America Muneera maintains her cultural practice but is slowly acculturating into the 'American way', as later reflected in her statement that she does not keep her head down as she used to do in Yemen. In an earlier conversation Muneera mentioned that her identity was 'Yemeni American':

> Over here I'd be focussed and I don't talk to them [the boys]. I walk away from them. I don't get my head down like this. I make myself proud of myself that I'm wearing my scarf and I'm Muslim. For the boys over here, I talk with them for homework and things.

It is interesting to note that, though Jordan and Yemen are both Arab-speaking countries, they differ in terms of dress code, food and dance. Jordan is more westernised than Yemen. The last wife of the late King Hussein of Jordan was the US-born Queen Noor of Syrian, English and Swedish descent, while his second wife, Princess Muna (mother of the current king, Abdullah II), was born in Britain. And the present queen of Jordan, Kuwaiti-born Queen Rania is seen dressed in western clothing. But Yemen still remains conservative. Most Yemeni women wear the black *burqa* and the *niqab*. In the US too, where there is a Yemeni concentration, young girls can be seen wearing the *burqa* and the *niqab*. Unfortunately, the cultural practice of honour killing occurs in both countries.[47] Honour killings are mostly carried out by brothers or fathers of women who have had sex outside marriage or run away from home with their lovers.

Cultural casualties?

The practice of arranging the marriage of Muslim daughters at an early age is still carried out by some first-generation immigrants residing in the West, irrespective of their ethnic background. Some researchers such as Fauzia Ahmad and Nazli Kibria have found that the concepts of *izzat* and *sharam* play a major role in South Asian Muslim communities in Britain and the USA. Some immigrant parents assume that if they do not arrange the marriages of their daughters (and in some cases sons) to people of their same community, then the parents would be discredited by their community members. In many cases, arranged or forced marriages turn out to be successful, but sometimes arranged marriages end up in a divorce.[48]

In this study, I found that the casualties of arranged marriages were not only confined to young South Asian Muslims; they were across the board. For example, US-born Zohra (30, US born of Palestinian background, national identity: Muslim American) was married to her cousin in Palestine at the age of sixteen, but this arrangement ended in a divorce. Zohra said:

> I could not click with him. He has the mentality of the Middle Eastern [people] and I was grown up here so it was hard for us even after ten years to click together.
>
> And I tried to make the best out of it [our marriage] and I tried to make him more

civilised because he never went to school and it was hard for him to accept that I do go to school. He wanted me to stay home and cook and clean and that's it. But honestly I have more energy to deliver to my community and I wanted to support myself and . . . and you know he wasn't okay with it . . . so I could not [be] surrounded [by] his ignorance . . . some of them get married just for American citizenship. (Interview, New York, February 2010)

Another participant, US-born Zainab (28, Palestinian, national identity: Arab American), spoke of identity:

Going through everything I went through, growing up I was identified as Arab and not as American, and then when you realise when you're among Arabs you don't feel you're an Arab, you feel more American. So I guess American Muslims have a different identity. I'm like Arab American and I think it's a different identity than just being all American or all Arab.

Zainab was married at the age of eighteen to a Palestinian, but the marriage lasted only a few years. She said:

He wasn't willing to compromise at all. He said, 'If you disagree with me, then too bad.' You know, [he wanted me to] just keep my mouth closed or whatever and then it got really physical . . . hostile. Well, I think he's a bit psycho. I think that being born and raised in a refugee camp might have affected him in a bad way.

Fortunately, both participants – Zohra and Zainab – had support from their family members, and were also employed in Islamic institutions.

Post-9/11 casualties?

After the 9/11 tragedy, Muslim parents have been more inclined to anglicise their children's names, such as changing Mohammad to Martin, so that their children may be better accepted by the wider society. One of my Muslim acquaintances told me that her daughter's name was Mehjabin and she (the mother) pondered whether to anglicise the name because her daughter was bullied at school and taunted as 'bin Laden'.

   A US-born woman of Pakistani background, Khojesta (30, an educator), thought that her marriage break-up was a casualty of the post-9/11 repercussions. Khojesta's parents had migrated to the USA in the 1960s, and since there was no Islamic school in her neighbourhood she attended a public school. She sometimes felt 'awkward' because she was the only Pakistani in the school, surrounded by 'a lot of Russians, a lot of Mexicans, and a lot of Irish'. Khojesta said that her parents 'were pretty strict but they also were very open minded about education; however, they didn't really encourage us to have friends so we didn't socialise that much'. She recalled how her mother used to take her (and her siblings) to the public library every week and since then she has enjoyed reading. 'I read *Wizard of Oz*, I read Baby-Sitters Club, I read Sweet Valley High. I mean, you know, I read all of the famous [series]. Agatha Christie, I love her mysteries' (interview, New York, January 2010). Khojesta was married to an overseas-born Muslim man of Pakistani heritage, but the marriage ended in a divorce. Khojesta observed:

> I don't think it's far fetched to say that 9/11 had a huge impact on my marriage. My husband was a private consultant, he depended on relationships in order to get his job, earn employment, so I felt like he kind of lost his identity because he felt like he had to stop being Muslim because it was a matter of paying the bills. It was only a single-income home so I think that affected us tremendously.

Khojesta said that her husband had 'tendencies towards being religious, but after 9/11 he kind of felt like he couldn't reconcile his identity. Because of his accent it was even more difficult for him to be a part of western society.' After going through an unpleasant experience in her marriage, Khojesta was confused about her own identity when she said:

> I still struggle as a second-generation American, but I'm starting to reconcile my Muslim identity with my American identity and on top of that my Pakistani identity . . . Six years ago I would totally disconnect myself from being Pakistani or American.

Young Muslim men

Psychologist Amber Haque observed that for Muslim youths facing two cultures – western culture in school and Islamic culture at home – life can be very stressful and that can affect their mental health. For example, at public schools, students are generally expected to comply with cultural norms in dress code, food habits, socialisation and even proper English accent. Public holidays, such as Easter, Halloween and St Valentine's Day, do not exist in Islam, and Muslim children are often in a dilemma when their parents do not approve of participation in these events, such as eating Easter eggs, dressing-up for 'trick or treating' at Halloween, and going out on St Valentine's Day. Further complications arise among Muslims during adolescence when dating is the social norm for their non-Muslim friends. In order to fit in with their school social circle, young Muslims may wish to have friends of the opposite sex. But they are supposed to stay away from activities that entail mixing with the opposite gender. As with some other religious groups, selecting partners for marriage is a very serious issue for young Muslims because parents prefer them to marry within their own cultures.[49] In this study some Muslim youths said that, even though they did not like their parents' decisions on some aspects of their life, such as marriage or career choice, they listened to them.

It's my parents' terms

A male participant, Akbar (22, US born of Bangladeshi background, national identity: Bengali American), said that he could not pursue his ambitions because of his parents' decision:

> Actually to be honest the only reason I'm going in a science major and becoming a dentist is because of my parents, because I had no intention of doing this. I had a chance of working on BMW when I was sixteen. I was going to get hired and I was supposed to go to Germany and work for them but my parents denied it and I also had a spot at MIT but they wouldn't let me go so I'm stuck with this. (Interview, Maryland, March 2010)

In this context, the non-western 'collectivist self' came to the fore. Through the 'collectivist self' individuals may enhance their family's social standing, meet the expectations of family members and feel indebted to their parents, who have made enormous sacrifices to raise and support them. Sometimes quite reluctantly, young people such as Akbar abide by their parents' decisions. But this is another cultural practice that is not exclusive to Muslims. For example, a Chinese student's desire to achieve academically is likely to be socially rooted, and not to be concerned with a 'me' personality.[50]

Cultural dilemmas

Several participants in this study expressed cultural dilemmas. For example, Sharukh Ali (male, 18, US born of Pakistani heritage, national identity: Pakistani American) is the younger of two brothers in his family with a father who had to retire seventeen years ago because of his severe health condition. His mother was also sick but she had to look after the family. Sharukh Ali said, 'My older brother is into drugs. So my mother is very stressed out. She wants to get me married' (interview, Michigan, May 2010). When I asked Sharukh Ali how his brother gets money for the drugs, he replied, 'Sometimes he does construction work.' When I asked about the drugs and how they operate, Sharukh Ali replied:

> My brother smokes marijuana. Marijuana is a very advanced drug. I mean it started off a long time ago, but nowadays there's new ways of developing, of getting high. It's not basically the marijuana, it's the chemical in it, THC, that will get somebody high, and there are different standards of weed, marijuana. I mean just the names that it's given you can tell it's been around. I mean you can call it marijuana, cannabis,

reefer, joint, blunt, spliff, doobie and . . . Marijuana is not really as bad as alcohol is, because marijuana, it just tends to like make people forget stuff. Like they get high, their eyes get low, they'll get red, you can smell it on them, they'll laugh sometimes. It'll make people really, really hungry. But gradually, it kills brain cells in your body.

When I asked Sharukh Ali if it was popular among the young people, he replied, 'It's very, very common, yeah. A smoke but then again is that it is just a cigarette in disguise. It's basically a cigarette with a flavour.' When asked how young people get the drugs, Sharukh replied, 'There are illegal spots. Around here you're not supposed to be selling, but just now there's a system, there's every way to corrupt the system.'

Speaking about his leisure time activities, Sharukh Ali said:

I just study and play basketball. I listen to rap just to hear what they got to say. Because I mean I got a brother that is also kind of living a rapper's lifestyle and it's kind of interesting to hear their lyrics and see what will cause them to do something like that, or kind of give me idea how to help my brother. And my brother is not really bad, just he doesn't like to listen. He wants to have things his own way, and buy drugs. Like he doesn't pop pills. He doesn't drink. He just smokes a lot of weed.

Sharukh Ali's brother was perhaps a casualty of being the oldest son of first-generation immigrants. Due to their low education levels and lack of English language skills, immigrant parents use their children as interpreters, which can be stressful for the children. Also, young immigrants' relocation and acculturation can lead them to hang out with the wrong crowd. In this case, Sharukh Ali was trying to compensate for his older brother by agreeing to get married at a very young age (even before pursuing his career):

I'm going to Pakistan this summer. I'm going to choose a wife, and I'm going to get engaged. Then I'm going to get to know her, so it's not a complete stranger to marry, and hopefully it'll be according to a Muslim tradition and engaged, marriage . . .

When I asked Sharukh Ali, 'So do you think you will have a good adjustment with your wife, who will have a different culture?' he replied:

No, I'm going to get really along with her 'cos I think that I understand people. I don't really, like, go for looks and I think it's all about the personality. And just get married, make my dad happy. Let him see at least one of his kids standing on his two feet before he passes away. Give him a little something in life.

The drug problem is not exclusive to young Muslims. It is a problem for youths of all backgrounds. Adolescent drug use is a serious public health concern in the United States, especially among high-risk ethnic and racial groups. In

2005, 26.5 per cent of youths aged 14–15 years and 41.9 per cent of youths aged 16–17 years had tried an illicit drug. The prevalence of adolescent substance use has been found to be particularly high among Hispanic and Latino youths,[51] and immigrant youths are also susceptible to the use of illicit drugs. For one reason or another, they tend to ignore parental authority and discipline and thereby become more prone to substance use. The young people also want to 'fit in' with the wider society and that could lead to further tension with their parents. The substance use could be an individual choice, but anti-social peer pressure is another factor in the use of drugs among immigrant youths.[52]

Asian Americans, such as Filipinos, Chinese, Koreans, Vietnamese, Indonesians, Indians and Pakistanis, might use alcohol or illicit drugs for several reasons. First, in adopting the host culture some young Asian immigrants resist the overly protective nature of their parents and succumb to the pressure of acculturation from the host society. As Molly Moloney et al. observed, 'Caught between two competing and often conflicting cultures – their own or their parents' "traditional" culture and their newly adopted culture – young immigrants may turn to drugs and alcohol as "coping mechanisms" to reconcile potentially conflicting pressures.'[53] Furthermore, in some cases immigrant parents face economic hardship and take full-time jobs, which do not allow them to monitor how their children are faring in school. Another factor is loneliness, anxiety and depression along with the inability to fit in to the host culture.[54]

In the midst of such social concerns, some Muslim parents (like some other non-Muslim groups) choose homeschooling for their children. In the next section, I examine the homeschooling system among Muslim families and consider whether it is helpful for social cohesion within the wider society.

Muslim youths' homeschooling

According to Priscilla Martinez, Muslim families are among the fastest-growing homeschoolers in the United States. Martinez observes the following reasons why Muslim families choose homeschooling for their children:

- to provide a better education compared to public and private faith schools
- for special-needs children who require specific learning attention
- for flexible school attendance (if they need to spend time travelling)
- to save their children from bullies, drugs, gangs and guns.[55]

Homeschoolers have to follow the curriculum of the education board; however, Muslim families think that they can include more Islamic education through homeschooling. There are arguments for and against homeschooling. Parents in favour argue that through homeschooling their children learn unique Islamic values and ethics. It also enables their children to socialise more with the Muslim community and the wider society through volunteering and community services, activities at local libraries, recreation at the YMCA, sporting activities, field trips and boy/girl scout programmes, and in mosques. Those against homeschooling claim it prevents children from socialising and integrating with the wider society. They argue that children are slower to develop their social skills and social negotiation skills when confronted with major events outside their cultural space. There are other challenges such as bullying in regular schools. By keeping children in isolation (homeschools), the children do not learn to cope with challenges.[56]

Through my fieldwork, I met one male Muslim university student who was involved with the Muslim Students' Association in a university. He was not interested in participating in my survey, saying, 'I haven't much to say because I was homeschooled.' By this he either implied he was not aware of happenings in the wider society, or simply that he was not confident enough to speak up. Later, I interviewed an educator of homeschooled children who spoke about the pros and cons of the system. Ayub, aged twenty-five, a Muslim convert of Caucasian American background (national identity: Muslim American), had a Master's in special education and a degree in education. He served students in both public schools and private tutoring and had this to say about homeschooling:

> I worked to help a few families with homeschooling. They were not happy with the public schools and there was no private school that was within distance.
>
> We based our homeschooling on a curriculum that was available. I found it for the particular situation we were in to be a tremendous success because most of the students, you know, had completed two grade levels in one year. So they were moving at a very fast pace because it was an individualised education. (Interview, Massachusetts, December 2009)

Ayub continued with his opinion:

> The reason big schools don't pursue individualised education is because it costs a lot of money to do it. This particular family had the money and resources to hire certi-fied and licensed teachers ... I wouldn't say it is good or bad, it's really a case-by-case basis. I've seen it really work well, and I've seen it really not do so well.

Ayub observed that in a homeschool setting there needed to be effort from all sides: the student's learning attitude, the parents' expectations and the educator's efforts. On its social aspects, Ayub said, 'Interactions with peers – they get plenty of it during most of the day, they have activities scheduled throughout the day as a school ... with groups, YMCA, boy scouts, swimming teams, you name it.' On communication, Ayub observed:

Interaction within the class is always dynamic. We have a discussion on a topic and hear other people's opinions and ideas but it is somewhat lost in homeschooling. So there's big plusses and minuses. I'm pretty neutral on the homeschooling issue.

Ayub also spoke about the social, spiritual, emotional, academic and physical development of young home-schooled children:

I've seen homeschooling do it very well and very poorly, and I've seen plenty of public schools and private schools do it very well and very poorly. I don't think it's the concept itself, I think it's how it's done.

From an educator's point of view, Ayub has explained the positive and negative aspects of homeschooling. Homeschooling is also popular with people of other ethnic, racial and religious backgrounds. From my research point of view, however, homeschooling can hinder Muslim youths' development of their bicultural skills. In the current geopolitical environment, where Muslims are considered as the 'other' by a certain section of the wider society, it is important that youths interact with the wider society through debate and sport. Interaction and integration are more likely to occur through regular schools.

Conclusion

In this chapter, I have examined several issues young Muslims face in the course of their development. The participants of this study were mostly second-generation Muslims who were endeavouring to cope with their parents' cultural expectations and to 'fit in' with the wider society. Sometimes the cultural expectations from their parents and the wider society were discrepant. Their parents were mostly first-generation Muslims living in a diaspora, and some hoped to return to their 'home' one day. Most wanted their children to adopt the parents' ethnic culture. On the other hand, the parents needed help from their children to improve their language skills. Often parents struggled to find jobs and were not fitting into the host society. In the face of these tensions second-generation Muslims were trying to be a part of the host society. In the entire process of enculturation and acculturation, it is obvious that the young people need to acquire bicultural skills so that they can be competent in both cultures. A balance between the two cultures is possible if parents allow and even encourage their children to be a part of the host society through education, sport and socialisation with their non-Muslim peers.

There are some issues within the Muslim community, such as Sunni–Shia relations and patriarchal tendencies, that need to be addressed for the sake of a cohesive society. Of course, some Muslim women unfortunately bear the oppression of men but overall their strong family foundation is adding to the mosaic of American society. The wider society should recognise the importance of cultural diversity and encourage immigrants to retain their languages and those aspects of their culture that are lawful. And surely the host nation would enhance its international standing by allowing Muslim women their choice of attire.

Notes

1. Stuart Hall, 'The Question of Cultural Identity', in *The Polity Reader in Cultural Theory* (Cambridge: Polity Press, 1994), p. 122; Anita Jones Thomas and Sara E. Schwarzbaum, *Culture and Identity: Life Stories for Counselors and Therapists* (Thousand Oaks, CA: Sage, 2006), p. 5.
2. David Matsumoto and Linda Juang, *Culture and Psychology*, 3rd edn (Belmont, CA: Thomson Wadsworth, 2004), p. 301.
3. Ibid., pp. 134, 156.
4. Ibid., p. 155.
5. Ibid. pp. 135–54.
6. Hazel R. Markus and Shinobu Kitayama, 'Culture and the self: implications for cognition, emotion, and motivation', *Psychological Review* 98 (1991), pp. 224–53; Matsumoto and Juang, *Culture and Psychology*, pp. 301–2.
7. Alberto Melucci, 'Identity and Difference in a Globalized World', in Pnina Werbner and Tariq Modood (eds), *Debating Cultural Hybridity: Multi-cultural Identities and the Politics of Anti-racism* (London: Zed, 1997), pp. 58–69; Gary S. Gregg, *Culture and Identity in a Muslim Society* (Oxford: Oxford University Press, 2007).
8. Gregg, *Culture and Identity in a Muslim Society*, p. 19.
9. Melucci, 'Identity and Difference in a Globalized World', p. 64.
10. Ibid. p. 65.
11. Seyyed Hossein Nasr, *The Heart of Islam: Enduring Values for Humanity* (San Francisco: HarperSanFrancisco, 2002), pp. 65–6.
12. Ibid.
13. Ibid. pp. 68–70; see also Jane I. Smith, *Islam in America*, 2nd edn (New York: Columbia University Press, 2010), p. 119.
14. Jocelyne Cesari, *When Islam and Democracy Meet: Muslims in Europe and in the United States* (New York: Palgrave Macmillan, 2004), p. 95.
15. Haneef James Oliver, *The 'Wahhabi' Myth: Dispelling Prevalent Fallacies and the Fictitious Link with Bin Laden*, 2nd edn (Toronto: TROID, 2004), p. 62.
16. Cesari, *When Islam and Democracy Meet*, p. 51; Shaykh Muhammad Hisham Kabbani, *Illuminations: Compiled Lectures on Shari'ah and Tasawwuf* (Fenton, MI: Islamic Supreme Council of America, 2007), pp. 24–5.
17. Cited in Kabbani, *Illuminations*, p. 23.
18. Sayed Moustafa Al-Qazwini, *Inquiries about Shi'a Islam* (Costa Mesa, CA: Islamic Educational Center of Orange County, 2000), pp. 4–9.

19. Nasr, *The Heart of Islam*, pp. 70–2; see also Smith, *Islam in America*, pp. 30–1.
20. Liyakat Nathani Takim, *Shi'ism in America* (New York: New York University Press, 2009), p. 90.
21. For further details on separate theological schools of thought among Muslims in the Indian subcontinent, see Nahid Afrose Kabir, *Young British Muslims: Identity, Culture, Politics and the Media* (Edinburgh: Edinburgh University Press, 2010), p. 60.
22. Takim, *Shi'ism in America*, p. 23; Smith, *Islam in America*, p. 63.
23. Takim, *Shi'ism in America*, pp. 133–6.
24. Ibid., pp. 119–20.
25. See also Takim, *Shi'ism in America*, pp. 140–1.
26. Smith, *Islam in America*, pp. 78–103; see also Herbert Berg, *Elijah Muhammad and Islam* (New York: New York University Press, 2009).
27. Smith, *Islam in America*, p. 84.
28. Ibid. p. 91.
29. Ibid., p. 96; see also Takim, *Shi'ism in America*, p. 197.
30. Jamillah Karim, *American Muslim Women: Negotiating Race, Class and Gender within the Ummah* (New York: New York University Press, 2009), p. 32.
31. Anna Bowers, 'The Search for Justice: Islamic Pedagogy and Inmate Rehabilitation', in Yvonne Y. Haddad, Farid Senzai and Jane I. Smith (eds), *Educating the Muslims of America* (Oxford: Oxford University Press, 2009), pp. 179–207, see pp. 184–5.
32. Ibid.
33. 'Gallup survey finds Muslims are younger, more racially diverse', *Christian Century*, 21 April 2009, pp. 18–19.
34. *Muslim Americans: No Signs of Growth in Alienation or Support for Extremism*, (Washington, DC: Pew Research Center 2011), http://www.people-press.org/files/legacy-pdf/Muslim-American-Report.pdf, accessed 15 May 2012.
35. Ibid., p. 18.
36. Ibid., p. 17.
37. Ibid.
38. Jobs are often classified as non-professional or professional, though the distinction between the two can be vague. Jobs are considered professional if they require specialised knowledge and advanced skills in a particular area. Teachers, engineers and doctors are all considered professionals. Most jobs classified as professional by the US Bureau of Labor Statistics require an associate or higher degree. Non-professional jobs do not require a college degree and usually provide on-the-job training. See Susan Stopper, 'Non-professional vs. professional jobs', eHow website, http://www.ehow.com/info_8140675_nonprofessional-vs-professional-jobs.html, accessed 15 May 2012.
39. See Randa Abdel-Fattah, *Does My Head Look Big in This?* (Sydney: Pan Macmillan Australia, 2005).
40. Further discussion on education and employment can be found in Chapter 6.
41. Asra Q. Nomani, *Standing Alone at Mecca: An American Woman's Struggle for*

the Soul of Islam (San Francisco: HarperSanFrancisco, 2005); see Smith, *Islam in America*, p. 186.

42. Smith, *Islam in America*, p. 136.

43. Ibid. p. 137.

44. See also Sondos M. S. Islam and Carl Anderson Johnson, 'Correlates of Smoking Behavior among Muslim Arab-American Adolescents', *Ethnicity and Health* 8:4 (2003), p. 322.

45. I have discussed mosques' restrictions and women in my previous work. See Kabir, *Young British Muslims*, pp. 62–4.

46. Yvonne Yazbeck Haddad, Jane I. Smith and Kathleen M. Moore, *Muslim Women in America: The Challenges of Islamic Identity Today* (New York: Oxford University Press, 2006), p. 17. See also Nazli Kibria, *Muslims in Motion: Islam and National Identity in the Bangladeshi Diaspora* (New Brunswick, NJ: Rutgers University Press, 2011), p. 66.

47. '"Honour killings" laws blocked', BBC News website, 8 September 2003, http://news.bbc.co.uk/2/hi/middle_east/3088828.stm, accessed 16 May 2012.

48. Fauzia Ahmad, 'The Scandal of "Arranged Marriages" and the Pathologisation of BrAsian Families', in N. Ali, V. S. Karla and S. Sayyid (eds), *A Postcolonial People: South Asians in Britain* (New York: Columbia University Press, 2008), pp. 272–90; Kibria, *Muslims in Motion*, p. 72; Kabir, *Young British Muslims*, pp. 66–71.

49. Amber Haque, 'Religion and Mental Health: The Case of American Muslims', *Journal of Religion and Health* 43 (2004), pp. 45–55.

50. Matsumoto and Juang, *Culture and Psychology*, p. 307.

51. Karla D. Wagner, Anamara Ritt-Olson, Daniel W. Soto, Yaneth L. Rodriguez, Lourdes Baezconde-Garbanati and Jennifer B. Unger, 'The Role of Acculturation, Parenting, and Family in Hispanic/Latino Adolescent Substance Use: Findings from a Qualitative Analysis', *Journal of Ethnicity in Substance Abuse* 7:3 (2008), pp. 304–27.

52 Ibid.

53. Molly Moloney, Geoffrey Hunt and Kristen Evans, 'Asian American Identity and Drug Consumption: From Acculturation to Normalization', *Journal of Ethnicity in Substance Use* 7:4 (2008), pp. 376–403, see p. 379.

54. Ibid., p. 388.

55. Priscilla Martinez, 'Muslim Homeschooling', in Haddad, Senzai and Smith (eds), *Educating the Muslims of America*, p. 110.

56. Ibid., pp. 115–20.

CHAPTER

3

WHAT DOES IT TAKE TO BE AN AMERICAN?

An American is someone who is either born in the United States, or is a permanent resident or a citizen and has developed an attachment to the USA through his/her length of stay in the country. Anthony Smith observed that, in the western model of national identity, nations are seen as cultural communities whose members are, if not homogeneous, united by common historical memories, myths, symbols and traditions. Even when new immigrant communities equipped with their own historic culture and traditions have been allowed into a host country, it has taken several generations before their descendants are absorbed into the circle of the 'nation' and its historic culture. Smith also identified land or attachment to land, its rivers, coasts, lakes, mountains and cities as important. These attachments become 'sacred' as people live in a place for generations, and this bond can create people's national identity.[1] Kwame Appiah noted, however, that identity is not determined by a specific amount of time or number of generations, but how quickly one can adapt to the host country's way of life. That is, according to Appiah, Americans are people who speak the English language and know something about American sports such as baseball and basketball. Americans are also familiar with American consumer culture and brands such as Coca-Cola, Nike, Levi-Strauss, Ford, Nissan and GE. They have seen Hollywood movies and know the names of some actors, and 'even a few who watch little or no television can probably tell the names of its "personalities"'.[2]

Speaking of the positive side of American society, Selcuk Sirin and Michelle Fine observed that Muslims in the United States have one of the highest rates of citizenship in a nation that embraces diversity and has the reputation of being a 'melting pot'. America allows the coexistence of many cultures such as Irish Americans and African Americans.[3] Appiah pointed out that the US is a country where citizens are remarkably diverse with respect to religious belief and practice and, nevertheless, share in the public world. 'Orthodox Jews and devout Sunni Mulims walk around together on 34th Steeet in New York City, and they don't attack one another. If they do, the state knows what to do about it.'[4] Similarly, American citizens with diverse backgrounds exercise their voting rights and enjoy the 'democratic and judicial processes of a liberal society'.[5] Some scholars, however, believe that since 9/11 and the enactment of the Patriot Act in October 2001, some Muslims have suddenly become regarded as the 'other'.[6] Tony Gaskew and Louise Cainkar observed that it has become more challenging for Muslim youth to negotiate their identities because they are perceived as a potential threat to the wider society.[7]

In this chapter I examine why and how the participants in this study constructed their identity. Firstly, I discuss their responses to questions about their identity (summarised in Table 3.1). Secondly, I examine the patterns of multiple and dual identities and determine the factors that may have dictated these identities. Thirdly, I evaluate why some respondents chose to have a distinct identity: collective national, ethnic or religious, and finally I discuss whether sport (an integral part of biculturalism) had any impact on the participants' identity. I have discussed the importance of biculturalism in youth identity in the Introduction and Chapters 1 and 2. Most of the participants of this study were bicultural. That is, they spoke the English language, listened to western music and watched English-language television programmes; some read English-language novels, engaged in contemporary politics (further exhibited in Chapters 5 and 6) and watched and participated in mainstream sports; and they also retained all or some of their ethnic and religious practices.

Table 3.1 shows that 58 participants spoke of their multiple identities (which sometimes included religion), 144 participants spoke of their dual identity (with or without the mention of Islam); 51 spoke of their single ethnic identity; 65 spoke of their collective/group identity; 36 participants mentioned only their religious identity; 19 participants spoke of their American identity; and 6 participants had other identities. In the next and subsequent sections, I examine the patterns of identity and try to find out why the participants discussed their identity/identities in a particular manner and to understand their placement in the American society.[8]

Multiple identities: identity is contextual

In this study, fifty-eight participants (of whom forty-three always added Islam and fifteen sometimes added religion) spoke of their multiple identities. On multiple identities, Amartya Sen observed that in everyday life a person sees himself belonging to various groups through his citizenship, residence, country of origin, gender, class, profession, food habits, interest in music and sport and social commitments. Each of these collectivities to which this person simultaneously belongs gives him a particular identity. So a person can live his or her

Table 3.1 Patterns of identity

Questions asked: How would you define your identity/sense of belonging? Would you consider yourself American? Or Afghan/Iraqi/Moroccan or Muslim, etc.?		
Number of participants	Responses	Key points
16 male, 27 female	Multiple identities: national, ethnic/racial and religious	Muslim first then African American; Muslim first and foremost, then Arab American; South-African American Muslim; Muslim Sri Lankan American; Muslim Black Haitian; Muslim American of Yemeni descent; 'American Muslim who came from Palestine'; 'Muslim first because I have memorised the Quran, then white and then Pakistani'; Muslim American Egyptian; Afghan American Muslim; Muslim Pakistani American; Muslim American Guyanese.
5 m, 10 f	Multiple identities (with or without the mention of religion)	Few identities; Muslim multi-racial; Canadian American Somali; Pakistani German American; Greek Italian Muslim American; Arab Italian Muslim American; Muslim Ethiopian American, a woman; Miami Cuban Turkish American; 'Muslim first, three-fourth American, one fourth British of Burmese heritage'; 'I am mostly American, I am Muslim, half Arab, and I am also something of a nerd'; French, American, Arab and Muslim.
21 m, 23 f	Dual identity: national/ethnic and religious	American Muslim; Muslim American; just Muslim from Sudan; Albanian Muslim; Muslim Guyanese; Muslim Palestinian; Indian Muslim; Muslim Yemeni; Muslim Algerian, Bengali Muslim; Muslim Egyptian; Muslim first then Pakistani.
49 m, 51 f	Dual identity: national and country of origin	American Iranian; Palestinian American; Pakistani American 50:50; 'American Bengali but my mom says that I have to be only Bengali Muslim'; 99 per cent American and 1 per cent Pakistani; American *Desi*; Guyanese American; American Tanzanian; 'half American and half Puerto Rican'; Syrian American; Iraqi American; Trinidadian American; American Yemeni; Lebanese American; Bengali English.
4 m, 2 f	Collective identity: African American	New migrant visibly white from Algeria, second generation from Sudan; great-grandparents from Louisiana, traditional African American.

Table 3.1 (*continued*)

Questions asked: How would you define your identity/sense of belonging? Would you consider yourself American? Or Afghan/Iraqi/Moroccan or Muslim, etc.?

Number of participants	Responses	Key points
16 m, 19 f	Collective identity: Arab American	'Arab American, if people want to know which country I'm from, then I will tell Palestine'; 'Arab American but 75 per cent American'; 'Arab American: 75 per cent Palestinian and 25 per cent Colombian'.
5 m, 9f	Collective identity: wider ethnic/racial group	Only Arab; Arab Muslim; more Arab; African Muslim; American Kurdish; half African American and half Puerto Rican.
2 m, 5 f	Collective identity: dual nationality/ ethnicity	Pakistani Kashmiri; Yemeni Arab, Filipino Egyptian; part Pakistani, part Cuban.
0 m, 3 f	Collective identity: regional	Middle Eastern; south Asian Kashmiri; Middle Eastern European.
16 m, 35 f	Single ethnic identity	Just Afghan girl; still Moroccan; just Pakistani, pure Bengali, Lebanese 100 per cent; only Guyanese; Iraqi; Yemeni; 'still connected to Somali tribe'; '100 per cent Turkish'; 'I don't want to be an American'; 'very Palestinian, very human'.
18 m, 18 f	Single religious identity	Just Muslim; practising Muslim in America; 'Muslim but my mom yells that I have to be a Bengali'; 'Muslim and servant of Allah'; 'I'm a man of God (Allah); 'I'm Muslim, kind, loving and friendly'; 'I don't consider myself as African American nor solely American. American history is full of oppression. I'm only Muslim'.
11 m, 8 f	Single national identity: American	100 per cent American (Pakistani origin); only American (West African origin); 'Most of the time I feel American' (Bangladeshi origin); 'My mother and grandmother were Native Americans'; American/African American convert; only American (Yemeni background).
4 m, 2 f	Other	'My identity is my family'; human being first and foremost; citizen of the world; 'I used to say that I'm only Muslim'; 'American history is all of oppression and I am now reconciling my identity'.

life through multiple identities.⁹ In this study, I found that, when participants spoke of their multiple identities, they spoke of certain issues from their lived experience such as experiences at workplaces or educational institutions. For example, Ameena (female, 20, US born, Egyptian origin) comfortably spoke of her multiple identities:

> I feel I am part of everything. I identify myself as an American, an Arab, a Muslim and a female and so there are a lot of identities that I carry with me every day. I can't say that one takes precedence over the other. (Interview, Florida, March 2010)

On her Arab identity, Ameena said at home she spoke Arabic with her parents, had Middle Eastern cuisine, and enjoyed listening to Arabic music. She said, 'So I guess the cultural aspect of it makes me Arab.' On her American identity, Ameena said, 'My first language is English and I speak it every day at school. I study it, and I listen to all the English songs, so that also makes me American.' She continued: 'My everyday religious practices, wearing the *hijab*, praying, fasting, make me a Muslim.' On her feminine identity, Ameena said:

> I definitely connect with all the women's issues that are going on around the world, even in the US too. Especially with my job here, we do address women's issues, you know, domestic violence. And even at the mosques that I attend, they are always seeking for people to help women in need financially or if they have psychological needs, so there is always a sister in the community that needs another sister to help her. So I always try to help them.

On her sporting interests, Ameena said that she watched the Super Bowl. She watched her brothers play American football in high school. She also followed the World Cup and the African Cup, and she played soccer and volleyball with her friends at the weekend. She added, 'I watch basketball too and since I live in Miami and I go to school in Miami, I support the Miami Heat. They are a basketball team.' Through her office, Ameena took an active part in raising funds for the earthquake victims in Haiti, and she was appreciative of the celebrities who were donating and contributing to that cause. Ameena concluded, 'I really commend them for that and going there personally and helping and building homes despite their busy and fancy life. They are taking time, you know.'

Sen wrote that identifying with others, in various different ways, can be extremely important for living in a society, and multiple identities involve loyalties. For example, in Ameena's case, her multiple identities revealed her loyalty to various categories: ethnicity/race (Arab), citizenship/nationality (American), religion (*hijab*), local/state (Miami Heat), feminism (helping women) and humanitarianism (Haiti). Sen said, 'Belonging to each one of the membership groups can be quite important, depending on the particular context.' However, he noted that 'when they compete for attention or priorities over each other, the person has to decide on the relative importance to attach to the respective identities, which will, again, depend on the exact context'.[10] That is, if Ameena chose her exclusive American identity over her Arab identity, it would be relative to her experience of a certain event.

The second participant, Fariha (female, 16, US born, American-Palestinian background) said, 'I am mostly American, half Arab, and I am Muslim and I am also something of a nerd, I guess' (interview, Michigan, May 2010). Fariha was not interested in sport, but she liked walking and dancing and wanted to try swimming but thought that her *hijab* was a barrier to such sport. Fariha's American and Muslim identities were revealed when she criticised Michael Roskin, the author of a school textbook she was using for a comparative study of government.[11] Fariha observed, 'Roskin takes a strong American stand and is basically comparing them [other governments] to our own government and the author gives the impression that all countries, even the UK and Germany, they are all inferior to us.' Fariha's reference to '*our* government' and 'inferior to *us*' revealed her Americanness. But her Muslim identity came to the fore when she said:

> There are lot of things that just strike you, it's all subtle, and I think that when you're talking about Muslims, I remember he [Roskin] had a whole page on whether Saddam was incompatible with the modern world and when he was discussing the Iranian government, it's just like a lot of little things like that. And I remember once, for instance, he said Muslims practice honour killing and wife beating.

Since Fariha mentioned Roskin's book, I read it to see what information the author provided to his readers (particularly high school and university students). I found that Roskin has indeed made stereotypical comments in his book. For example, he wrote, 'As in Britain and France, some Muslims want Islamic family law to govern such traditional practices as wife beating, instant divorce, and "honor killings" of unchaste women.' Next, Roskin said, 'Muslim families have many children, sometimes eight or more. Some Russians fear that their stagnant numbers will be swamped by a tide of inferior peoples.' Roskin continued, 'In some Muslim countries (not Iran), such customs as the seclusion of women, the veil, and female genital mutilation are pre-Islamic and were absorbed by Islam.'[12]

In my previous research, I have addressed how some media sources label some cultural practices, such as honour killings, as an exclusively Muslim practice, but honour killing is very much practised by some non-Muslims in places such as India. Similarly the practice of female circumcision is a cultural practice in some African countries.[13] Identifying certain cultural practices in textbooks as the 'Muslim other' is not helpful.

Finally, Murad Ali (male, 18, overseas born, Egyptian background) said that he was 'an Egyptian, American and a Muslim'. He explained, 'My culture, my originality, my parents, I'm born in Egypt, I'm naturally Egyptian. I could say I am American because I was able to change my mindset . . . I'm more open minded.' Murad Ali was very much into sport. He revealed his American connection when he said:

> I don't know why America is trying to help other countries when it's so screwed up itself right now. You have so many illegal immigrants destroying the country, it's half Hispanic. The population of Hispanics is growing so rapidly. And they're living on the government's money so the government is paying for them to have more kids and repopulate the country and that's stupid, that's pointless. I'd rather have 100 educated people than 10,000 retards. (Interview, New York, January 2010)

Murad Ali was concerned that if the number of uneducated people increased, it would be a burden on the US government.[14] He worked part time in a grocery shop and he expressed his concern about how some people (including Muslims) drove expensive cars such as BMWs and yet bought food with food coupons, thereby 'cheating the system [the government]'. Even though Murad Ali spoke of his multiple identities, his interview conversation mostly revolved around 'being a good American citizen' and 'not cheating the system'.

Dual identity

Identity is negotiable

A plurality of participants (144) cited their dual or hyphenated identities, which meant that they were simultaneously identifying with two cultures. Homi Bhabha observed that people accepting two cultures are flexible in negotiating every situation, thereby locating their culture in a 'third space'.[15] Sometimes one's response can be deliberate, sometimes spontaneous or unintentional. In a duality, one's cultural mind can crystallise while responding to certain events. As Bhabha said, 'The process of cultural hybridity gives rise to something different, something new and unrecognisable, a new era of negotiation of meaning and representation.'[16] For example, a participant in this study, Sami (male, 17, US born, Sudanese origin) said that his identity was 'just Muslim from Sudan'. He was born in the USA but had visited Sudan many times. He was also involved in Muslim community services and liked travelling and sport.

Sami's identity meant that he was culturally a Sudanese Muslim. He observed the Muslim way of life (prayers, fasting, *halal* food, no alcohol) and felt connected to Sudan through his frequent visits there, together with Sudanese cuisine and the Arabic language. Sami's Sudanese identity was reflected when he spoke of the Sudanese president, Omar Bashir: 'A lot of media have gone against Sudan and overexaggerated that he was responsible for killings and all this raping and stuff but I guess Omar Bashir handled it well.' When I asked him about the teddy bear incident in Sudan, Sami replied:

> About the British lady naming the teddy bear Muhammad . . . They [the Sudanese government] shouldn't have put her in jail . . . because she's not Muslim so she doesn't know what's *harram*. She did that by an accident. All they had to do was explain to her and maybe if they want emigrate her back to her country. (Interview, New York, January 2010)

In November 2007, a 54-year-old British international school teacher at Unity High School in Sudan, Gillian Gibbons, was charged with 'inciting religious hatred'. In Sudan, where the legal code is based on *shariah* law, it is considered an insult and illegal to give the name Muhammad to an inanimate object. The charge was that by giving this name to a toy bear in her second-grade class, Ms Gibbons insulted Islam. She was arrested in Sudan and faced the prospect of up to six months in jail, a fine and forty lashes for blasphemy. Later, Ms Gibbons was spared the lashes, and the president of Sudan pardoned her after two British Muslim members of the House of Lords, Baroness Warsi and Lord Ahmed, pleaded for clemency on her behalf.[17] So Sami's 'third space' was a negotiation or reconciliation with western culture (though he did not mention his American connection) which helped him to think rationally on the matter.

Identity is situational

The second participant, Karishma (female, 15, US born, Sudanese origin) said that she was 'Sudanese American':

> I'm in the middle, half and half. I really love my Sudanese culture – it's beautiful. I think it's very unique and I like to be a unique person. But also since I'm in America I feel like I'm almost American; it's alright, I guess. (Interview, Massachusetts, November 2009)

Karishma related her Sudanese culture to her food and language. Karishma's American side was revealed when she said, 'I like to play basketball, I like to watch football. I'm trying to learn how to play soccer . . . I like the Patriots of course.' Karishma's identity appeared to be situational with an intense need to fit in to American youth subculture.[18] When I asked Karishma about her lip ring, she replied, 'I don't want people to think all Muslims are crazy, like all they do is pray, pray and pray. I want to show them a different side. We can get piercings; we can do all this stuff in Islam.' Karishma went on to criticise the American media:

> American media it's not great like I would expect it to be. They keep pushing on Muslims, saying that they're all bad, and there were a couple of incidents – like we

were going on the train and then, you know, non-Muslims kept saying 'Oh, Muslims are terrorists' and I don't really like to be called that at all.

Karishma's experience coincided with and may have arisen from news that the alleged terrorist Tarek Mehanna was arrested in Boston in October 2009 (see further discussion in the Arab American section of this chapter). Karishma continued telling her experience of racial profiling:

> I don't think it's the Muslims' fault . . . I think it's just the media. Like if someone wearing *hijab* or a man with a really long beard, if you go to the airport . . . I remember we went to the airport and they always have to check us, as if we had a bomb in our pockets or something. We would go through the detectors and the alarm doesn't go off but then they have to check us. I think if we didn't wear *hijab* or if we cut our beards that wouldn't have happened in the first place.

Experiences of racial profiling were discussed by other participants whose identities varied from single to dual or collective (discussed later). Apart from the concept of racial profiling, in this study I found that the desire to fit in ('a third space') with the broader community was a common attribute of Muslim youths.

Identity is spontaneous

Deeba (female, 25, US born, Iranian background), identified herself as American Iranian. Deeba was a sports fan and watched soccer, American football and basketball. Her favourite teams were the New York Knicks and the Boston Celtics. Deeba enjoyed swimming and gymnastics until the age of twelve, less so when she started wearing her *hijab*. However, she continued to play soccer in her *hijab*. Though born and raised in the US, Deeba was aware of the bitter relationship between Iran and the USA since the downfall of the Shah of Iran and the rise of the Islamic Revolution. Deeba's 'third space' appeared to be spontaneity. When I asked Deeba how she felt when Iran was so much in the news, she replied:

> I kind of find it really interesting with politics and it's been over 30 years, how much the Iran and American relationship is. But you know, both countries are very smart about their tactics with each other. If one says something, the other has to retaliate and so on . . . Because most of the Iranian people and the American people just absolutely love each other . . . Yeah, it's the government. (Interview, Massachusetts, December 2009)

Deeba also observed that negative American news was highlighted in the Iranian newspapers and vice versa. For example, the American media would be critical of Iran for its abuse of human rights against homosexuals. But negative news about Americans does not get equal space in the US media:

> If you open up the newspapers in Iran, you know the doctor that they killed, for example, in Atlanta, Georgia some time ago, because he had an abortion clinic; it wasn't a huge deal in the United States [but was a big news story in Iran]. They kind of put a damper on it, but what I'm saying is that both governments [and the media] know how to play the cat and mouse.

In 1973 abortion was legalised in the USA. Since then some anti-abortion activists have resorted to violence against abortion clinics and doctors. But this information (as Deeba observed) does not capture news headlines or is not reported as continuously in the US as other news. Since 1993 four American medical doctors who conducted abortions have been killed by anti-abortion activists: David Gunn and John Bayard Britton in Pensacola, Florida; Barnett Slepian in Buffalo, New York; and George Tiller in Wichita, Kansas.

Iran featured in the US (and other) media over the controversial re-election of President Mahmoud Ahmadinejad in June 2009. His opponent, Mir-Hossein Mousavi, issued a statement saying that the election results were a 'charade', and urged his supporters to fight the decision but without any acts of violence. This resulted in massive post-election street protests. However, the powerful Iranian Guardian Council formally certified the re-election of President Ahmadinejad to a second four-year term, saying there was no validity to charges of voting fraud.[19] Perhaps Deeba's Iranian identity persuaded her to take the side of the Guardian Council when she said that there is also corruption in the US election process but it was never in the news:

> Yeah, the old [guard], I'm not very familiar with Iranian politics . . . But the funny thing was . . . I started asking myself how come five years ago I didn't go around saying 'Where did my vote go for John Kerry [opponent of George W. Bush]?', you know?

The 2000 US presidential election was controversial. In this election, George W. Bush ran on the Republican ticket against Democratic candidate Al Gore. The election was flooded with allegations of voter fraud and disenfranchisement, particularly in Florida. Eventually, the US Supreme Court gave the state of Florida's electoral votes to George W. Bush.[20] This meant that, although Gore held a slim popular vote victory of 543,895 (0.5%), Bush won the electoral college 271–266, with one Al Gore elector abstaining. The 2004 US presidential election (like 2000) was also decided by one state. Ohio's twenty electoral votes gave President Bush his margin over his Democratic Party opponent, Senator John Kerry.[21] Deeba's hometown was in Ohio so her opinion on the 2004 election result may have some validity. Through her Iranian 'self'

Deeba thought at least there was a democratic process in Iran as demonstrated by the Iranian public protests on the streets, but when there was a reasonable doubt over George W. Bush's election results, Americans were reluctant to go onto the streets and protest:

> I came to ask myself, why didn't Americans, why didn't we pour out onto the street and ask the United States government 'Where did my vote go?' But at the same time it goes to show how far Iran has come, that [this] generation was able to go out onto their street and ask those questions.

The remark 'Why didn't *we* pour out into the streets?' reflect Deeba's Americanness, though she was constantly going back and forth with her comparison of Iran with the USA.

On the topic of homosexuality, Deeba commented:

> What was funny was when President Ahmadinejad had mentioned that we don't have any gay people in the country, the next day on NPR all these gay people are coming out and they're saying 'Yeah, I'm gay, I'm gay'! So that's the thing, it's like okay if there are homosexuals in Iran, maybe ten years from now they might be open about it . . . it goes back to even like ten years ago as an American if you were gay . . . it wasn't even a spoken thing in the United States.

It is also interesting to note here that Deeba used 'we' to refer to Iranians, which was obviously indicative of her collective Iranian identity.

In 2007 during his visit to the USA, President Ahmadinejad gave a talk at Columbia University in New York. He proposed a conspiracy theory when he asked the university audience to look into 'who was truly involved' in the 9/11 terrorist attacks, defended his right to question established Holocaust history, and denied there were gay Iranians. He elicited laughter and boos from the audience when he said, 'In Iran, we don't have homosexuals, like in your country.'[22] Though Deeba spoke of her identity as Iranian American (and defended her Iranian identity), she spoke of her ordeal of 'being Muslim and American' at airports. She said that in the USA 'they would stop me and say "Okay, can you step over here? We have to search you." Then they have this glass-like box and you go in there so they can see you through the machine.' However, in a Muslim country, Deeba found that they practise 'an extreme form'. She said:

> When I was in the United Arab Emirates in the airport . . . and it's a Muslim country, technically, and they [female security] pulled me aside and they told me to take off all my clothes . . . Again being Muslim, being American, you're sandwiched in between because if you go with your American passport to a Muslim country they're going to treat you the same way that they're being treated here . . . So it makes the situation harder but, like I say, you just have to take it with a grain of salt.

However, the case in point is that identity is always in motion, so the subconscious 'self' may spark up as a spontaneous reflection when one's country of origin is questioned or ridiculed. Also, certain aspects of identity that were not explicitly spoken about (for example, Karishma and Deeba's Muslim identity) came up in the conversation when identity was in crisis, particularly at airports.

Collective identity: African American identity

Francesca Polletta and James Jasper observed that collective identities can be expressed in cultural materials such as common names, narratives, symbols, speech patterns, clothing, customs and traditions. Cultural collective identities can also be formed beyond any common cultural materials through emotional connections (in this case with the African continent). And they may be imagined rather than experienced directly. They are fluid and relational and emerge out of a desire to discover pre-existing bonds, interests and boundaries. It is a process by which individuals try to make sense of broader social interests.[23] Kwame Appiah observed that the 'African American identity (like all other American ethno-racial identities) is centrally shaped by American society and institutions: it cannot be seen as constructed solely within African American communities, any more than whiteness is made only by whites'.[24] Appiah observed that an oppositional character/institution or an 'opposing self' is necessary for the formation of an identity. So a conventional 'white' American society would produce an African American community. Though the African American community has moved on since the Black Power and Civil Rights movements,[25] several researchers have shown that some African Americans still occupy a marginalised position in American society.[26] In my study, however, the participants who identified themselves as African Americans revealed their diverse connections.

Emotional attachment

A first-generation participant, Mesbah, of Algerian background (male, 30, overseas born, educator) migrated to the USA in the 1990s, and he looked visibly 'white', but defined his identity as 'African American I would say, even though I'm not dark. I feel like I belong to Africa more than I belong to Algeria itself' (interview, Massachusetts, November 2009). Mesbah was religious. He was not interested in sport but he listened to religious music, such as *nasheeds*. He said, 'The one I listen to, if I have time of course, I don't know if you know Mishary Rashid Alafasy from Kuwait.'

Mesbah identified himself as 'African American' because he felt connected to the African continent but when he spoke of *nasheeds* he preferred a Kuwaiti singer. It appeared that he was comfortable with a transnational *ummah* connection. However, Mesbah was not alone. I found that a few second-generation young Americans such as Somali Americans would define themselves as 'African Americans', though they were non-traditional African Americans (with no enslavement history in the USA). The US census form has 'African American' in the 'race' category, so some people may classify themselves accordingly. Also, the new immigrants of African background may feel comfortable with their collective African identity because of their diasporic placement in America. They may have an emotional attachment to Africa and a wish that one day they will return 'home'.[27]

Race/colour

A third-generation participant, Adam, of Jamaican background (male, 16, US born), said that his African American identity was linked to his race: 'I was born in America and so were my parents, but both of my grandfathers were born in Jamaica. My African connection is because of my skin colour.' Next, he expressed his connection to sport through his race:

> I have fondness for football as well but I much prefer basketball. Oh, Celtic, Boston Celtics! Because they have three of my favourite players on that team, yes. Kevin Garnett, Paul Pierce and Ray Allen, and . . . and a fourth is Rajon Rondo. They're all African American. (Interview, New York, November 2009)

At the time of the interview Adam looked Muslim because he was wearing the *kufi* (though it is a traditional cap for men in west Africa irrespective of their religion). Adam said that he attended a *madrasah* when he was young, and when he was not attending school (during school break) he attended an African American mosque during *Ramadan* and for Friday prayers. About his friends, Adam said:

> Well, I have friends who are Arab, I have friends who are from Pakistan, I have friends who are African American, I have friends who are Hispanic. I have friends who are Chinese and I have friends from all over.

Some social identity theorists state that external factors (power, politics of difference) or internal factors (similar ingroup feeling) can lead to the construction of one's identity.[28] In Adam's case, his roots (heritage) and visibility (blackness) played leading roles in the construction of his identity. Also, in his interview, Adam did not specifically mention if he had any white American friends. This factor could have impacted on his restricted African American identity.

Religion

Mariyam, of African American origin (female, 22, US born), said that her identity was African American. However, most of the time during her interview she spoke about Islam and how to be a 'good Muslim'. Mariyam converted to Islam because she intended to marry a Muslim man. The marriage did not take place but she was happy that she had converted. Mariyam wore the *hijab*. She said that she used to be a cheerleader and also played soccer but now she has abandoned playing soccer because in some sports, she says, 'You have to shake hands with men.' She liked swimming and was a fan of the New England Patriots American football team and the Boston Red Sox for baseball. On music, Mariyam said:

> Music is *harram* and I'm trying to stop but there's one CD I keep listening to. The name of this group is New Radicals and the name of the song 'You Get What You Give'. It's about rich people always dressed up and they have closed hearts, they don't care . . . So this is the music I listen to and I like it but I'm trying to really cut back because there's maybe two swears in it . . . He says the A-word for your butt. [The song includes the words 'This whole damn world can fall apart . . . We'll kick your ass in']. (Interview, Massachusetts, November 2010)

According to Mariyam (and a few other participants in this study) listening to music is *harram*. Mariyam said, 'Music is *harram* because Satan made the trumpets.' The topic of listening to music, however, has been contentious among Muslims. The British pop singer Yusuf Islam, formerly known as Cat Stevens, stopped singing shortly after his conversion to Islam in 1977. He was told by his Islamic teachers that music 'represents frivolity and time wasting', but since then he came to understand that music can serve a purpose. He thought that music can be healing when he noticed Bosnian Muslims, who had lost everything else during the war in Yugoslavia, listened to music to maintain their sanity.[29] Whereas some Muslims, such as the mystical Sufi sect and the Turkish 'whirling dervishes', consider music to be part of 'the very essence of Islam', others, for example ultra-conservative Muslims such as the Salafis, feel it is 'intoxicating' and distracting from meditation and spiritual concentration (I discuss music further in the Conclusion). Mariyam had some ultra-conservative Muslim friends from an Arab background, so she was perhaps influenced by their thoughts.

Visibility: men

Ehsan, of African American/Native American/Spanish background (male, 19, US born), was bearded and visibly Muslim; he wore the white Arab *jilbab* and *kufi*. Ehsan identified himself first as an African American, and second as a Muslim American. Ehsan was not a sports fan but he listened to music. 'Actually hip-hop, I also like a little soft rock, alternative rock, classical, R&B. Yeah, I do listen to hip-hop.' Ehsan spoke passionately of Palestine, which I thought was an awkward African American connection:

I love the country Palestine. I feel for that country so much basically because [of] all the things that they're going through. Actually, my best friend, he's Palestinian. So he's also led me to love the country even more, just because of how he loves it and his passion for his country. (Interview, Michigan, April 2010)

Ehsan's Palestinian connection came through his social group, especially a college friend who was a Palestinian. Ehsan's friend visited Palestine and shared with him the difficulties the Palestinians face in their everyday lives. And Ehsan revealed his Muslim identity when he said:

Being Black and Muslim can be difficult. So I can walk down the street here [in a Muslim majority suburb] with a turban and my *thob* or whatever, and I feel comfortable, I feel safe. But walking down my street, because there are not very many Muslims on the side of town where I live, it's kind of difficult because they'll say something like 'Why is that on your head?' or 'Terrorist' or things like that.

The Mosque Study Project of American mosques in 2000 found that African Americans comprised 63 per cent of the converts to Sunni Islam and 68 per cent of those African American converts were male.[30] A few other African American participants in this study who were visibly Muslim said that they were often misunderstood by the wider society because of their colour and Islamic visibility. In his study on African American young Muslims, Richard Brent Turner observed that since 9/11 the mainstream backlash against Muslims has also been directed against African Americans. However, the post-September 11th media coverage has been focused on the immigrant communities, particularly Middle Eastern people. The social and political perspectives of African American Muslims, who constitute roughly 30 per cent of regular mosque participants, have largely been ignored.[31]

Visibility: women

Aisha, of an African American/Native American background (female, 33, US born), identified herself as 'Black American Muslim'. Aisha converted to Islam through marriage. Regarding this conversion Aisha says, 'I had no idea about Islam . . . And how I came to *din* [faith] was [through] my [former] husband . . . I heard him call the *azan, alhamdulillah*, I took my *shahada* that day and was covering that same day.' Aisha was a single mother of four children, and she said that she was not a TV person, 'I'm more of a movie person but I am a writer (writing a book)'. Aisha thought that being black and Muslim was difficult:

I suffered a lot because of Islam. Where I worked at the time . . . when I first became Muslim and I started covering, the first thing my boss said was, 'How long are you going to wear that thing?' And I said, 'What thing? . . . This is a part of who I am . . . and I've been working for your company as an accountant for seven years, I'm still the same person . . . I feel like you're starting to discriminate against me and if that's discrimination then I need you to talk to my lawyer.' (Interview, Virginia, December 2009)

Aisha continued, 'And if I may add, there is prejudice even in Islam.' She talked of her experience with the mainstream Sunni Muslims:

You can take this as my opinion, a Pakistani Muslim who won't accept a black Muslim or don't think that you should even be Muslim, so that's very difficult. I've experienced every day and even during *Ramadan* . . . I was in the mosque at *Ramadan* to serve the people to feed them and, *alhamdulillah*, Allah made a way for me to do that, but because I was black some people wouldn't take the food from me.

When I asked Aisha about her identity, she replied:

We went from being coloured to black to African American; we went through all these changes of 'who we are'. It's one thing to be an American; if you're American and non-Muslim it's pretty much accepted. To be a black American is different, it's several variances. To be a black American is very difficult even before Islam. It's even more difficult being American, black and Muslim. I've added not only that I'm an American or black American but now I'm a black American who covers and is Muslim.

In her study on Muslim women of South Asian and African American backgrounds, Jamillah Karim found that sometimes African American Muslim women (and men) are forced to isolate themselves from South Asian Muslims because of the latter's lack of acceptance of the former. African American Muslims have been historically stigmatised as having low educational levels, living in poor neighbourhoods, and being unemployed or underemployed, so this distances them geographically from South Asian or other Muslims. Typically, these African Americans choose to pray in African American mosques 'not because they feel excluded from immigrant mosques, but because they prefer a space that radiates distinctly African American Muslim heritage'.[32] There is also a general consensus among African Americans that immigrant Muslims are obsessed with the ordeals of their fellow Muslims in Iraq or Afghanistan and unsympathetic to the plight of African Americans in terms of poverty and their overall marginalised position in American society.[33] However, Aisha was educated and had the confidence to integrate into the immigrant Muslim community, even though she faced resistance from some of them.

Collective identity: Arab American identity

Participants in this study with an Arab heritage defined themselves either as 'Arab' or 'Arab Muslim', or as 'Arab Americans'. Amaney Jamal noted that some Arabs endorsed their collective Arab American identity because of social and cultural factors and the political situations of their country of origin. Through various institutions – family, Arab and Islamic schools, social and cultural organisations and social networks – Arab Americans continue to reproduce their Arab identity characteristics in the US.[34] Nadine Naber further noted that Arabs are a heterogeneous group; for example, there are Lebanese, Iraqis and Sudanese, but they are conflated by the media and Hollywood movies into one homogenous 'Arab' group.[35] Other scholars have observed that Arab stereotypes in the media, such as 'backwards', 'murky oil sheikhs' and 'terrorists', could be a compelling reason to endorse a collective Arab American identity.[36] (I discuss media stereotypes further in Chapter 4.) Steven Salaita wrote that the constant 'othering' of Arab Americans since 9/11 is reinforcing the tendency of the Arab population in America to endorse a unifying Arab American identity.[37] As the social theorist Richard Jenkins said, 'Individuals, in using stereotypical categories to define themselves, thus bring into being human collective life. Individuals will self-categorise themselves differently and the contingencies with which they are faced.'[38] In the following subsections, I examine the construction of an Arab-Muslim, Arab American identity and how it is manifested.

Arab to Muslim Arab: same social group

Hameed, of Egyptian origin (male, 15, US born), identified himself as an 'Arab': 'I just like to classify myself as Arab 'cos the fact, it's like pointing out that I'm Egyptian; actually it causes [division], the other Arabs like Palestinians go against us and I think Arab in general is better' (interview, New York, November 2009).

Hameed attended an Islamic school where he felt if he retained his ethnic (Egyptian) identity he would be distinctive among his school friends, who were mostly Arabs of other nationalities. Hameed said that if he retained his Egyptian identity, the Palestinians may 'go against us'. It was not quite clear whether the Egyptian political situation had any impact on this statement. Egypt has long been an ally of Israel, so for that reason a few Egyptian students, who formed a minority in the school, may have felt marginalised and therefore decided it was necessary to adopt the broader 'Arab' identity. Hameed was fond of basketball and lived in a predominantly Arab area.

Safwan, of Palestinian background (male, 16, US born), attended the same Muslim school and said that he felt 'Muslim Arab'. Safwan was born in the USA but was raised in Palestine, where he spent ten years. He also went to Palestine every year with his family. He has seen the hardship of the Palestinians in Palestine, though he is from the peaceful part of Palestine, Ramallah. Safwan speaks fluent Arabic and listens to Arabic music. When I asked him if he had a girlfriend, Safwan replied, 'No, we don't . . . it's *harram*.' I asked him, 'You listen to which music – is it hip-hop, rap?' Safwan replied, 'More of cultural music . . . there's a lot but the one I mostly listen to, his name is Naser el Fares, he's also from Palestine, Ramallah.' Safwan later explained the kind of songs Naser el Fares sings. 'Ah well, it's more of like wedding songs, but it's the day before the wedding, we have this party for the men that they do at night . . . he sings *dabke falasteeny*.' *Dabke* is the cultural Arab dance for wedding occasions and a *dabke falasteeny* is a specific Palestinian variant. Regarding his identity, Safwan said:

> I feel I'm more of a Muslim Arab, yeah. I speak the language. I was born here and my parents are from there. Well, we feel that there is no difference; in the end we're all Arabs, it's the same thing, just different places that we live in. (Interview, New York, November 2009)

Instead of identifying exclusively as Palestinian, Safwan chose the broader Arab-Muslim identity, perhaps because it suited his ideology to 'fit in' with his school's broader social circle. Safwan enjoyed swimming and lived in a predominantly 'white mainstream American' suburb.

Arab American: a lot of outside pressure

Habib, of Libyan origin (male, 16, overseas born), was not into sport but he liked reading. Habib attended a public school. At home he spoke Arabic. I asked Habib, 'Your Libyan Arabic, is it similar to Palestinian Arabic or Iraqi Arabic?' He replied, 'Yeah, kind of. It's a little bit different, but it's still basically Arabic. We would understand each other.' Regarding his identity, Habib said:

> I would say 'Arab American' because it's important that I'm from Libya but when you talk to other Americans you just say 'Arab American', because if you tell them 'Libyan' they're not going to like it . . . They immediately relate you to Gaddafi. There's a lot of pressure. You have to think what you have to say before you say it. (Interview, Michigan, April 2010)

Habib spoke about the then Libyan leader, the controversial Colonel Muammar Gaddafi. 'Well, I personally, my family at least, we don't really support him, so what we think he is doing is wrong and the media talks about how it's wrong, we agree with them pretty much.' Habib also referred to the Lockerbie plane bomber Abdelbaset Ali Mohmet al-Megrahi's cancer diagnosis. Habib said,

'They said that he had cancer or something, so they were going to let him out of jail.' It was interesting to note that a second-generation Libyan American youth was well informed about incidents related to Libya.

In January 2001, al-Megrahi was convicted of killing 270 people by blowing up Pan Am Flight 103 over Lockerbie in 1989. However, in August 2009, he was freed from prison in Scotland on compassionate grounds because he was said to be suffering from terminal prostate cancer. Al-Megrahi returned to Libya but there was strong protest in some of the US media. During that period I was in the USA for my research on young American Muslims' identity. So I expected to find a situation of unease for people of Libyan/Arab background, even if they did not support such terrorism. Megrahi died on 20 May 2012, nearly three years after his release from prison.

The question of loyalty

Two participants, Bakr and Murtaza, volunteered to sit for an interview together and identified themselves as Arab Americans. Bakr, of Syrian background (male, 18, US born) said, 'I would say I'm an Arab American you know, I am half-half, like in blood too' (interview, Michigan, April 2010). Bakr has visited Syria several times with his parents, so his Americanness comes from the place where he was born and raised and his Arabness from his heritage. Murtaza's explanation was that his father has lived in the US for a long period and has endorsed both Arabian and American culture; so, like his father, he chose to identify himself as Arab American. Murtaza also said that Palestine was still an occupied territory, so there was no point for him to endorse an alternative Palestinian identity.

Both Bakr and Murtaza were keen on sport, which reflected their American identity. Bakr played basketball and he supported the local team, the Detroit Pistons, whereas Murtaza preferred American football and supported the Minnesota Vikings. But when it came to joining the army, their Arabness came to the surface. They spoke of the Arab American festival that takes place in Dearborn every year:

> We just have it on the street. They just close it down from Greenfield to Schaffer and the whole street is just music and festivals and stuff. They bring in the rides and stuff and . . . It's free and they have it in July. Yeah, it gets bigger and bigger every year.

They explained how the US Army and the CIA are keen to hire Arabs/Muslims at this event:

> I think it was like the last two times the US Army and the CIA were there. They have business booths . . . they want to hire translators. It's a bad thing because you are translating for countries that you are originally from, you know. It's kind of like a

double [-crossing] thing . . . And you are from the other countries so, just stay away from the army, just totally stay away from it, the whole thing.

Both Bakr and Murtaza were concerned that unemployment was very high in Michigan (about 15 per cent) and that it was difficult to find work. However, their Arab identity was preventing them from seeking employment in the US security forces. It should be noted that in 2010 the number of military person-nel on active duty in the US armed forces was 1.46 million.[39] Yet in the same year, there were only 3,500 Muslims in the US military which constituted a tiny minority (0.24 per cent) of the total active duty personnel in the US armed forces.[40]

It is the media

Finally, Amjad, of Jordanian background (male, 18, overseas born) said this about his identity:

With the people I am [with], I mean it [my identity] changes, it differs. I was raised here in America even though I was born in Jordan and at home I have an Arab iden-tity of course. I still retain, you know, both Arab and American identity. (Interview, Massachusetts, November 2009)

To my question 'How do you connect yourself to your American identity?', Amjad replied:

Oh, sports-wise, for example, [a] competitive background that I feel that has been instilled in me being raised here. Education-wise . . . as American culture, they are very competitive, they're very strict with their education, like everyone always seeks to be the best in their field and excel. I feel that has also been instilled in me living here. That, you know, you believe maybe not so much in what used to be called the 'American Dream' but more in that there's always an opportunity and just how you see it; it all depends on how you see it.

Amjad's American identity was reflected in his sports and education. Amjad's Arab identity appeared when he was critical of the media.

I don't feel the media is really impartial when portraying Muslims . . . for example, Tareq Mehanna, the person who was arrested from Worcester [Massachusetts], he taught in Worcester and I believe he lived in the Boston area . . . The media focused more on what he was alleged of doing, and they really didn't focus on the qualities of the person himself . . . I mean it was one isolated incident but then by displaying it nationally the whole world started . . . they view one person, they exercise that view upon the group, that's all.

Amjad meant that the media can sometimes portray a Muslim so negatively that the whole world comes to view all Muslims negatively. In 2008, Tarek Mehanna, an American-born Muslim of Egyptian background, graduated from the Massachusetts College of Pharmacy, where his father was a professor. In October 2009 Mehanna was arrested in Sudbury, Massachusetts on charges that he was planning a 'violent *jihad*' against US politicians and American troops in Iraq and conspired to shoot randomly in shopping malls. He is alleged to have conspired with two other men. However, some Muslims felt that Mehanna was innocent and that the government was trying to foment Islamophobia.[41]

Single ethnic identity

Stuart Hall observed that identity is fluid and is subject to change under different circumstances. It is produced through specific historical and institutional structures. However, it can also emerge within the play of specific modalities of power, and thus is more a product of the marking of difference and exclusion. Sometimes it can be a sign of unity (without internal differentiation) versus the external 'other'.[42] Social identity theory indicates that sometimes differential treatment by the majority group may lead to an 'outgroup' sentiment, which may impact on one's identity formation.[43] Also, immigrants living in diasporas may desire one day to return 'home' and therefore they remain strongly connected to their ethnic culture.

I'm only Guyanese

Qutb (male, 18, US born, Guyanese background) identified himself as 'only Guyanese'. He was born in the USA and had never been to Guyana but said, 'Yeah, my parents are Guyanese so I would consider myself Guyanese . . . 100 per cent.' I asked him, 'Do you socialise more with the Guyanese community?' Qutb replied, 'Not really, I socialise with a very diverse type of people in New York and through high school, but my connection is through family.' On his leisure time activities, Qutb said, 'As a child, no I haven't played much sport . . . Leisure time is mostly with computers' (interview, New York, January 2010).

In the Australian context, in 2004, Elsa Germain conducted research on 400 young people of minority cultures, aged twelve to nineteen. The participants were of indigenous or non-English-speaking backgrounds. Germain found that the participants who had lighter skins or looked white would identify themselves with the Anglo-Australian identity and describe themselves as 'white', whereas the visibly ethnic participants would adopt a bicultural identity rather than their exclusive cultural identity. However, some visibly ethnic youths, such as the Torres Strait Islander respondents, felt they did not 'belong' and were more likely to acknowledge their cultural roots because that appeared natural.[44] Similarly, Qutb chose to link his identity with his family, so it manifested itself through his choice. However, the next two case studies are of participants whose identity was constructed through the 'othering' of the wider society.

I'm a Bangladeshi, 100 per cent

Maimuna (female, 30, overseas born, Bangladeshi background, educator) identified herself as 'Bangladeshi 100 per cent'. Maimuna migrated to the USA in 2007, so she still felt very connected to her country of origin. Also, Maimuna was upset about her perceived 'outgroup' treatment. She said:

> I just want to share with you one of my bad experiences in [the] time of my citizenship interview. I went to the immigration office and I was wearing my *hijab*. The lady immigration officer asked me some questions and she also interviewed my husband but I think it's not normal [questions]. My husband has [a] beard and [the] first question was if we were married. After that she asked me two more questions: 'Are you involved in [any] terrorist group and do you donate to a Muslim terrorist group?' This is humiliating or this is racism, whatever you say, I think so. And the other question: 'Do you hate any group?' She specifically asked me, 'Do you hate Jewish people?' I said, 'No. Why should I hate the Jewish people? I came here from Bangladesh and, do you know, we are new here, we are struggling to establish ourselves, we have no time to hate any people. We are struggling in language or culture, everything. We have to adjust ourselves with this culture.' It was so embarrassing. (Interview, Michigan, April 2010)

The question 'Are you involved with a terrorist organisation?' is written on the immigration form which everyone coming to the USA or Australia has to fill out. For security reasons, this question is necessary, though Maimuna thought that she and her husband were asked this question because they were visibly Muslim. However, the question asking if Maimuna (and her husband) hated Jewish people was subjective. A Muslim appearance (for example, the *hijab*) can have an impact on some people. In this context, I would like to share my mother's experience at an immigration/customs office in the USA. She was travelling with me from Bangladesh to the USA. She looked Muslim. She was wearing a *sari* and a scarf over her head. At the airport immigration counter (for incoming passengers) we were asked to go to the immigration office, which was also located at the airport. My mother and a non-Muslim black woman passenger were waiting in their wheelchairs for the immigration/custom officers to call them (for visa reasons). They kept my mother waiting for more than an hour and let the other woman leave within a short time. I was surprised that while both women were wheelchair (special assistance) passengers, my mother was treated differently. It was also offputting when the immigration officer asked me if I spoke English, though I did not look visibly Muslim (I did not wear any conspicuous Islamic dress). They simply associated me as the 'other' because I was with my mother.

A certain topic was a common concern for some participants, though their national identities differed. For example, Maimuna expressed concern over the new immigration laws passed in Arizona:

> Now [the] immigrant issue in Arizona is a burning question. I mean President Obama attracts the young generation, he has magnetic power, just everybody [is] focused on how Obama is doing good. Sometimes I think people forget to judge if he is doing good or bad. I think after ten years or twenty years history will tell whatever he did good or bad, not now.

Maimuna did not explain Arizona's new immigration law, but she questioned whether President Obama had any say over it. Bushra, another participant (female, 18, overseas born), explained the law. She mentioned her identity as 'Bangladeshi Muslim American', yet like Maimuna she was also concerned about the law:

> The governor passed – I'm not sure who the governor is, but she passed the immigration laws in Arizona, which means that they're going to try to limit the number of immigrants in their state, within their borders. And the cops, the authority, the police are now allowed to pull over anyone who's suspected of being an immigrant. And at all times Arizona residents or anyone visiting in the state of Arizona must carry paperwork, legal paperwork, such as a passport and a birth certificate to prove that they are American residents. And, if not, they can be jailed up to six months. (Interview, Michigan, May 2010)

On 23 April 2010, Arizona Governor Jan Brewer signed into law what many call the toughest bill on illegal immigration in the country. The bill makes it a crime to stay in Arizona illegally, requires all aliens to carry immigration paperwork, and levies sanctions against employers who knowingly hire illegal workers. Facing criticism that the law would legalise racial profiling, the Arizona legislature modified the law on 1 May 2010. It now states that police officers cannot use race as the sole grounds for suspecting that someone is in the country illegally. On 27 May, the talk radio host Glenn Beck said on his show that '64 per cent of Americans support the Arizona immigration law'. And a Pew Research Center poll conducted between 6 and 9 May 2010 found that 59 per cent approved the law.[45]

Though the immigration law in Arizona may impact on Hispanics, Muslim leaders observe that it will also impact on Muslims. A Muslim leader in Michigan, Dawud Walid, said, 'Since legal status in America cannot be

Figure 3.1 Racial profiling. *From* Muslim Observer, *6 May 2010*

ascertained by looking at persons' skin colour or religious attire, this bill becoming law has the potential of targeting Latinos and Muslims from various national backgrounds'[46] (see Figure 3.1). President Obama was also critical of the Arizona law when he said that it threatened 'to undermine basic notions of fairness that we cherish as Americans, as well as the trust between police and our communities that is so crucial to keeping us safe'.[47] However, this law was passed by the Arizona state senate, so President Obama could not overhaul it.

Why I am a Somali

An overseas-born participant of Somali origin, Zaker (male, 24, educator), migrated to the USA at the age of four, where he was raised and educated, but when asked he said, 'I am a Somali.' Zaker was very passionate about American sports but at the same time he felt very connected to his country of origin, even though he has never visited Somalia since migrating to the United States. Zaker said, 'We have a region called XXX, that's where my tribe lives. And it's a very interesting place where actually now they say there is more genocide than Darfur.' Like many immigrants, Zaker was concerned about the ordeals of his people back home. Zaker showed me his key ring, which had an emblem of his clan on it, and said, 'You can see my key tag, and on 21 September we have this thing called, like, World Peace thing.' Zaker added, 'Yeah, World Peace Protest, and then that day I want to actually have all these people come out. Like learned people, people like you who don't know what XXX [my tribe, its people and their ordeal] is all about.'

Zaker criticised the US media for profiling the Somali people as 'pirates' and was critical of the American government's handling of the case of a fifteen-year-old Somali pirate, Abduwali Abdukhadir Muse. Zaker said that in Somalia normally the pirates send 'a guy to deliver a message'. In this case they sent Muse to a US ship on the Somali coast, and he was captured and sent to the US for trial. Zaker observed:

> However, that fifteen-year-old, I believe personally, should have gone to court in Somalia, should receive his punishment in Somalia, you know, because he's a Somali citizen. You cannot bring an American boy to Somalia and say, 'We're going to put you in court.' If America has free speech, freedom of anything, I am willing to say that was wrong, you know? What I believe about pirates is they're little boys, fifteen-year-olds, seventeen-year-olds, uneducated, that are trying to find food. Why they're doing that is because that's the way to bring money home. (Interview, Massachusetts, November 2009)

It was reported that on 8 May 2009, Muse led a gang of four pirates who attacked an American ship, the *Maersk Alabama*, demanded a ransom of $2 million, and took the captain hostage. Muse was wrestled down, tied up with a wire, and later brought to the USA for trial. The three other pirates involved in this attack were killed by Navy Seal snipers in a rescue mission for Captain Richard Philips of the *Maersk Alabama*. However, New York civil rights lawyers have questioned the legality of Muse's being in American custody rather than Kenyan, which has an international agreement to prosecute terrorists, and whether his prosecution was lawful given the uncertainties surrounding his age.[48] In May 2010 Muse was convicted of the hijacking of the *Maersk Alabama* and the kidnapping of its captain. He was sentenced to nearly thirty-four years in prison.[49]

As Zaker continued his interview, he said that he had been a victim of racial profiling by the FBI at a time when he was representing the USA as an elite national icon in another western country:

> My mother called me crying, tears and like, 'Where are you, what are you doing, are you up to no good?' . . . And they're [the FBI] in my home harassing, and my mom lost 18 pounds 'cos she was worried. They asked her, 'Where is your son? What does he do? Do you know anything about him?' He [the agent/investigator] never came

out with anything . . . I got a lawyer and then my lawyer had to call him and clear that up but there was nothing to clear. Like why you're harassing this guy – because he's a Somali, because he's a young Muslim? How many Americans that are not black, not Muslims are there doing things?

On the topic of the USA Patriot Act, Zaker spoke of his ordeal when he was at a US airport:

Until this search and FBI and all this . . . I'm still shocked, you know? I'm a young, educated African American man, who never thought about nothing but good about life now. But when I see all these searches, all these discriminations, breaking your privacy, you know, not having human rights, basically I don't have any privacy. I think I lost rights, my human rights were violated here in America, where the man [at the airport/border security] was telling me that you've got to tell me how much money you make. I can't refuse to answer because he's going to have me there another eight, ten hours, you know? He takes my cell phone and keeps it like five, six hours; he gets my laptop; he gets my videos; he takes basically my wallet . . .

Speaking about . . . missing flights, there were times that I missed flights and I had to spend the night over at the airport, wait until the next day because of searching.

As revealed through his interview, Zaker felt connected to his country of origin, Somalia. Zaker's connection to his Somali community was revealed through his social work with young Somalis and, finally, his dream was that Somalia would get US approval and that one day he would visit Somalia. While speaking of racial profiling, Zaker speculated that he was victimised because he was 'black', 'African American' and 'Muslim'.

Sometimes US security officials can go overboard with their searching of the visible 'other', but it must be acknowledged that some Somali Muslims have become a security concern. For example, it was a matter of great concern for the Somali Muslim community and the wider American society when in 2008 some young Somali Americans from Minnesota went to Somalia to join the *jihadi* al-Shabaab group led by Ahmed Abdi Godane. It is alleged that al-Shabaab had alliances to Anwar Alwaqi's al-Qaeda in Yemen and to the Pakistani-based al-Qaeda terrorist network, that it had up to 3,000 fighters and a batch of American recruits. And al-Shabaab had been branded a terrorist organisation. In 2008, a 26-year-old first-generation Somali American from Minnesota, who had been trained by al-Shabaab, carried out a suicide bombing against the Somali government. And in 2009 Burhan Hassan, a seventeen-year-old Somali American also from Minnesota, went to fight with al-Shabaab and was killed in Somalia.[50]

I believe that security is important but when it takes the form of stereotypes, it is not helpful. For example, in his interview Zakir also said that sometimes at US airports, he was asked which tribe he belonged to, and at times in his neighbourhood, people yelled 'Pirate!' at him.

Religious identity

Only Muslim identity

Some female participants in this study said that they did not have any alternative but to assume an Islamic identity because that is what their parents wanted by sending them to Islamic schools or youth clubs. Some said that they assumed an Islamic identity because of peer pressure; for example, in a public school or university if they did not wear the *hijab* then their Muslim friends who wore the *hijab* would view them as the 'other'.[51] Others have chosen a Muslim identity of their own accord; for example, Afrosa (female, 15, US born, Bangladeshi background) said, 'I feel more Muslim because American people, they do different sort of things. Muslims follow everything their parents say and the Quran, that's what I follow' (interview, Michigan, April 2010).[52]

In the British context, however, Avtar Brah observed that sometimes the discourses and practices of Islamophobia can lead Muslims to specific religious identification and connect them to the Muslim *ummah* nationally and transnationally. Furthermore, conflicts in global sites such as Iraq, Chechnya and Kashmir increase their sense of grievance on behalf of all Muslims.[53] In my study, I found that some participants' connection to a Muslim identity was through either ethnic or religious ingroup feelings (discussed next).

'I'm Muslim'

Shimaz (female, 15, US born, Pakistani origin) said, 'I'm Muslim, not Pakistani, and not American.' Shimaz was struggling with her ethnic identity because she was not brought up in her parents' country of origin. She felt comfortable with her Muslim identity because she spent her time in an Islamic environment and attended an Islamic school. Shimaz said that she watched American football with her brothers on the TV, and that she was a fan of the Pittsburgh Steelers. However, she did not connect herself with an American identity because she observed that mainstream society, particularly the media, was treating Muslims as the 'other'. She expressed this dilemma as she spoke about the controversial Afia Siddiqui case:

> Afia Siddiqui actually was in Boston, she was a doctor there. And you know, they [the media] twisted her story around because she went to Pakistan to visit her mom with her children and when she was in a cab to go back home, her car was stopped and she had no idea why she was being stopped or anything. They took her children away from her and they separated her away from her family . . . and the media put

her in some mental place. And they changed the story around over and over again, but apparently she is guilty of holding a gun [to] a CIA agent . . . They [the media] want to give Muslims a bad name and they just feel so negative about us. (Interview, Maryland, February 2010)

The Guardian reported that Afia Siddiqui disappeared from Karachi in 2003 and reappeared in Ghazni, Afghanistan in 2008. It was alleged that there was a dispute in a police station in Afghanistan and the US accused Siddiqui of trying to shoot two soldiers and two FBI agents. She was sent to the US in 2009, tried and in 2010 sentenced to eighty-six years in jail.[54] Consequently, in Pakistan Siddiqui became a *cause célèbre*. Critics and supporters in Pakistan compared her case with that of the FBI contractor Raymond Davis. Despite allegedly killing three Pakistani citizens, Davis was set free to return to the US in January 2011.[55] In April 2011 Raza Rabbani, a senator for Sindh in the Pakistani parliament, commented in a US report about the following US major violations of human rights: the Siddiqui case; killing people in drone attacks; using power in Iraq and Afghanistan; and the inhuman manhandling of prisoners, which continues at the Guantánamo camp (despite corrective measures announced by President Obama).[56] Both the cases (Siddiqui and Davis) are complex, but the point I would like to make is that incidents that connect to ingroup identity can play a major role in people's identity formation. Especially noteworthy is that in this study only some participants of Pakistani origin discussed the Siddiqui case, which again shows their ingroup ethnic (Pakistani) connection.

I'm Muslim, 'Slave of Allah'

Faizul (male, 24, overseas born, Bangladeshi background) migrated to America with his parents when he was eight years old. He attended a public school with other students of diverse backgrounds. He eventually became an educator and was involved with Islamic organisations. Regarding his early life, Faizul said that he stopped lying and stopped hanging around with the wrong friends. He confessed, 'I used to work in a bar, and I needed to get away from all those bad things. So I became a better individual, morally and ethically.' On his entertainment choice, Faizul said that he listened to music 'but the clear clean ones'. In sport, Faizul likes ice hockey: 'I like [the Detroit] Red Wings a lot and I only watch them; other than that I try to keep away because it's very addictive . . . They lost 2-0 for now but we'll come back, *insh'Allah.*' Faizul defined himself as a Muslim, and provided several reasons for his exclusive Muslim identity. First, he related himself with religion:

I consider myself a slave of Allah, working for Allah towards any human being . . . if there's an accident outside my road, or outside right now in the building, I'm not going to sit here and identify this individual as Christian or Jew, I'm going to identify them as human and that is why Allah has sent Prophet Muhammad [PBUH] to serve the humanity. (Interview, Michigan, May 2010)

Then he expressed his ideological battle with the American system: the American media, the FBI, American foreign policy and American democracy:

If my ideologies or my beliefs come in contradiction of what American ideologies are, I'm sorry, I'm going to take my belief before my culture. American media is always negative on Muslims. For example, whenever they're allowed they would make fun of prophets and messengers but whenever you make a comment about Israel they're really mad and they're really scared . . . CNN an example, Fox too.

Further on the media, Faizul said, 'For example, look at what's going on at Guantánamo. There are so many tortures and oppression but none of it the media showed, nobody revealed it.' Faizul thought the American media did not provide accurate international news, saying, 'Look what happened in Iraq, in Afghanistan. They always hide things, they always do undercover things. Why should I believe what they tell me about [the] Fort Hood shooting [see Chapter 4]?' Then Faizul spoke of an FBI raid on some Christian militia in March 2010 and compared it with the heavy-handedness of the FBI in the Imam Luqman case: 'Well, hello! What happened to Iman Luqman? How come you guys [FBI] shot him down? Nineteen times, yes. It doesn't make sense. Logically, it doesn't make sense.'[57]

The question of the FBI's shooting of the African American Imam Luqman was also raised by other participants who lived in Michigan. In October 2009, Imam Luqman Ameen Abdullah was shot a total of twenty times (incurring twenty-one wounds, from which he died) during a raid by federal law enforcement agents on a warehouse in Dearborn. The autopsy on Imam Luqman found that he was hit twice in the chest, four times in the abdomen, twice in the groin, four times in the left hip and side, seven times in the left thigh, once in the scrotum and once in the back. A federal indictment alleged that Imam Luqman led a radical separatist mosque and a stolen-goods ring, and that he had opened fire during their raid on a stolen-goods operation. However, Dawud Walid, executive director of CAIR Michigan, questioned why, if Imam Luqman had been killed instantly, he was found handcuffed.[58]

Faizul also expressed his Islamic identity through other points:

I didn't vote. My parents voted; I didn't vote and I don't want to support the system in any way. Because I believe for me to even support such a system that does not give any kind of fairness, like I said, there's no free education, there's no free health care system. It's not providing me anything and I don't believe in democracy because it's against my belief. Islam says sovereignty belongs to God, it doesn't belong to humanity . . . So if American ideology contradicts this, if people cannot see clearly that it is doing wrong to humanity, then I don't know what I can put my emphasis on.

Faizul was not only critical of US domestic and foreign policies; he was critical of Muslims living overseas who failed to work for their fellow Muslims. When I asked him if he had watched a recent Bollywood movie, *My Name Is Khan* (which was critical of the US government's racial profiling after 9/11), Faizul replied, 'I'm kind of against certain movies, such as *My Name Is Khan*.' Faizul explained his distaste for the movie: 'Personally I think Shahrukh Khan [the lead actor in *My Name is Khan*], who is very famous out there, could do a lot for Muslims but I don't think he's doing enough.' Once again Faizul linked his Islamic identity transnationally when he said:

> Shahrukh Khan is not doing enough for the Muslims because if he was to, at least he should have stood up for the Gujarati Muslims at that time when they were getting slaughtered in 2002. I don't think he was doing anything about it.

Faizul was referring to a conflict between Hindus and Muslims in India. On 27 February 2002 a train bound for Ahmedabad, the largest city in Gujarat, was set on fire and fifty-eight passengers, including twenty-six women and twelve children, were burnt to death. It is alleged that *kar sevaks* (Hindu volunteers) had harassed Muslims travelling on the train and provoked them to carry out this heinous crime. This tragedy led to violence in Gujarat: from 28 February to 2 March 2002, sixteen of Gujarat's twenty-four districts suffered organised armed mob attacks, in which 2,000 lives were lost, 270 mosques and religious and cultural monuments were destroyed, and the Muslim community of Gujarat suffered an enormous loss worth 35 billion Indian rupees.[59] Faizul concluded by praising the journalist Yvonne Ridley:

> Look at her experience with the Taliban. What is her response? Yvonne Ridley, the British news reporter, when she went to Afghanistan, she got caught by the Taliban [on 28 September 2001]. In [the] ten days they were holding on [to] her, and in [those] ten days [with] the treatment they give her, she came back and became Muslim. She said, 'I couldn't believe these people treated me so right, they wanted me to eat, they locked me up in a room, they gave me the keys to the room and they said, "This is your room."' She was shocked by the [considerate] way they treated her, you know.[60]

'Americanness'

When I asked the African American participant Ehsan 'What is it to be an American?' he replied, 'To be an American, first, I guess you would have to love this country. It's like [you would] follow the traditions of America – sports on Sundays, apple pie, baseball, national pastimes . . . Yeah, like baseball' (interview, Michigan, May 2010). Some participants in this study identified their Americanness in other ways.

Two different worlds

Haneef, of Pakistani background (male, 17, overseas born), migrated to the USA in 2001. He spoke Urdu, and was fond of multicultural food: '[I like] Pak food . . . but my mom likes to cook English foods; she cooks Italian food, and watches the Food Network.' Haneef had restrictions at home on watching television: 'At home my dad allows no TV because nobody does their homework, and then when he calls for something they don't go and listen so they just keep watching TV, so that's why he said it affects the education.' On his identity, Haneef said, 'I will say American 100 per cent,' giving the following reasons for his connection to the USA:

> Because everything is over here, education is much better than over there. They [Pakistani education system] give you a lot of work. Here teachers are very nice, they're very polite to you and . . . [In Pakistan] it's more congested, that's what I say . . . more pollution. (Interview, New York, November 2009)

Haneef attended a public school in New York and worked part time in a fast food shop. When I asked if there was a mosque in his neighbourhood, Haneef replied, 'No, I don't go to any mosque.' Regarding sport, Haneef said, 'I play handball with my friends. Sometimes I watch [the] Super Bowl. I support the New York Giants.' Haneef spoke of the walk that he did to raise money for cancer research: 'They [the Pakistanis/Muslims] should try to help as this is, like, their country. I never feel I'm a foreigner. I never feel different, so they should try to help this country to take it up, rise it up [*sic*].' Haneef added, 'I'm going to do engineering to help this country out. Yeah, it's an open country.'

Haneef chose his identity as American perhaps because he felt connected to the wider society through his part-time work and his voluntary work (the cancer walk), he felt more integrated with the wider community through his public school, and because he appreciated the American education system and sport.

No discrimination

Other reasons given by participants who felt very American (though some of them were visibly Muslim, for example bearded men in long Arabic attire, or women wearing *hijabs*) were:

- They were born in the US.
- They had been living in the US for a long time.
- They were fluent in English.
- They worked in mainstream American shops and other businesses.
- They had an American girl/boyfriend.

Faiq, of Somali background (male, 17, overseas born), attended an Islamic school in Florida but felt very American because he migrated with his parents at a very early age and had never been to Somalia. He sometimes went to Minnesota, where there is a large Somali community, but he only stayed there for a couple of weeks, so that did not impact on his identity. Faiq worked in a fast food store with mainstream Americans. He spoke about basketball, mentioning the names of some players he was fond of, such as the NBA player Kevin Durant. Faiq said that as a Muslim he never felt discriminated against:

> I just speak English. So unless they know my first name, they can't tell I'm Muslim. And no one discriminates me because I'm Muslim, thank God. I don't get any of that. Neither does my brother. It's a little harder for my sisters, because they're *hijabis*. And when they go out they sometimes get looks. And it's uncalled for. They don't do anything. They get dirty looks and they're girls and they're sensitive. So I just tell them 'Don't let them bother you'. (Interview, Florida, March 2010)

It's an open society

Nawaz, of Yemeni background (male, 19, US born), said, 'I'm straight American. I'm an American citizen. I feel connected to America, 100 per cent.' Nawaz said that his grandfather and father had lived in the US most of their lives. However, Nawaz was concerned that his father would arrange a marriage for him, so he secretly became engaged to a Colombian Muslim girl (which his parents would not approve of). Nawaz said, 'If I go back to Yemen, I'm for sure getting married [to a Yemeni girl], but I don't want to go back though' (interview, Michigan, April 2010). Nawaz was keen on sport, including soccer, basketball and American football. In my research on young British Muslim identity, I found some Muslims disapproved of their children getting married outside their clan, and considered that having friends of the opposite sex was *harram*. It seems that Nawaz constructed his Americanness through his historical connections and having a girlfriend in the 'open and free' American society.[61] In having to contend with two cultures, Nawaz preferred his Americanness.

It's my culture

Parvez, of Pakistani American origin (male, 24, US born), said:

> I realised how American I was when I travelled . . . I'm attached to this particular
> part of America, I guess as my homeland. I went to Saudi Arabia last year [for teach-
> ing] and really I felt like, oh, you know what, I really missed my home because three
> months away from home is the longest I've ever been and I missed the American
> holidays. You know, fall for us is apples and pumpkins and Thanksgiving and
> Halloween, Christmas and like, over there, none of that. It gets a little bit cooler but
> it's not the same, you know. (Interview, Massachusetts, November 2009.)

Parvez's mother was a mainstream white American and his maternal grandparents (with whom he was closely connected) were non-Muslims. So he
enjoyed the American cultural celebrations such as Halloween and Christmas,
which are forbidden in Saudi Arabia. Parvez was not interested in sport but he
enjoyed music and he was passionate about learning languages. He said, 'I love
international music. There's this one Arabic musician, Algerian, Cheb Khaled.
I like his music a lot. I love Brazilian music, rock music.' He was very transnational in his love for music. Parvez also took pride in performing the *hajj*
while he was in Saudi Arabia. However, his identity construction was mainly
influenced by American culture.

No choice but to be American

Aimal, of Lebanese-Greek origin (female, 17, US born) said, 'I play tennis, volleyball, I used to surf but I don't do that any more. I wrestle. I work out every
day. I go to the gym. I just probably say I'm American.' When I commented 'I
see you are wearing the scarf (*hijab*)', Aimal responded:

> I started wearing one this year. I am new to Arabs. I've never been around Arabs
> my whole life. Honestly, when I first moved to this school, I was scared, because my
> cousin died in September 11, and I had it in my head that Arabs were terrorists. That's
> what I had the vision of when you hear so many things from different Americans. I
> came here and my dad was like, 'I want you guys near your culture, near your people.
> In this school you are going to have to start putting on the scarf.' I mean, I got really
> mad, I didn't want to put it on. I didn't want to be around different Arabs, because in
> my head Arabs were not a good thing. Especially because my relative got killed on the
> airplane on September 11, you know. (Interview, Michigan, May 2010)

Aimal feared that she would be viewed as the 'other' if she looked Muslim. She
was forcing herself to be 'American' by being invisible through her western
clothing. It is important to note that at least 358 Muslims died in the World

Trade Center attacks,[62] but the irony is that sometimes the wider society (particularly some media) failed to emphasise that Muslims were also victims of the terrorist acts of the *jihadis* (who can be lethal but constitute a tiny minority of the 1.5 billion Muslim population worldwide).

To be American is my choice

In contrast to Aimal, Daniel, of Palestinian origin (male, 19, US born), felt that it was important to be American and at the same time to express one's Islamic culture. Daniel (also a sports fan) said that he felt American at a cultural level:

> Culturally speaking, on a more superficial level, I'm an American simply because that's where my sense of humour, my interest in clothing, stuff like that is American. Although I do obviously enjoy foreign cultures, but if I was to identify myself culturally it'd be American. (Interview, Florida, March 2010)

When I told Daniel 'But you are wearing Arab dress', Daniel replied, 'I wear it occasionally simply because I like to establish among the college population there are people wearing this [who] can still be people who speak English fine, who you can interact [with] and have normal interactions.'

Sport and identity

So far in this chapter, while discussing the identity of the participants, I have argued that the issues that are important to young American Muslims range from voluntary embracing of their identity through heritage and social groups, to various internal and external factors impacting on their identities. I have also examined their other interests (apart from their studies or work), and found that sport has impacted profoundly on the construction of their identity.

Andrew Parker and John Harris argued that identity is generated both internally (within ourselves) and externally (through our social involvement with other people), and sport demonstrates how people see themselves as well as how others view them. Therefore, sport can be a very important source for the construction and display of identity.[63] For example, a person who follows suburban baseball may identify more with the wider white community than a person who is interested in basketball since the latter is more associated with an inner city (black) culture. Speaking of the importance of sport, Tony Schirato observed that when young people participate in organised sports such as soccer, netball, athletics, cricket and baseball, or in games without codified rules such as touch rugby or kickball, 'they are being subjected at some level to a form of socio-cultural training (learning to win, to compete to struggle and overcome)'.[64] Sport also empowers them and raises their self-esteem, helping them to overcome various forms of tension such as racism, and ethnic- and class-based prejudice, as well as cultural restrictions.

In the British context, Parker and Samaya Farooq found that British-born Pakistani males in a Muslim school, aged fourteen to nineteen, negotiated their identities at different levels: internally, they wanted to be better Muslims by practising Islam, offering prayers, reciting the Quran etc., but on an external level they valued self-esteem (through exercise in school), the rational self (through following the *Hadith*); the disciplined self (through adhering to the rules of sports) and the united self (through the unity and cohesion of playing sport). The students had six hours of physical education per week, with an emphasis on team sports such as hockey, basketball, soccer and cricket.[65] To sum up, Farooq and Parker argued that 'physical activity provided a social environment in and through which the production of the ideal "self" could be achieved'.[66] In other words, through sport, young Muslims can negotiate their identity and in times of crisis can maintain their sanity.

Furthermore, young people who encounter everyday racism, or cultural restrictions, may find sport an antidote for their anxiety. For example, in my previous research on young British Muslim identity,[67] I found many participants were fond of Manchester United, and their favourite player was Cristiano Ronaldo (who played for Manchester United from 2003 until 2009 and since then has played for Real Madrid). So in the midst of politicians' debates on Muslim women wearing the *niqab*, and support for certain parts of *shariah* law, many young Muslims were embroiled in the world of sport. So in this study, I also questioned the participants on their interest in sport. Their responses were varied (see Table 3.2).

Analysis

Table 3.2 shows that out of 379 participants, 259 (68 per cent) watch sport. Out of a total of 167 male participants, 142 (85 per cent) watched sport, and out of 212 female participants 117 (55 per cent) watched sport. And many of the participants who watched sport also played sport, particularly basketball. Out of 259 participants (both male and female), 165 participants (64 per cent) watched basketball or American football. That is, 91 participants (35 per cent) watched basketball and 74 participants (29 per cent) watched American football. Forty-eight participants (18 per cent) watched soccer, 18 participants (7 per cent) watched baseball and 28 participants (11 per cent) watched other sports.

It is interesting to note that some of the participants who played sport did not watch it – probably because sports like volleyball, handball, kickball, table tennis, badminton, bowling, swimming, gymnastics, golf and cricket were not regularly shown on American TV. For example, Omran said, 'I have a black belt [in the] traditional kung fu of Indonesia. I play soccer, I play badminton and of course I do jogging' (male, 16, US born, of Sudanese origin, national identity: Muslim American, interview, Florida, February 2010). Some participants enjoyed watching or playing sports that are more popular in their country of origin:

- Riaz (male, 20, US born of Guyanese background, national identity: Guyanese American): 'In Guyana it is mostly played cricket, so I watch cricket.'
- Aysegül (female, 15, US born of Turkish origin, national identity: Turkish): 'I support the Turkish soccer team.'
- Erphan (male, 19, overseas born of Iraqi origin, national identity: Iraqi American): 'Soccer . . . My father was a soccer player.'
- Sadat (male, 18, US born of Palestinian background, national identity: Palestinian): 'After work I like to go out with my cousins and play cards.'

In some cases, young participants showed their loyalty to their local teams; for example, Ata (male, 16, national identity: African American), said, 'Like sports and everything? Yeah. Basketball: my favourite is the LA Lakers. But being I'm from Detroit, the Detroit Pistons' (interview, Michigan, May 2010). Anis (male, 16, Pakistani origin, national identity: more American) said, 'I support my local team, Ravens from Baltimore; I am a fan of Ray Lewis, Ravens, football' (interview, Maryland, January 2010). It is interesting to note that, though the participants identified themselves in various ways, when they affiliated themselves with sport they appeared to be very American; for example, Nazneen (female, 18, US born, Afghan origin, national identity: 'I consider myself an Afghan'), said:

I watch hockey, I love the big [Washington] Capitals. They were in Pittsburgh . . . Like the thing is, Capitals and the Pittsburgh Penguins, they were like big time rivals and we won.

Ever since I was young . . . my dad would just watch it and I'm pretty sure it was 1996 or 1998 when they first went to the play-offs and they were so close to winning the Stanley Cup, which is like the big cup. And they lost, I'm pretty sure, to the Pittsburgh Penguins, and ever since then they were just big time rivals. (Interview, Virginia, January 2010)

Anwara (female, 15, US born, Pakistani origin) identified herself as Muslim: 'I'd say I'm 100 per cent Muslim 'cos I wouldn't want my culture or anything to mix in with my Islam and my religion.' However, when the discussion of sport came up she said, 'I love to watch basketball, soccer and baseball' (interview, New York, January 2010). Some female participants said that they became fond of sport because their family members, father or brother (and in a few cases husband) watched and they joined them in watching sport. Another participant, Rabab (female, Ivory Coast origin, national identity: 'Muslim first,

Table 3.2 'What sport do you support or watch?'

State	American football	Baseball	Basketball	Soccer	Other	Not interested
MA: 36 participants (21 m, 15 f)	5 m, 2 f New York Jets, New England Patriots	1 m, 2 f Boston Red Sox, Philadelphia Phillies	5 m, 1 f New York Knicks, Boston Celtics, Los Angeles Lakers, Chicago Bulls	6 m, 0 f Morocco, Manchester United	2 m, 0 f Track meet, karate	2 m, 10 f Cut down on sports, waste of time, no time
NY: 80 participants (30 m, 50 f)	8 m, 10 f New York Giants, New England Patriots	3 m, 6 f New York Mets, New York Yankees	5 m, 4 f Los Angeles Lakers, Boston Celtics	7 m, 6 f Brazil, Turkey; Egypt–Algeria games	3 m, 3 f Cricket	4 m, 21 f Play sport but do not watch it
VA: 26 participants (7 m, 19 f)	3 m, 5 f Washington Redskins, Dallas Cowboys	0 m, 2 f New York Yankees	3 m, 0 f Los Angeles Lakers	0 m, 1 f Spain, Barcelona	0 m, 1 f Cricket	1 m, 10 f Write, play sport but do not watch it, listen to music
MD: 35 participants (15 m, 20 f)	9 m, 6 f Washington Redskins, Baltimore Ravens, New Orleans Saints	0 m, 0 f	2 m, 2 f Washington Wizards, Cleveland Cavaliers, college team	2 m, 3 f Manchester United	1 m, 1 f Olympics	1 m, 8 f Watch at times, no sports, waste of time

State / participants	American football	Baseball	Basketball	Soccer	Other sports	Comments
FL: 96 participants (51 m, 45 f)	9 m, 3 f Dallas Cowboys, Pittsburgh Steelers, New England Patriots, Miami Dolphins, Orlando Predators, New York Jets, Indianapolis Colts, Tampa Bay Buccaneers; Super Bowl	1 m, 2 f Florida Marlins, New York Mets	26 m, 7 f Miami Heat, Los Angeles Lakers, Orlando Magic, Houston Rockets, Dallas Mavericks, Boston Celtics, Cleveland Cavaliers, Phoenix Suns	1 m, 6 f Real Madrid	3 m, 2 f Motor racing, ice skating, volleyball	11 m, 25 f Have 2 jobs, lost interest and now into religion, grew up in music, only Indian movies
MI: 106 participants (43 m, 63 f)	8 m, 6 f Detroit Lions, New England Patriots, Minnesota Vikings, Indianapolis Colts, Atlanta Falcons, Tennessee Titans, New Orleans Saints, Dallas Cowboys, Oklahoma Sooners, Pittsburgh Steelers; flag football	0 m, 1 f Detroit Tigers	19 m, 17 f Los Angeles Lakers, Detroit Pistons, Cleveland Cavaliers	5 m, 11 f Brazil, Argentina; FIFA World Cup; Iraqi and Yemeni teams	5 m, 7 f Detroit Red Wings (ice hockey); tennis, kickball, wrestling, cricket, ice skating, ice hockey	6 m, 21 f At times soccer, 'I am a bookworm', no time for sports.

Note: Some participants mentioned multiple games that they watched:
MA: American football and baseball (4 m, 1 f)
NY: American football and baseball (2 m, 0 f); basketball and soccer (2 m, 0 f); baseball, basketball and soccer (2 m, 1 f)
VA: basketball and soccer (1 m, 0 f); American football, baseball and soccer (2 m, 0 f)
MD: American football, basketball and soccer (2 m, 0 f)
FL: American football and basketball (2 m, 0 f); basketball and soccer (1 m, 0 f); American football, basketball and soccer (1 m, 0 f)
MI: American football and basketball (1 m)

then African American'), said, 'I really love basketball. I don't like regular football, but I like flag football. I love Cleveland Cavaliers (basketball) and my favourite player is LeBron James' (interview, Michigan, May 2010). As discussed earlier (e.g. in Adam's case), in some cases African Americans take great pride in connecting themselves with African American sportspersons.

Sport helps to resolve difference between colour, race, creed and class. It is normally in the sports field that one can see a black sitting beside a white, a Muslim beside a non-Muslim, all cheering for their respective teams. In outlining the role of sport in the identity-making process, Jeremy MacClancy observed that through particular forms of expression, sport helps to define a community. And sport provides people with a sense of other people's social identity.[68] Some people's identity may be already established but, when they show their passion for a particular sport or sports, they reflexively take on an additional identity, which for hardcore fans may be their primary identity.

David Ogden and Michael Hilt noted that most African Americans pre-ferred basketball because it has become a part of their culture, giving them a sense of collective identity. Almost 80 per cent of American basketball players in the NBA are black, compared to 13 per cent in major league baseball. Many more black youths than white youths are encouraged in schools to play basketball because it is seen as the 'best and shortest trip' out of their unde-sirable socioeconomic condition. And by seeing many black NBA players, black youths feel encouraged; it boosts their self-esteem and helps their social mobility.[69] In this context, it is worth mentioning that President Obama plays basketball.

However, my study shows that basketball is not confined to an African American identity. Ninety-one (35 per cent) Muslim Americans of diverse backgrounds spoke highly of basketball (followed by American football; see Table 3.2) and many of them said that their favourite team was the Los Angeles Lakers and their favourite player Kobe Bryant. Ogden and Hilt observed that through basketball games both black and white youths develop a 'sense of cultural power' by wearing basketball apparel and Nike shoes (as worn by the players), thereby reinforcing their masculine identity.[70] Basketball is not exclusive to masculine identity, however: thirty-one female participants said that it was their favorite sport (in some cases jointly with American football). My study also showed that the next preferred sport of Muslim Americans was American football. Participants who lived on the east coast (Massachusetts, New York, Maryland and Virginia) mostly preferred teams in their region, for example, the Patriots and the Redskins. In Florida and Michigan, the choice of team was varied, but some tended to support their local teams. The Super Bowl was a popular event among the sports lover participants in all states.

In the last 150 years, baseball has been considered America's 'national pastime' but it appears that basketball has gained supremacy worldwide, with approximately 450 million people playing the game, and, for the 2007–8 NBA

Figure 3.2 Kobe Bryant. Los Angeles Clippers v. Los Angeles Lakers, 25 March 2011. Result: Clippers 104, Lakers 112. Bryant scored 37 points. *Lisa Blumenfeld/Getty Images Sport.*

season, there were 1.76 billion TV viewers. In 2008–9, the Sporting Goods Manufacturers Association said (based on their recent survey) there were 25.9 million regular basketball players in America, making it the most played sport, with baseball and outdoor soccer ranked second and third.[71]

In my survey, the soccer fans (48) were more numerous than baseball fans (18) (see Table 3.2). I am not sure why such a variation exists among young Muslims. Perhaps soccer is more popular because it is also played in their country of origin, and watching soccer has become a cultural and family event. Whatever their ranking of sport, young peoples' involvement in any sport/ games should be viewed as 'cultural capital' (competence that is conducive to membership of a cultural community). Sport can impact on identity, and it is very important as a healing process and helping with the development of young Muslims' self-esteem.

Conclusion

As can be seen in this chapter, the identity responses of participants were varied: multiple, dual or hyphenated, collective and single. When participants discussed certain issues, either they spoke from their personal or lived experience or their opinions were based on observation. In most discussions, the topic of the 'media' popped up and this may have impacted on their identity. I agree with other social identity theorists that identity is always in motion, and that it is formed through various factors, such as heritage, social group, family and community environment, ingroup feelings, and recognition and approval from ingroups (Muslim community) and outgroups (wider society). When identity confronts an 'opposing self', the 'self' can crystallise instinctively, and when people see similarities their identity can polarise into a collective identity.

While interviewing the participants, I asked them about their hobbies or extracurricular activities and I found that most participants appeared to be bicultural (balanced with a foot in each culture), with their American identity often linked by participation in American sports (such as basketball). However, this chapter could serve as a cautionary tale for Muslims and the wider community to work together to address their impending issues, and to create a productive bicultural society for young citizens. This proposition will be discussed further in the concluding chapter.

Notes

1. Anthony D. Smith, *National Identity* (London: Penguin, 1991), pp. 11–15.
2. Kwame Anthony Appiah, *The Ethics of Identity* (Princeton, NJ: Princeton University Press, 2005), p. 116.
3. Selcuk R. Sirin and Michelle Fine, *Muslim American Youth: Understanding Hyphenated Identities through Multiple Methods* (New York: New York University Press, 2008), p. 3.
4. Joshua J. Yates, 'Making Sense of Cosmopolitanism: A Conversation with Kwame Anthony Appiah', *Hedgehog Review*, Fall 2009, pp. 42–50, at pp. 44–5.
5. Ibid., p. 45.
6. See Chapter 1 for detailed discussion. See also Jocelyne Cesari, *When Islam and Democracy Meet: Muslims in Europe and the United States* (New York: Palgrave Macmillan, 2004); Yvonne Yazbeck Haddad, Jane I. Smith and Kathleen M. Moore, *Muslim Women in America: The Challenges of Islamic Identity Today* (New York: Oxford University Press, 2006), p. 28; Selcuk R. Sirin and Michelle Fine, 'Hyphenated Selves: Muslim American Youth Negotiating Identities on the Fault Lines of Global Conflict', *Applied Development Science* 11:3 (2007), pp. 151–63; Yasmin Moll, 'Screening Faith, Making Muslims: Islamic Media for Muslim American Children and Politics of Identity', in Yvonne Yazbeck Haddad, Farid Senzai and Jane I. Smith (eds), *Educating the Muslims of America* (Oxford: Oxford University Press, 2009), pp. 155–77; Sally Howell and Amaney Jamal, 'The Aftermath of the 9/11 Attacks', in Detroit Arab American Study Team, *Citizenship and Crisis: Arab Detroit after 9/11* (New York: Russell Sage Foundation, 2009),

pp. 69–100; John L. Esposito, *The Future of Islam* (New York: Oxford University Press, 2010); Jane I. Smith, *Islam in America*, 2nd edn (New York: Columbia University Press, 2010).

7. Tony Gaskew, *Policing American Muslim Communities: A Compendium of Post 9/11 Interviews* (Lewiston, NY: Edwin Mellen Press, 2008); Louise Cainkar, *Homeland Insecurity: The Arab American and Muslim American Experience after 9/11* (New York: Russell Sage Foundation, 2011).

8. The interviews were tape recorded. The anonymity of the participants is maintained.

9. Amartya Sen, *Identity and Violence: The Illusion of Destiny* (London: Allen Lane, 2006), pp. 4–5.

10. Ibid. p. 19.

11. Michael Roskin, *Countries and Concepts: Politics, Geography, Culture*, 11th edn (Boston: Pearson Longman, 2011).

12. See Roskin, *Countries and Concepts*, pp. 234, 335, 552. This phenomenon of stereotyping Muslims or Arabs in textbooks is not new. In 1971, when researching social studies textbooks used in schools in Ontario, authors McDiarmid and Pratt found the words most often used to describe Muslims were 'infidels', 'fanatical', 'great', 'devout' and 'tolerant', whereas the words used to describe Christians included 'devoted', 'zealous', 'martyr', 'great' and 'famous'. In a survey of elementary and junior high social science textbooks used in the Californian educational system, Ayad al-Qazzaz found that though the nomadic Bedouin life accounts for only 5 to 8 per cent of the total Arab population, in the textbooks this information is provided as something normal in Arab society. This generalisation about Arabs as Bedouin people impacted on the school students. Consequently, in a survey of 251 junior and senior high school students, al-Qazzaz found that more than half of them viewed Arabs as a desert people. See Baha Abu-Laban, 'The Canadian Muslim Community: The Need for a New Survival Strategy', in Earle H. Waugh, Baha Abu-Laban and Regula B. Qureishi (eds), *The Muslim Community in North America* (Edmonton: University of Alberta Press, 1983), pp. 75–92; Jacqueline S. Ismael and Tareq Y. Ismael, 'The Arab Americans and the Middle East', *Middle East Journal* 30:3 (1976), pp. 390–405.

13. Nahid Kabir, 'Representation of Islam and Muslims in the Australian Media, 2001–2005', *Journal of Muslim Minority Affairs*, 26:3 (2006), pp. 313–28, see pp. 314–15; Nahid Afrose Kabir, *Young British Muslims: Identity, Culture, Politics and the Media* (Edinburgh: Edinburgh University Press, 2010), p. 137.

14. Similar concern was expressed by Samuel Huntington in his book *Who Are We? The Challenges to America's National Identity* (New York: Simon & Schuster, 2005) when he said that if the 'bilingual and bicultural society' was allowed to grow then the cultural identity of mainstream American Anglo-Protestants would be threatened. Huntington's earlier book, *The Clash of Civilizations and the Remaking of World Order* (New York: Simon & Schuster, 1996), has generated a lot of controversy in academia for its antagonistic views towards Muslims.

15. Homi Bhabha, *The Location of Culture* (London: Routledge, 1994).

16. Jonathan Rutherford, 'The Third Space: Interview with Homi Bhabha', in Jonathan Rutherford (ed.), *Identity: Community, Culture, Difference* (London: Lawrence and Wishart, 1990), pp. 207–21.

17. Anne Applebaum, 'Teddy bear tyranny', *Washington Post*, 4 December 2007, p. A21.

18. The desire of young Muslims to fit in with the wider society has been discussed by other scholars. For example see, Shabana Mir, '"I Didn't Want to Have That Outcast Belief about Alcohol": Muslim Women Encounter Drinking Cultures on Campus', in Haddad, Senzai and Smith (eds), *Educating the Muslims of America*, pp. 209–30.

19. Michael Slackman, 'Iran's Guardian Council certifies Ahmadinejad election victory', *New York Times*, 30 June 2009, p. 4.

20. 'Controversial Elections', FairVote website, http://archive.fairvote.org/e_college/controversial.htm, accessed 17 May 2012.

21. 'America Votes 2004', CNN website, http://us.cnn.com/ELECTION/2004/index.html, accessed 17 May 2012.

22. 'Ahmadinejad speaks; outrage and controversy follow', CNN website, 24 September 2007, http://edition.cnn.com/2007/US/09/24/us.iran/, accessed 17 May 2012.

23. Francesca Polletta and James M. Jasper, 'Collective Identity and Social Movements', *Annual Review of Sociology* 27 (2001), pp. 283–305, see pp. 285, 298.

24. Appiah, *The Ethics of Identity*, p. 107.

25. Black Power was a political movement that grew up in the 1950s and 1960s to express a new racial consciousness among African Americans. It sought to improve the economic conditions of the black community but did not encourage assimilation/integration with 'white' society. This movement led to the development of a 'black' identity but the negative side of this movement was that some African Americans resorted to violence. However, later it developed into the non-violent Civil Rights movement led by Martin Luther King. In 1964, President Lyndon B. Johnson signed the Civil Rights Act and in 1965 he signed the Voting Rights Act, thus granting emancipation to African Americans.

26. See Obiagele Lake, *Blue Veins and Kinky Hair: Naming and Color Consciousness in African America* (Westport, CT: Praeger, 2003); Richard Brent Turner, 'Constructing Masculinity: Interactions between Islam and African-American Youth since C. Eric Lincoln, *The Black Muslims in America*', *Souls* 8:4 (2006), pp. 31–44; Anita Jones Thomas and Sara Schwarzbaum, *Culture and Identity: Life Stories for Counselors and Therapists* (Thousand Oaks, CA: Sage, 2006), pp. 11–29.

27. See Obiagele Lake, 'Towards a Pan-African Identity: Diaspora of African Repatriates in Ghana', *Anthropological Quarterly* 68:1 (1995), pp. 21–36.

28. For example Richard Jenkins, *Social Identity*, 3rd edn (London: Routledge, 2008).

29. 'The Cat's comeback from rock star to Muslim devotee . . .', *Globe and Mail*, 22

May 2000, p. R1; see also Smith, *Islam in America*, pp. 175–6.

30. Ishan Bagby, Paul M. Perl and Bryan T. Froehle, *The Mosque in America: A National Portrait – A Report from the Mosque Study Project* (Washington, DC: Council on American–Islamic Relations, 2001), p. 21, cited in Turner, 'Constructing Masculinity', p. 32.
31. Turner, 'Constructing Masculinity', p. 40.
32. Jamillah A. Karim, 'To Be Black, Female, and Muslim: A Candid Conversation about Race in the American *Ummah*', *Journal of Muslim Minority Affairs* 26:2 (2006), pp. 225–33, see p. 229.
33. See for example, Jamillah Karim, *American Muslim Women: Negotiating Race, Class and Gender within the Ummah* (New York: New York University Press, 2009), pp. 43–4; Gaskew, *Policing American Muslim Communities*, pp. 118–27.
34. Amaney Jamal, 'Inside and Outside the Box: The Politics of Arab American Identity and Artistic Representations', paper prepared for 'The Role of the Arts in the United States', Immigrant Communities Working Meeting, Princeton University, 1–2 June 2006, pp. 3–4, http://cmd.princeton.edu/papers/wp0604a.pdf, accessed 24 May 2011. See also Andrew Shryock, 'The Moral Analogies of Race', in Amaney Jamal and Nadine Naber (eds), *Race and Arab Americans before and after 9/11: From Invisible Citizens to Visible Subjects* (Syracuse, NY: Syracuse University Press, 2008), pp. 81–113.
35. Nadine Naber, 'Ambiguous Insiders: An Investigation of Arab American Invisibility', *Ethnic and Racial Studies* 23:1 (2000), pp. 37–61, see p. 43.
36. Edward Said, *Covering Islam: How the Media and the Experts Determine How We See the Rest of the World*, rev. edn (London: Vintage, 1997); Yvonne Yazbeck Haddad, 'American Foreign Policy in the Middle East and Its Impact on the Identity of Arab Muslims in the United States', in Yvonne Yazbeck Haddad (ed.), *The Muslims of America* (New York: Oxford University Press, 1991), pp. 217–35; Caroline R. Nagel and Lynn A. Staeheli, 'Citizenship, Identity and Transnational Migration: Arab Immigrants to the United States', *Space and Polity* 8:1 (2004), pp. 2–23; Naber, 'Ambiguous Insiders'; Jamal, 'Inside and Outside the Box'; Shryock, 'The Moral Analogies of Race'; Haddad, Smith and Moore, *Muslim Women in America*.
37. Steven George Salaita, 'Ethnic Identity and Imperative Patriotism: Arab Americans before and after 9/11', *College Literature* 32:2 (2005), pp. 146–68.
38. Jenkins, *Social Identity*, pp. 112–13.
39. 'United States Armed Forces', Wikipedia, http://en.wikipedia.org/wiki/United_States_Armed_Forces, accessed 24 May 2012.
40. 'Muslims already pray at Ground Zero', *Korea Times* website, 5 September 2010, http://www.koreatimes.co.kr/www/news/opinon/2012/05/160._72545.html, accessed 18 May 2012.
41. Laura Crimaldi, 'Many rally for alleged terrorist', *Boston Herald*, 13 November 2009, p. 3.
42. Stuart Hall, 'Introduction: Who Needs "Identity"?', in Stuart Hall and Paul du

Gay (eds), *Questions of Cultural Identity* (London: Sage, 1996), pp. 1–17, see p. 4.

43. Henri Tajfel (ed.), *Human Groups and Social Categories: Studies in Social Psychology* (Cambridge: Cambridge University Press, 1981); Jenkins, *Social Identity.*

44. Elsa R. Germain, 'Culture or Race? Phenotype and Cultural Identity Development in Minority Australian Adolescents', *Australian Psychologist* 39:2 (2004), pp. 134–42, see p. 140.

45. Lukas Pleva, 'Glen Beck says President Obama is out of step with the nation on Arizona's immigration law', *St Petersburg Times*, 3 June 2010.

46. 'Say no to Arizona type profiling law in Michigan', Dawud Walid's blog, 28 February 2011, http://dawudwalid.wordpress.com/2011/02/28/say-no-to-arizona-type-profiling-law-in-michigan/, accessed 18 May 2012.

47. Randal C. Archibold, 'Arizona enacts stringent law on immigration', *New York Times*, 24 April 2010, p. 1.

48. 'Somali pirate on trial in US court', Institute for Security Studies website, 12 May 2009, http://www.iss.co.za/iss_today.php?ID=1197, accessed 18 May 2012.

49. Ron Scherer, 'What will US do with 15 Somali pirates after fatal hijacking?', *Christian Science Monitor*, 25 February 2011, http://www.csmonitor.com/USA/Justice/2011/0225/What-will-US-do-with-15-Somali-pirates-after-fatal-hijacking, accessed 18 May 2012.

50. 'Baby Bin Ladens', *Dominion Post*, 8 January 2011, p. 21; David Usborne, 'Cries of McCarthyism over US Muslim hearing', *The Independent*, 11 March 2011, pp. 26–7.

51. Kabir, *Young British Muslims*, p. 98; Nazli Kibria, *Muslims in Motion: Islam and National Identity in the Bangladeshi Diaspora* (New Brunswick, NJ: Rutgers University Press, 2011), p. 72.

52. For similar views, see also Jasmin Zine, 'Safe Havens or Religious "Ghettos"? Narratives of Islamic Schooling in Canada', in Haddad, Senzai and Smith (eds.), *Educating the Muslims of America*, pp. 39–66.

53. Avtar Brah, 'Non-binarized Identities of Similarity and Difference', in Margaret Wetherell, Michelynn Laflèche and Robert Berkeley (eds), *Identity, Ethnic Diversity and Community Cohesion* (London: Sage, 2007), pp. 136–45, see pp. 144–5.

54. Declan Walsh, 'Explosives plot: neuroscientist was at heart of al-Qaida cell, files claim', *The Guardian*, 26 April 2011, p. 7.

55. 'Raymond Davis and norms of justice', *PakTribune* website, 7 March 2011, http://paktribune.com/articles/Raymond-Davis-and-Norms-of-justice-236956.html, accessed 24 May 2012.

56. 'Foreign funding in education intact: Rabbani', *Daily Post* (Lahore, Pakistan), 10 April 2011.

57. I discuss the points raised by Faizul, such as the fact that the media did not label the Christian militia that planned to attack the police force as 'terrorists', in detail in Chapter 4. I discuss the civilian casualties in Afghanistan and Iraq and the

Guantánamo Bay ordeal in Chapter 6.

58. George Hunter and Doug Guthrie, 'Detroit imam autopsy raises ire', *Detroit News*, 2 February 2010, p. 3.

59. Zeenath Kausar, 'Communal Riots in India: Hindu–Muslim Conflict and Resolution', *Journal of Muslim Minority Affairs* 26:3 (2006), pp. 353–70, see p. 359.

60. See also Helen Carter, Rory McCarthy and Rebecca Allison, 'British journalist freed', *The Guardian*, 9 October 2001, p. 1.

61. Kabir, *Young British Muslims*, pp. 64–6, 78; see also Smith, *Islam in America*, pp. 139–44.

62. Esposito, *The Future of Islam*, p. 30.

63. Andrew Parker and John Harris, 'Introduction: Sport and Social Identities', in John Harris and Andrew Parker (eds), *Sport and Social Identities* (Basingstoke: Palgrave Macmillan, 2009), pp. 1–14, see pp. 3–4.

64. Tony Schirato, *Understanding Sports Culture* (Los Angeles: Sage, 2007), see p. 17.

65. Samaya Farooq and Andrew Parker, 'Sport, Religion and Social Identity: Physical Education and Muslim Independent Schooling', in Harris and Parker (eds), *Sport and Social Identities*, pp. 109–31.

66. Ibid., p. 121.

67. Kabir, *Young British Muslims*.

68. Jeremy MacClancy (ed.), *Sport, Identity and Ethnicity* (Oxford: Berg, 1996), pp. 2–3, cited in Parker and Harris (eds), *Sport and Social Identities*, pp. 6–7.

69. David C. Ogden and Michael L. Hilt, 'Collective Identity and Basketball: An Explanation for the Decreasing Number of African-Americans on America's Baseball Diamonds', *Journal of Leisure Research* 35:2 (2003), pp. 213–27, see pp. 217–22.

70. Ibid., p. 221.

71. Bryan Curtis, 'The national pastime(s)', *New York Times*, 1 February 2009, p. 5.

REFLECTIONS ON THE AMERICAN MEDIA

The most talked-about subject in this study was the media. Some of it was unsolicited, but most was generated from the question 'What do you think of the American media?' The question evoked intense discussion and a lot of emotion. Many respondents said that the media in general portrayed Muslims negatively, while some mentioned a particular media outlet and provided anecdotes. In Chapter 3 I pointed out that most of the respondents claimed to have dual or multiple identities, but when they spoke about issues that were 'near and dear' to them, their ethnic or religious identities came to the fore. As I discussed in Chapter 1, emotion and identity are interrelated. Sometimes people create their ingroups by choice – they desire to stay with their own cultural group – and sometimes external factors, such as the media and mainstream politics, lead to the creation of ingroups. The creation of strong ingroups may lead to less interaction with the wider society, which slows progress towards social cohesion between the two groups.

Between 14 and 22 July 2011, the Pew Research Center in Washington, DC conducted telephone interviews with 1,033 Muslims (both male and female, aged eighteen and over). Among several questions (discussed in other chapters) they asked: 'Do you think that coverage of Islam and Muslims by American news organisations is generally fair or unfair?' About 55 per cent of respondents thought that the media coverage of Islam and Muslims by US news organisations was generally unfair. Back in 2007, when the same question was asked (to a different sample), about 57 per cent of American Muslims regarded the US media as 'unfair'. In 2011, 30 per cent observed that the news coverage was fair, while 25 per cent said it depended on the news or were unsure.[1] American-born Muslims (about 63 per cent) were more likely than their overseas-born counterparts (50 per cent) to observe that the media coverage of Muslims was 'unfair'.[2]

The difference between the Pew Research Center's survey and my fieldwork is that, though the number of participants (1,033) was much larger than the number in my study (379), their survey was conducted over the phone, so there was less opportunity for discussion. Most of my participants elaborated their views on the American media (see Table 4.1 below). Another difference is that the Pew Research Center included only adult participants (eighteen years and over), and they did not provide a breakdown of male and female participants. In my study the total number of participants was 379 (167 male, 212 female, mostly US born); and of these 188, or almost exactly half, were young participants, aged fifteen to seventeen (74 male, 114 female), with the remainder being eighteen and over. Overall, the majority of participants (about 78 per cent) observed that the American media was unfair (further analysis of Table 4.1 follows later). Finally, the most important difference was that by the time I interviewed my participants a relationship had been formed; therefore, respondents may have been less guarded in their responses than in the Pew survey.

In this chapter I first discuss some academics' observations on the American media. Secondly, I report the patterns of my 379 participants' responses on the topic of the media (summarised in Table 4.1). Thirdly, I discuss the major pattern emerging from the participants' responses and examine some print media coverage[3] of the Fort Hood shooting and some other subsequent incidents to assess whether the young Muslims' view that the media is 'biased' is justified. Fourthly, I examine the Christian–Muslim dichotomy in media reporting by discussing the Christian militia incident in Michigan. Finally, I examine participants' positive comments on the media.

Academics' observations on the media

In *Covering Islam*, Edward Said observed that there are many troubling incidents associated with the Muslim world, such as the killing of 240 American marines by a Muslim group in Lebanon in 1983, the Lockerbie bombing of Pan Am Flight 109 in 1988, and Ayatollah Khomeini's *fatwa* against Salman Rushdie in 1989; but when the western mass media applies a blanket label of 'Islam' to an event, either as an explanation or indiscriminately to condemn 'Islam', this is usually a form of attack against the Islamic world.[4]

Here is a sample of studies that have been published on the print media. In 1984 E. Ghareeb noted that some prestigious newspapers, such as the *Washington Post*, portrayed Muslims as terrorists.[5] In 1999 Ahmadullah Siddiqi observed that over the past several years some newspapers and magazines had identified Islam as the most significant threat to the liberal democracies of the West. These included *The Economist* (1992), *Time* (1993), the *New York Times* (1993), *US News & World Report* (1993) and the *Chicago Tribune* (1995).[6] Siddiqi noted that the western media 'have always pointed out that "Muslim men" were implicated in the World Trade Center bombing, [but] never did the media say that the suspects in [the] Oklahoma City bombing were Christians'. Siddiqi stated that the media were responsible for the back-lash towards Muslims after the bombing of the Murrah Federal Building in Oklahoma City on 19 April 1995. Immediately after the bomb blast, radio and television started reporting that people of Middle Eastern origin were the prime suspects. Many experts and Congressman David McCurdy appeared on the media speculating that the bombers were of Middle Eastern origin.[7] But later the suspects arrested were found to be 'white, Christians from the Midwest, not from the Middle East'.[8]

Jack Shaheen also observed that, although Timothy McVeigh was an Irish Catholic, no one mentioned his ethnic or religious background. The Oklahoma bombing was immediately related to Middle Eastern suspects in news broad-casts, even on moderate TV channels such as ABC and CBS. Before 9/11, when nineteen Arab Muslims killed about 3,000 Americans, Arabs and Muslims were already regarded as threatening people, but afterwards it was assumed that all 1.3 billion Muslims were the 'other'.[9]

Saud Joseph, Benjamine D'Harlingue and Alvin Wong analysed the *New York Times* from 2000 to 2004, observing that even before the 9/11 Twin Towers attacks it represented both Arab Americans and Muslim Americans as the 'other'. It is interesting to note that Arab Americans were portrayed largely as Muslims, even though the overwhelming majority are Christians. This tendency to conflate both groups into one 'collective', essentialised iden-tity continued after 9/11, when Sikhs were also included under the label 'Arab American'.[10] For example, after 9/11 the *New York Times* reported the reper-cussions for Arabs, Muslims and Sikhs under the headline 'Attacks and harass-ment of Arab Americans increase'.[11] It is difficult to say whether the conflation of American Muslims (and Sikhs) with Arab Americans was a result of cultural ignorance on the part of the media, or whether it was an institutional bias that all Arabs are the 'other' (a bias that has been fuelled by the Israeli–Palestinian conflict).

Immediately after the 9/11 tragedy, through its reporting, the *New York Times* questioned Muslim Americans' loyalty. For example, in his report 'In U.S., echoes of rift of Muslims and Jews', columnist Laurie Goodstein quoted a girl who commented:

'I'm Arabic and Palestinian and I have just one thing to say,' said Yasmeen Hindi, 19, a customer at Uptown Deli Grocery. 'I feel bad, but Americans have to understand something: If we're going to get killed, they're going to get killed back. Stop support-ing the Israelis.'[12]

By extracting this quotation, the reporter implied that some Muslims were outraged at US foreign policy towards its ally Israel (so the 9/11 terrorist act was tacitly justified). Goodstein thereby suggested it was reasonable to doubt whether Muslim Americans were loyal citizens.[13]

Jane Smith has observed that some mainstream Americans are concerned that an increase in Muslim migration may 'lead to the growth of radical cells or even to advocacy of *shari'a* law', and this fear has been induced by some media, such as radio talkback programmes, TV shows and videos.[14] In 2005 about twenty-eight million copies of a documentary film, *Obsession: Radical Islam's War against the West*, were distributed free of charge on DVD.[15] In the film Islam was equated with Nazism under the label of 'Islamofacism'. It ended with a map of the world capped with a swastika, followed by scenes of carnage caused by 'Islamic radicals'.[16] Such fear-mongering tactics, together with some of the most prominent American Christian evangelical leaders' portrayal of Prophet Muhammad (PBUH) as a terrorist and Islam as an evil religion in the media, have not been helpful.[17]

Participants' opinions of the media

Analysis

The first five rows of Table 4.1 show that a large number of participants (203) had negative perceptions of the American media. The next sixteen rows, 6 to 21, also reveal the negative perceptions of ninety-one participants of the US media, and some of them provided specific examples, such as the Fort Hood shooting. Rows 22 ('MSNBC') to 29 ('some good and some bad') provide a different picture. Here fifty-two participants offered a positive or somewhat positive view. Row 30 reveals that eight participants emphasised that if Muslims hope for a better society then they themselves also have a role to play in improving their image (discussed in the Conclusion). The last row shows that twenty-five participants had no comments on the media. Overall, out of 379 participants, 294 (77.5 per cent) had negative views on the American media. In the following section, I discuss some of the key responses of the participants.

Participants' observations

Most of the participants in this study were critical of the American media in general and of the Fox channel in particular. Some participants mentioned Fox 5 (Boston, New York and Washington, DC) while others mentioned Fox 2 (Detroit and Florida). Though the participants defined their identities differently, they were unanimous in their views on Fox. For example, Zeenat (female, 16, US born of Bangladeshi background, national identity: Bengali) had this to say:

> What I was really shocked about was in Fox 5 News during the elections they were
> not afraid to say that they had a problem with Obama being Muslim or coming from

Table 4.1 Key points of responses to question 'What do you think of the American media?'

	Number of participants	Responses	Key points
1	29 m, 24 f	Media is biased	There's a lot of bias in reporters, especially in Fox News, against Muslims or against Democrats.
			Fox is more to the Republican side and CNN is more Democrat/liberal.
			Fox 5 was anti-Obama during election time.
			During election time, 'Muslimness' became an issue.
			I think Fox News is really racist.
			Fox News is far from being 'fair and balanced'. If anything, they're the complete opposite.
			I can't stand the O'Reilly show [*The O'Reilly Factor*].
			Media does not bring Muslim experts to talk on Muslim issues 'who lived it'; they bring non-Muslims to speak instead, or they would bring Muslims without *hijab* to speak.
			I don't watch CNN.
			CNN portrays Muslims negatively.
			Media should 'double-check' the news.
			Fox News, I think they're just the most Islamophobic people like ever! Fox and CNN, those are the big ones.
			Media is bad since 9/11.
			Media needs to do more research, e.g. CNN.
			(Most participants were critical of Fox News)
2	22 m, 30 f	'Muslim' equals 'terrorist'	'Muslim' equals 'terrorists'.
			They say, 'Muslims are terrorists. Arab Muslims are terrorists'.
3	25 m, 19 f	Media labels 'Muslims'	Muslims are labelled as Muslims but Christians who commit any crime are not labelled. Media does not label the non-Muslims, e.g. the Virginia Tech guy.
4	19 m, 15 f	American media (in general)	Media sometimes goes overboard.
			American media is self-centred.
			Media is controversial.
			Media is very messed up.
			Media is very negative.

			Media should not disrespect someone's religion.
5	8 m, 12 f	Media lies; media is not trustworthy	Media is misleading, confusing. Media needs to be fair. Media is subjective, e.g. Al Jazeera and western media. Media constructs an image. Media feeds ignorance. Media in general is not doing a very good job. It is just the news channel that makes us look bad. Media bias in Palestinian context. Media exaggerates. They are always brainwashing people. They make fun of 'us'. Media is to just kind of scare people. Another example is Tiger Woods: 'media slaughtered him'. Media is propaganda. It is lying to the whole world, the world's going to take it the wrong way then Media twists things, e.g. the case of Afia Siddiqui (discussed in Chapter 3). To be honest, I stay away from the media.
6	2 m, 6 f	Fort Hood incident	It is the 'Muslim again'.
7	1 m, 9 f	Double standards	The IRS plane crash in Austin, Texas: no mention of terrorists or religion.
8	5 m, 8 f	They make us look stupid	They make us look bad.
9	4 m, 3 f	Media distortion	First-hand observation. Media distorts, makes a bigger picture of a small incident.
10	2 m, 1 f	It disrespects our religion	Media caricatures our religion, our Prophet Muhammad (PBUH), e.g. *South Park* TV programme.
11	0 m, 2 f	Media should show our positive side	Media should show our positive side, e.g. Project Downtown, Haiti project, Tallahassee meeting etc.

Table 4.1 (*continued*)

	Number of participants	Responses	Key points
12	1 m, 2 f	Watch news for a laugh!	Fox is garbage. We sometimes watch it to have a good laugh. Fox is a joke.
13	1m, 2 f	Somali context	Media portrays Somalis as 'pirates'.
14	2 m, 5 f	Media is one-sided	Media is one-sided, e.g. Palestinian context. Media can mark a place negatively. Media can damage people's lives.
15	2 m, 2 f	Middle East/ Arab context	Arabs are shown as 'uncivilised' in the movies, in TV shows as well.
16	3 m, 6 f	Print media	*Washington Post* sensationalises a lot. They can do damage. *Boston Globe* was antagonistic to Muslims. *New York Times* was against Obama. *Daily News* and *New York Post* are the 'worst'.
17	3 m, 2 f	Digital media	They make fun of Muslims. They show Muslims are violent. Digital media also portrays Muslims badly.
18	1 m, 4 f	Media is Jewish	The media is on their side because the media are the Jews.
19	1 m, 0 f	Media is very politically based	I believe in conspiracy theories.
20	1 m, 6 f	Media is commercial	Media is commercial, to sell better. Media has portrayed all Afghan women as illiterate.
21	2 m, 2 f	Radio talkback	WTKK (conservative), NPR (intellectual, stimulating). *Rush Limbaugh Show* is terrible.
22	0 m, 1 f	MSNBC	*Schnitt Show* is negative towards Muslims. It is better than the others. It is more open and accepting of Muslims.

23	1 m, 1 f	CNN	I only watch CNN. CNN is getting better.
24	3 m, 1 f	*Daily Show*	*Daily Show* (from Comedy Central) is sarcastic but better than CNN, Fox.
25	1 m, 5 f	Other channels	I watch BBC, which is more reliable. I listen to NPR, it is educational. Local channels are better. I do watch Al Jazeera. I try and watch BBC the most.
26	5 m, 1 f	Al Jazeera	Al Jazeera English shows the truth. Al Jazeera is better news. It gives a global picture, but the American media limits itself.
27	2 m, 0 f	Internet	It is a better option for accurate news.
28	9 m, 10 f	Positive comments	Cultural education of reporters, media is getting better. American media is better than Egyptian media (American media shows weather and all other stuffs such as accidents, but Egyptian media always speaks of soccer!). Media can be inadvertently positive. Through our interviews in the media, people get a good picture of Muslims. Muslims leaders are in the media. It is changing for the better.
29	3 m, 9 f	Some good, some bad	Some channels are racist against Muslims, some try to understand our religion. Media is moderate. People should do research and find about Islam. Media is OK.
30	1 m, 7 f	We have obligations too	Work for a better society. We also should try to improve our image.
31	8 m, 17 f	No comment	I don't watch a lot of stuff. I don't follow the news: they went to Iraq, call people 'terrorists', destroy the place, too disturbing Not interested in the media.

Note: Sometimes participants offered multiple views, such as on *The Daily Show*, CNN and Fox, in their discussions.

Muslim roots. I feel like people don't care about if they're being racist . . . It's like an open thing that Muslims are hated and they're looked upon as terrorists. (Interview, New York, February 2010)

Doubts about whether Barack Obama was a Muslim were portrayed by other media as well, for example in the *New York Times* (discussed further in Chapter 6). The next participant, Fuad, of Egyptian background (male, 17, US born), said that he was a 'Muslim American Egyptian'. But he reflected his broader Arab identity when he said, 'If one Palestinian kills a Jewish person, they would say terrorist Palestinians kill Jews. If the Jewish army [*sic*] kills thousands of Palestinian women and children and men, they won't say the full story . . . I think it was Fox' (interview, Florida, March 2010). Sohaib (25, overseas born of Pakistani background, national identity: several identities) spoke from his personal experience:

> Fox News is notorious to take a very conservative approach. When I was president of a Muslim students' association [in a different state] . . . the *O'Reilly Factor* show, they try to bring Muslim students on, but what they do is they always sort of back them into a corner and they're always asking them questions that will sort of lead them to say something that they want them to say. Something . . . that they can pounce on. So the Fox News Channel is not a great channel when it comes to objective news . . . Muslim issues, or issues pertaining to Muslims. (Interview, Massachusetts, November 2009)

For one participant, Aaqib (male, 22, overseas born of Bangladeshi background, national identity: Bangladeshi American), Fox News has become a laughing stock:

> I do think the media sometimes tend to go overboard, they exaggerate a story and it just fuels the fire . . . I wouldn't call them a news source; nowadays they're an entertainment source. Yeah so if I feel like laughing I'll turn to Fox and just have some fun. (Interview, New York, January 2010)

A Muslim leader, Yusef (male, 25, US born of Indian background, national identity: 'fifty-fifty'), spoke of his local newspaper from his firsthand experience.

> I don't think [the] *Miami Herald* is really connected to Muslims or even when they are, they don't really cover the stories. For example, after the earthquake in Haiti, we did 'Support a Muslim Day for Haiti'. There was no coverage, or when there was coverage they did a piece [but] that's after I called and called and called and called and then finally they covered it but they didn't put [a] picture . . . I mean, we had about forty or fifty young Muslims from different colleges and some high schools to come out and they volunteered . . . The newspaper merely mentioned that Muslims were doing stuff. (Interview, Florida, March 2010)

Anwar (male, 30, overseas born of Tunisian background, national identity: Muslim) said:

> [The] majority of the media is fairly biased against Muslims. Various small outlets that are most of the time independent outlets are outlets that would give you a story that makes more sense to you as a Muslim. The rest are fairly biased because there is conglomerates now of media in the United States and these conglomerates are huge. Rupert Murdoch is one of the greatest examples. He is the owner of Fox and many other outlets . . .
>
> When the press, the TV, the radio is giving the same word, people are going to listen to it and it may be a fat lie but you repeat a fat lie three times or more and people start believing in it . . . I think still there is somewhat of a much bigger negative view of Muslims because of this media. And to answer your question ['What do you think of the American media?'] simply, a majority of the media is against Muslims. (Interview, Florida, March 2010)

As noted in Table 4.1, the majority of the participants had negative views of the American media. When I was in the USA for this study, a few horrendous incidents occurred and I had a chance to make firsthand observations of how the media represented the news. The incidents were:

- the Fort Hood shooting incident, 5 November 2009
- the Times Square bombing attempt, 2 May 2010
- a pipe bomb blast on 10 May 2010
- the Arizona shooting incident, 8 January 2011

When my survey on the identity of young American Muslims commenced in late 2009, the shooting incident in Fort Hood, Texas had just taken place. While interviewing the participants on the media, discussion of the Fort Hood shootings arose. Most of the interviews were conducted by early May 2010, so the later topics (such as the Times Square bombing attempt) did not come up in the interviews. For the later topics, I resorted only to content/discourse analysis of the media. In the next section, I give a detailed discussion of the Fort Hood shooting incident and a brief discussion of the later events. The main focus of this examination was to check the validity of the participants' observation that the 'media is biased'.

The Fort Hood shooting incident, 5 November 2009

On 5 November 2009, Major Nidal Malik Hasan, a US Army psychiatrist, American born of Palestinian-Muslim background, aged thirty-nine, who had counselled soldiers involved in foreign wars, opened fire with two handguns on soldiers preparing for foreign deployment at the Fort Hood US Army post in Texas, killing thirteen and wounding thirty others. Responding to this shooting rampage, a civilian police officer shot and wounded Major Hasan. Hasan's cousin said that Hasan had been ordered to serve a term in Iraq but had resisted such a deployment for some time. The interviewees in this study did not comment on whether Hasan was a good or bad person, but they noted the different agendas of the media when an incident that is related to Muslims is mentioned. For example, Ali (male, 17, US born of Egyptian background, national identity: Arab American) said: 'Yeah, Fort Hood, once the guy did it they blamed Islam automatically but if a Christian guy does it they blame him but not the religion, so that just gets me pissed off' (interview, New York, January 2010). Nadira (female, 17, of Bangladeshi background, national identity: Bangladeshi Muslim) said:

> I notice on the TV, like a few days ago the guy, he shot down thirteen people at Fort Hood. What he did was very bad, I don't think it's right to kill people, but one of the news anchors said that it was the worst terrorist attack since 9/11 and I didn't agree with that. 'Cos a few years back in Virginia Tech . . . this Asian man, he shot down all those people, that was a terrorist attack too, but nobody labelled it as a terrorist attack because it wasn't done by a Muslim. They think only Muslims do terrorist attacks and I don't believe that – everybody from different cultures does that. (Interview, New York, January 2010)

The two respondents made observations on the media reports: Ali spoke of how Islam was emphasised after the Fort Hood incident, while Nadira recalled the Virginia Tech massacre, when a non-Muslim student, Seung-Hui Cho, killed thirty-two people and injured many others on the campus of Virginia Polytechnic Institute and State University in Blacksburg, Virginia before committing suicide on 16 April 2007, but the media did not emphasise either his ethnicity or his religion.

Bearing the views of the interviewees about the Fort Hood shooting in mind, for a week (6–13 November 2009) I examined six newspapers – *USA Today*, the *New York Times*, the *Boston Globe*, the *Boston Herald*, the *Daily News* (New York) and the *New York Post* – and analysed them for discourse and content. I found they all reported that Nidal Hasan was a Muslim through headlines or news content. While reporting news on Hasan, nonetheless, some newspapers maintained some moderation. It should also be noted that the next day, on 6 November, a similar shooting took place in Orlando, Florida. An unemployed engineer, Jason Rodriguez, aged forty, opened fire in his old office, killing one person and injuring five. When asked 'Why did you do it?' Rodriguez replied, 'Because they left me to rot.'[18] In *The New York Times* report, Rodriguez was portrayed as an angry man, but his ethnicity and religion were not mentioned. Also, the media reporting (both print and electronic media) on Rodriguez did not continue for days, as in the Hasan case. Hasan's story remained a cover page story for almost a week. A participant in this study, Mujeeb (male, 16, US born of Palestinian background, national identity: Arab American), observed:

> I think it's [the media] not in a good way, to be honest with you. I feel if a Muslim killed someone in America and a white guy killed somebody, the white guy will be one day on the news. The Muslim guy would be ten days on the news, and then they'll be more scared of him. They'll keep it always behind their head. American dude, two days in the hype and it's done . . . Yeah, if someone [Muslim] does something we get blamed. They make it like all Muslims do that. And that's not true. (Interview, Michigan, April 2010)

In the following sections I discuss how some print media made the Fort Hood tragedy a Muslim issue.

USA Today

USA Today reported: 'Nader Hasan, who described himself to Fox News as a cousin, said [Nidal] Hasan is a Muslim who went into the military against his parents' wishes.' His cousin further said that Major Hasan was a 'good American' who did not support wars in Iraq and Afghanistan.[19] It was emphasised even more in the next issue that the Fort Hood incident was a 'Muslim' issue, as the headline indicated: 'Top brass warn against anti-Muslim backlash'.[20] It reported that President Obama immediately cautioned Americans (possibly the American media) against saying that religion played a role in the attack or that it was 'terrorism'. Similarly, Army Chief of Staff General George Casey and Homeland Security Secretary Janet Napolitano expressed the same view as the president that Major Hasan's shooting case should not be made a religious issue. General Casey commented, 'Speculation could potentially heighten a backlash against some of our Muslim soldiers,' and Napolitano remarked, 'This was an individual who does not represent the Muslim faith.' The editorial of the same issue pointed out that warning signs were not detected when in 2007–8 Hasan justified suicide bombings at his lecture at the Maryland military medical college, and expressed his 'anti-American rants'.[21]

On 10 November 2009, in an article headed 'FBI: Fort Hood suspect had ties to radical imam', *USA Today* reported that Hasan exchanged emails with the terror suspect Anwar al-Awlaki.[22] The headline 'radical imam' implied again that the Fort Hood shooting was a 'Muslim' issue. An opinion piece by Lucinda Roy, nevertheless, compared the atrocities committed by Seung-Hui Cho at Virginia Tech with those of Hasan since they were similar crimes but in different places. Roy wrote, 'Mass shootings often appear to be the result of personal alienation, anguish and rage, but they can also be intensely political acts.'[23] The next day in another opinion piece, James Alan Fox and Jack Levin discussed whether the shooting incidents that took place around the same time at Fort Hood and Orlando were workplace related and cautioned that Hasan's shooting incident should not be regarded as a terrorist act.[24] In my examination of *USA Today*'s reporting on Nidal Hasan, I found the opinion pieces of the columnists discussed above tried to present reasonable explanations, which is important for the readers' rational thinking. An interviewee in this study, Parveen (female, 15, of Bangladeshi background, national identity: 'American Bengali but my mom says that I have to be only Bengali'), observed:

> I mean I don't blame American media for not understanding Muslims but I feel like they should at least take some time to see what's going on other than what, what's happened because . . . people just don't do that, there has to be some psychological factor behind it for . . . to cause someone to kill thirteen men just like that. (Interview, New York, January 2010)

Yet Major Hasan's religion really was a concern for some readers. For example, one person wrote to the editor:

> He [Hasan] was suspected of Internet postings on suicide bombers. He said he was 'Muslim first and an American second' . . . And the most disturbing supposed opinion of Hasan's was [that] the war in Iraq is 'a war against Islam' . . . I am wondering whether he was left alone for fear of a racial profiling charge, or an anti-Muslim complaint.[25]

New York Times

On its first day of reporting, the *New York Times* did not include the word 'Muslim' in its headline but its content created the reasonable suspicion that Major Hasan was a 'Muslim'. It reported:

> In one posting on the Web site Scribd, a man named Nidal Hasan compared the heroism of a soldier who throws himself on a grenade to protect fellow soldiers to suicide bombers who sacrifice themselves to protect Muslims . . . It could not be confirmed [by the FBI], however, that the writer was Major Hasan.[26]

The next day, the *New York Times* confirmed that the Fort Hood incident was a Muslim act. It reported that Hasan was 'an American-born Muslim of Palestinian descent, he was deeply dismayed by the wars in Iraq and Afghanistan but proud of his Army job. He wore Middle Eastern clothes to the convenience store and his battle fatigues to the mosque.'[27] Furthermore, 'he was trained to counsel troubled soldiers, but bottled up his own distress about deploying'.[28] The article also reported that General

George Casey had expressed concerns about a possible backlash against Muslims.

Over the next few days, the *New York Times* continued reporting on Major Hasan and in one instance he was pictured as a Muslim wearing Middle Eastern garments and a *topi* at the convenience store during the morning of his shooting rampage.[29] Another report said:

Muslim leaders, advocates, and military service members have taken pains to denounce the shooting and distance themselves from Major Hasan. They make the point that his violence is no more representative of them than it is of other groups to which he belongs, including Army psychiatrists.[30]

The president of the Islamic Society of North America, Ingrid Mattson, commented, 'I don't understand why the Muslim-American community has to take responsibility for him . . . The Army has had at least as much time and opportunity to form and shape this person as the Muslim community'. [31]

On 10 November 2009, the *New York Times* published five letters, one of which specifically labelled Islam as oppressive and murderous:

It is true that personal demons (delusion, rage and so on) are responsible for many of these incidents. It is also true that there are ideologies, including Communism, fascism, and yes, strains of Islam, that intellectually justify and even promote oppression and murder to achieve prescribed ends.[32]

The last item in this issue was an opinion by David Brooks, who was critical of the army's 'political correctness'. Brooks pointed out that on the fringes of the Muslim world some Muslims see 'a war between Islam on the one side and Christianity and Judaism on the other . . . They are the ones who go into the crowded rooms, shout "Allahu Akbar", or "God is great", and then start murdering.'[33] Brooks realised that for the moment 'political correctness' in the army was acceptable because otherwise Muslims might be singled out, but if this attitude continued then it would encourage self-radicalisation by 'individual[s] in the US as much as by groups in Tehran, Gaza or Kandahar'.[34] The opinion piece obviously made the Fort Hood incident an Islamic issue, and suggested that both Israel and the USA were victims of 'Islamic terrorism'. On 12 November 2009, a Muslim wrote to the editor:

As a Muslim American, I am not afraid to raise my voice against terror perpetrated in the name of Islam. I do worry about the political correctness that might have prevented Major Hasan's superiors from putting him under some kind of supervision despite the danger signs.[35]

Boston Globe

The first-day reporting of the *Boston Globe* revealed that Major Hasan was a Muslim. It reported that Faizul Khan, a former imam at a mosque that Hasan attended, said that he often spoke with Hasan about how Hasan wanted to find a wife.[36] It also reported that several years ago Hasan had been thinking of leaving the military 'after other soldiers harassed him for being a Muslim'.[37] The next day the paper reported how Sergeant Kimberly Munley, a civilian police officer, raced towards the gunfire and fired at Hasan, bringing him down by shooting him four times. Some army officials reported that Hasan shouted '*Allahu Akbar!*' (God is great) as he was shooting other officers.[38] The photograph of Hasan in his Islamic garments (in the convenience store) was published in this issue.[39]

The *Boston Sunday Globe* finally labelled Hasan 'Muslim' in its headline.[40] The new information in this report about Hasan was that he had once told his classmates that he was 'a Muslim first and an American second'. It also reported that the leader of the Islamic community in the region around Fort Hood, Osman Danquah, was concerned that Hasan did not integrate enough. Another headline, 'Fort Hood suspect reached out to radical imam', also profiled Hasan's religion.[41] The report was similar to that of other newspapers of the day, mentioning Anwar al-Awlaki's praise in his blog for Hasan: 'He is a man of conscience who could not bear living the contradiction of being a Muslim and serving in an army that is fighting against his own people.' It also mentioned that Hasan's family attended the Dar al Hijrah Islamic centre in Falls Church, Virginia, where Awlaki was preaching in 2001, and that two of the 9/11 hijackers also attended Awlaki's mosque. In the opinion page, however, there were four letters of which two were on the topic of 'Muslims'. Both these letters included positive views on Muslims serving in the US military.[42]

Boston Herald

The *Boston Herald*'s earlier issues had similar reports on Major Hasan. But on 9 November 2009, its headline 'Fort Hood suspect tied to 9/11 mosque' suggested that the Fort Hood incident was a Muslim concern. On 12 November 2009, the *Herald* reported:

> Family members . . . [suggested] that Hasan's anxiety as a Muslim over his pending deployment overseas might have been a factor in the deadly rampage.
>
> Hasan had complained privately that he was harassed for his religion and wanted out of the Army. But there is no record of Hasan filing a harassment complaint or formally seeking release from the military, the officials said.
>
> Doctors overseeing Hasan's training viewed him as belligerent, defensive and argumentative in his frequent discussions of his Muslim faith, a military official said.

Hasan was characterized in meetings as a mediocre student and lazy worker.[43]

An interviewee in this study, Seerat (female, 17, US born of Palestinian back-ground, national identity: Arab American), noted:

> And just because he's a psychiatrist that kind of went off and shot people, they could have said 'A psychiatrist from this, this, this was involved in a shooting'. They didn't have to say 'a Muslim psychiatrist'. I think, okay, when you say Muslim, that makes it sound as if it's every Muslim. You can't judge an entire category based on one person. It's not fair, and I don't find it fair. When there's rapists and murderers, you don't say a Christian or a Catholic or Jewish. You don't see that right before their name. No, they only do it for Muslims, or that's what I've noticed. And that's not right at all. (Interview, Florida, March 2010)

Thus Seerat observed the general media profiling of Muslims and, in particu-lar, that the *Boston Herald* had gone further by characterising a Muslim as a 'mediocre student and lazy'.

Daily News

The first page of the *Daily News* had a big headline 'Face to face with evil'.[44] It was accompanied by a photograph of Nidal Malik Hasan. Another headline at the bottom of pp. 6–7 read 'Hasan went to same mosque as 9/11 thugs', fol-lowed by a similar story, reported in other newspapers, suggesting that Hasan may have been connected to the 9/11 terrorists. The next day the editorial in the *Daily News*, entitled 'Fanaticism hits home', commented:

> It was increasingly apparent that the mass murder at Fort Hood by Maj. Nidal Malik Hasan is the latest in a line of attacks or attempted attacks by Americans radical-ized by fanatical Muslim ideology . . . That Hasan began his rampage . . . by saying *'Allahu Akbar'* or 'God is Great' is relevant to his crime . . . Hasan is the latest dot to connect in a picture of home grown radicalization. Another dot is Najibullah Zazi, the Denver man indicted here in an alleged bomb plot. Another dot is Tarek Mehanna, the Boston area man charged in a plot to kill, kidnap or maim people, including shoppers in U.S. malls. Another dot is Michael Finton, the 29-year-old convert to Islam arrested in an alleged plot to blow up a federal building in Illinois. Another dot is Hosam Maher Husein Smadi, the 19-year-old Jordanian arrested for hatching a similar plot against a Dallas skyscraper. Of late, there have been many such dots, and the U.S. ignores them at its peril. Perhaps the government did so in Hasan's case.[45]

The editorial was critical of the intelligence authorities for not detecting that Hasan was inclined to violence, even though he had exchanged emails with

Anwar al-Awlaki. The editorial was also critical of the CAIR spokesperson Ibrahim Hooper, who said:

> He could have just snapped from some kind of stress. The thing is, when these things happen and the guy's name is John Smith, nobody says, well, what about his religious beliefs? But when it is a Muslim-sounding name, that automatically comes into it.

The editorial reiterated that Hasan was 'swept along by the perversion of Islam – repeat, perversion – that has justified violence'.[46] Later, in a *Daily News* opinion column, Charles Krauthammer was critical of some media sources who did not label Hasan's case as connected with Islam:

> 'I cringe that he's a Muslim . . . I think he's probably just a nut case,' said *Newsweek*'s Evan Thomas. Some were more adamant. *Time*'s Joe Klein decried 'odious attempts by Jewish extremists . . . to argue that the massacre perpetrated by Nidal Hasan was somehow a direct consequence of his Islamic beliefs'.[47]

New York Post

The cover page headline of the *New York Post* on 9 November was 'Fort Hood massacre, mosque of evil, killer's 9/11 terror link'.[48] Although there was another headline relating to sport on top of the Fort Hood massacre, the words 'MOSQUE OF EVIL' were printed in such a big bold font that they dominated the news of the day. The paper reported, 'Fort Hood fiend Dr. Nidal Malik Hasan attended a Virginia mosque at the same time as two 9/11 hijackers – and authorities are now probing a possible link between the men, a source confirmed yesterday.' Another headline on page 5 read 'Killer prayed at mosque with hijackers'. It included similar information as the *Boston Globe* that Hasan had attended a Virginian mosque at the same time as the two 9/11 hijackers and that the mosque imam may have had ties with Anwar al-Awlaki. The overall presentation of the newspaper (with the headlines and photos) connected Islam with terrorism.

The next day, there was a large image (covering almost half the page) of Hasan in his Islamic attire and *topi* coming out of the convenience store.[49] The caption read: 'Ticking time bomb: Maj. Nidal Hasan in security-camera footage taken at a 7-Eleven just hours before his rampage.' Below the photograph was the headline 'Officials admit shrugging off gunman's e-mails to al-Qaeda'. The story reported:

> The FBI last night said Hasan – who faces a court martial – first turned up on its radar in December 2008.
> That's when 10 and 20 e-mails were sent by Hasan to several terror-related Islamic figures, including Anwar Aulaqi [*sic*], a radical imam from Virginia who has been

openly propagandizing for al Qaeda in Yemen and who had ties to several of the 9/11 hijackers.[50]

In the same issue, it appeared through the discourse on the editorial and the letters pages that Hasan was being tried by the media. The editorial was critical of the FBI and army investigators who had earlier ignored Hasan's case. It was appreciative of Senator Joe Lieberman, who speculated about Hasan's link to terrorism. It pointed out that 'one doctor who studied with Hasan said that he "would frequently say he was a Muslim first and an American second" '.[51] He and others reportedly complained to higher authorities but no action was taken against Hasan. The editorial quoted Hasan's classmate's comments: 'We questioned how somebody could take an oath of office and be an officer in the military and swear . . . to defend America against all enemies, foreign and domestic' with that attitude.[52] Out of thirteen printed letters to the editor there was only one that defended Muslims: 'To blame the whole Islamic world for a terrorist attack by one individual is wrong.'[53] Other letters were critical of Muslims, Islam and other media.

In the same issue (10 November 2009), columnist Ralph Peters was critical of the people (including those in the media) who advocated caution in labelling the attack as a Muslim or terror attack.[54] An opinion piece by Rich Lowry, which ran under Peters's column, was critical of *Time* magazine for blaming the stressful environment of Fort Hood and suggesting that the frequent deployments may have led to Hasan's act.[55] Lowry was also critical of a *New York Times* piece that raised the possibility that Hasan may have contracted post-traumatic stress disorder by treating patients who were very distressed. On 13 November 2009, in his opinion piece, Paul Sperry was critical of CAIR and some sections of the media that gave Muslims a voice during the Fort Hood crisis. Sperry wrote:

> For years, our media and government routinely accepted and even promoted the Washington-based Council on American–Islamic Relations as a legitimate voice of Muslim Americans, buying into its claim to be the Muslim ACLU.
>
> In fact, CAIR is a radical Saudi-funded front group founded by leaders of the terror-supporting Muslim Brotherhood to infiltrate Washington and defend extremists. More than a dozen of CAIR's leaders have been jailed or otherwise implicated in support of terrorism – yet its spokesmen until recently were welcomed in the highest corridors of power . . .
>
> In the wake of the Fort Hood killings CNN, PBS, Fox, MSNBC and other networks immediately put CAIR's leaders on the air – where they predictably insisted the attack had nothing to do with Islam and warned that any 'Islamophobes' who make that obvious connection are inviting violent 'backlash' against Muslims.[56]

Finally, in his opinion piece Bill O'Reilly concluded:

Fort Hood isn't a 'tragedy' … Hasan is a hater driven by a fanatical Islamic viewpoint … Americans are at risk because Muslim terrorists want to kill us. That doesn't mean most Muslims subscribe to jihad, but it does mean the problem is exclusively Muslim.[57]

Further analysis of the Fort Hood media coverage

Nizam (male, 20, US born of Bangladeshi background, national identity: 'I feel more American') observed:

Yeah, the Fort … Fort Hood kind of solidifies my argument as the news media [television] being a source of entertainment and what you will see, the first thing they show over and over again, repeatedly scene after scene – we're talking about this Nidal Hasan guy – he's shown buying a coffee. Well, the first week I thought it was a false story, just because they showed this man with an Arab suit, with Arab dress on, and him buying coffee. Now this is totally unrelated to the actual topic, which is him murdering thirteen people, now why would you show a Muslim man in a type of Arab dress when this is totally unrelated to the story? You have a crazy guy, not a Muslim, and they're showing that scene over and over … This is how they perhaps construct a Muslim image as the 'other'. (Interview, New York, November 2009)

While Nizam made his observation about the electronic media, I examined the Fort Hood news representation in the print media. For example, there were reports of prayers for the departed souls and the alleged gunman (Major Hasan) in a church, and some newspapers explicitly printed photographs of the church,[58] though there was no report of mosques where Muslims had prayed for the Fort Hood victims. For example, members of the South Florida Muslim community expressed their concerns, and prayed for peace and for the victims at Fort Hood in the Friday prayer (the day after the shooting incident) in the mosques of southern Florida. The president of CAIR South Florida, Muhammed Malik, also urged mosques to pray for the victims. Malik said, 'It is totally unacceptable in Islam; any person of conscience will condemn that and we condemn that.' A former Muslim American Navy officer, Yusuf Mendez, said, 'It is a tragedy. You know in the Quran it says whenever you kill one person you kill all mankind. It is our duty to safeguard the community in which we live.' Mendez also pointed out that tens of thousands of Muslims serve in the US military. The Muslim community in southern Florida organised a candlelight vigil on the following Monday, and they urged Christians and Jews to join them.[59]

In Chapter 3, I discussed that the number of Muslims serving in the US armed forces is low compared to the total population. In November 2009, the *New York Times* reported, 'Some 3,557 military personnel identify themselves as Muslims among 1.4 million people in the active duty population, according to official figures. [But] Muslim advocacy groups estimate the number to be far higher, as listing one's religious preference is voluntary'.[60]

Hasan's religion also sparked a lot of controversy on some mainstream American talkback shows across the country. For example, Jimmy Cefalo's radio show on 610 WIOD in southern Florida included some callers who commented on Muslims, for example, 'We are at war against people that declared war against us. We didn't declare war against them. They declared war against us.' Jimmy Cefalo asked his listeners, 'No Muslims should be allowed in the military, is that the idea?' A female caller replied, 'Exactly, they are going to turn on you anyway sooner or later.'[61] The executive director of CAIR, Nihad Awad, commented on MSNBC live news after the Fort Hood shooting incident:

> I am not really happy that his [Hasan's] religion is becoming the subject when we have crimes committed against our soldiers and against our civilians inside the United States and outside the United States and how the religion, if it plays by the motives of those who are committing these acts, it does not become a story in the United States press except when he or she is a Muslim and it is our unfortunate [*sic*] and even this guy uttered this word *Allahu Akbar*, God is Great . . . this is an isolated incident by a disturbed individual . . . This also reminds me of . . . the abortion bomb . . . he did it in the name of Christianity or Christian, he became the subject of the press . . . even if they claim their religious affiliation, I don't think we should play into their hands.[62]

Times Square bombing attempt, 2 May 2010

Time printed a detailed report on Faisal Shahzad's bombing attempt in Times Square in Manhattan:

> The explosion [if it had happened], lasting only a few seconds, would have created a thermal ball wide enough to swallow up most of the intersection. A blast wave would have rocketed out in all directions at speeds 12,000 to 14,000ft per sec. (3,700 to 4,300m per sec.); hitting the surrounding buildings, the wave would have bounced off and kept going, as much as nine times faster than before. Anyone standing within 1,400 ft (430 m) – about five city blocks – of the explosion would have been at risk of being hit by shrapnel and millions of shards of flying glass. The many who died would not die prettily . . . Indeed, shortly after the incident in Times Square, Pakistan's Tehrik-e-Taliban claimed it was behind the plot.[63]

Time's eight-page coverage discussed Shahzad's history in the USA and revealed that he lived in an affluent suburb but later lost his job. *Time* also justified the wars in Afghanistan and Iraq and drone attacks in Pakistan because 'while . . . drones in Pakistan have killed many would-be terrorists, those who continue to operate do so more independently', and gave the examples of Nidal Hasan

Figure 4.1 When is someone's religion relevant and newsworthy?
From Muslim Observer, *16 May 2010*

in Fort Hood and Umar Farouk Abdulmutallab, who allegedly attempted to blow up a flight as it approached Detroit in December 2009.[64] Overall, *Time* managed to generate fear among some readers as it published photographs of alleged and convicted terrorists (all bearing Muslim names), and mentioned that terrorist groups in Pakistan were working globally.[65]

The fears and concerns of both Muslims and non-Muslims were expressed later in letters to the editor. For example, Kenneth Lee wrote of his concern 'about the legal immigrants who want to harm us rather than the illegal immigrants who only want a job'.[66] Lynne Gaylor stated, 'We have always been a nation that is willing to help other countries, but what do we get in return? A stab in the back.'[67] At the same time the Faisal Shahzad incident made some American Muslims feel vulnerable. As Reem Bakker wrote, 'The worst thing that came from Shahzad's botched bombing is that it further damaged the reputation of Muslims in the U.S.'[68]

Another Muslim, Zoya Mehmoud, appealed to the wider society: 'Although the events in Times Square were certainly frightening, the political backlash against Pakistanis and Muslims was even more so ... Don't make us pay for the mistakes of others.'[69] Finally, a Muslim from Pakistan, Syed Naheer Ameer, wrote:

Time's article on the Times Square incident is rather biased. There was a great deal mentioned about the tragic loss of life that could have occurred if the explosion had taken place on May 1, but little about the many deaths suffered by civilians at the hands of drone missile attacks in Pakistan. Is a Pakistani life not worth the same as that of a U.S. citizen? You should be bridging the gap between Muslims and the West instead of heightening tension.[70]

Pipe bomb blast, 10 May 2010

On 10 May 2010 a pipe bomb was detonated at the Islamic Center of Northeast Florida (a mosque in the Southside district of Jacksonville). It went off during evening prayers, and it was powerful enough to send shrapnel flying 100 metres. Worshippers at the centre said they heard a loud noise outside the mosque and went outside where they found fire engulfing a rear emergency exit. The flames were put out with a fire extinguisher. The case was treated as a hate crime.[71]

An observer of both the Times Square and the pipe bomb incidents, Hesham Hassaballa, was surprised that the Times Square bombing attempt was considered an act of terrorism while the pipe bombing was first treated as a hate crime and later 'as a possible act of domestic terrorism'. Hassaballa commented, 'What if a pipe bomb exploded in Times Square? Or outside a church? Would this be called terrorism? Of course it would . . . and it should. So should this attack on the Jacksonville, FL mosque.'[72]

A year later, an alleged perpetrator of the pipe bombing, Sandlin Matthews Smith, of St Johns County, Florida, was shot and killed when he pulled a gun on agents who were trying to arrest him in Oklahoma.[73] When the mosque bombing incident happened in May 2010, I was in the US and keenly observed both the print and electronic media, but this pipe bombing surprisingly was not given as high a profile as other news such as the Fort Hood shooting incident.

Arizona shooting, 8 January 2011

On 8 January 2011, a 22-year-old man named Jared Loughner killed six people (including a child) and injured thirteen others (including Arizona Democrat Congresswoman Gabrielle Giffords). The shooting occurred when Giffords was talking to two constituents at a 'Congress on Your Corner' event outside a grocery store.[74] The electronic media selectively chose not to racially profile the perpetrator. And Fox News's *Glenn Beck* programme was sympathetic to the victims and apparently overprotective of the conservative leaders who were considered by some people to be inadvertent instigators of the shooting incident.

This man [the Arizona perpetrator] wasn't a right-wing nutjob. But he also was not a left-wing nutjob. He was just a nutjob.

There are people who are nuts and will do violent things and they will do them in somebody else's name because they're nuts. There's also people like the nineteen hijackers who took down the World Trade Center in the name of Allah. Is Allah responsible? Or, hey, how about the religion that these guys go to? No, no, no, no, no, no, we are told by the media. These nineteen hijackers – no, no, no.[75]

I found the analogy of the nineteen hijackers in the Twin Towers attacks completely irrelevant. It once again reminded the audience that 'we' are not a threat but 'they' [Muslims] are.

Christian–Muslim dichotomy in the media

Fifty-two participants in this study particularly observed that the American media has often portrayed Muslims solely through the prism of extremism and terrorism. The media discourse on Muslims tends to transpose Muslims as 'bad Muslims'. In most instances, when the perpetrators are not Muslims, the media do not identify their religion at all. Lateefa (female, 25, African American, national identity: American) observed:

> Every day someone's committing a crime, and most of the people in the United States ascribe to some religion, but it's never said a Christian does such and such and such, a Jewish person does such and such and such, but when a Muslim does it that's one of the first things they say, 'He is a Muslim', and to me that's, in itself, just bias. (Interview, Florida, March 2010)

For example, on 18 February 2010, Joseph Andrew Stack crashed a plane into the IRS office in Austin, Texas, where 190 employees were working. Stack was angry with the federal tax authorities. Apparently, he left a suicide note that criticised the IRS and declared: 'Violence is the only answer.' Apart from the pilot, there were no casualties. The Austin police chief, Art Acevedo, 'said there was no cause for concern and assured residents that it was an isolated incident'. The White House commented, 'The crash did not appear to be an act of terrorism.'[76] The media did not spend much time on this issue. Ten participants in this study (see Table 4.1) considered this episode represented a 'double standard' because there was no mention of 'terrorism' and no discussion of the religion of the perpetrator.

Muslim leader Zahed (male, over 30, African American, national identity: 'black American') mentioned that the radical Christian militia group Hutaree, charged with plotting to kill police in Michigan and wage war on the federal government, were not identified as Christians:

> We have, from not just right-wing TV like Fox National News, but even sometimes . . . local stations through ignorance misrepresent issues relating to the Muslim com-

munity or they use inaccurate nomenclature to describe us or news stories. Like, for example, they'll call a Muslim like this guy 'the Christmas Day bomber', and 'Islamic radical' or a 'Muslim terrorist', but then with the Christian militia group they won't even mention Christianity . . . Hutaree, this is just one example. (Interview, Michigan, May 2010)

I checked Zahed's comment about Hutaree (meaning 'God's warrior'), and found that on 28 March 2010 nine members of a Christian militia group in Michigan were indicted after a federal investigation into an alleged plot to kill a police officer and then attack the funeral with bombs in the hope of starting an uprising against the government. They were arrested following raids in Michigan, Indiana and Ohio. Hutaree's doctrine alludes to the end of the world: 'When the time comes for those without enough faith, they will fall to the Anti-Christ's doctrine. And it will make perfect sense to the whole world; even the elect.'[77] An online video depicted men armed with rifles dressed in camouflage and an arm patch with the Hutaree insignia of a red and brown cross flanked by diagonal brown stripes. It also showed gunmen practising shooting from behind a car, and conducting military manoeuvres in a wooded area.[78]

On 12 February 2011, I looked into the Factiva database (which has a wide-ranging collection of newspapers) and typed 'Hutaree' to see if it was associated with Christianity. There were 753 news items from 28 March 2010 to 27 January 2011. In my survey I found some overseas media in Australia, Canada, India, Thailand and New Zealand had printed headlines that included the words 'Christian militia'. But since my discussion is on American Muslims, I focused on the American media and found that only 2 per cent of the American media included the word 'Christian' or its derivatives in the headlines in their reporting. Here is the sample:

- 'God's warrior Christian militia' (*Nightline*, ABC, 29 March 2010)
- 'Christian militia members arrested; Tea Party still influential?' (*Campbell Brown*, CNN, 29 March 2010)
- 'FBI has 3 raids; Christian militia a reported target' (*St Louis Post-Dispatch*, 29 March 2010)
- 'Stepmother says she helped coax Michigan Christian militia member into surrender to FBI' (Associated Press Newswires, 30 March 2010)
- '"Christian warriors" indicted; help for homeowners; bullied to death?; Karl Rove heckled; Russian subway suicide attacks; forced to pay rent' (*CNN Newsroom*, CNN, 30 March 2010)
- 'Militant Christians held in murder plot' (*Financial Times* (USA), 30 March 2010)
- 'Michigan Christian militia group appears in federal court' (Voice of America Press Releases and Documents, 30 March 2010)

- 'Feds had eye on "Christian warriors"' (*Knoxville News* Sentinel (TN), 31 March 2010)
- 'Beware of false Christians bearing arms' (*Ventura County Star* (Camarillo, CA), 2 April 2010)
- 'Beware of false Christians bearing arms' (*Times Record News* (Wichita Falls, TX), 4 April 2010)
- 'Christian terrorists?' (*Christian Century* (Chicago), 4 May 2010)
- 'Violence cloaked in Christianity' (*Virginian-Pilot & Ledger-Star* (Norfolk, VA), 9 April 2010)
- 'Giving Christians a bad name' (*Las Vegas Review-Journal*, 11 April 2010)
- 'Christian terrorism' (*Abilene Reporter-News* (TX), 11 April 2010); also published in another newspaper: 'Pitts: Christian terrorism' (*Daily Camera* (Boulder, CO), 12 April 2010)
- 'Christian militia case defendant lived in Tukwila' (Associated Press Newswires, 14 April 2010)
- 'Christian bows out of hate-filled take on faith' (*Sunday News* (Lancaster, PA), 25 April 2010)
- 'U.S. "Christian militia" members on trial accused of plotting uprising against govt; advance media information; future news item; U.S. District Court for the Eastern District of Michigan' (*Precise Media Planner*, US District Court for the Eastern District of Michigan, Detroit, 9 December 2010).[79]

In the 753 Factiva American news items, I found some media outlets that were critical of Hutaree but refrained from using the word 'Christian' in their headlines. For example, *USA Today* reported:

> Charges that nine members of a Michigan militia group were cooking up a crackpot plot to kill police officers and wage war on the United States should come as a surprise to no one. We've seen this kind of lunacy before, most tragically with the 1995 bombing of the federal building in Oklahoma City.
>
> But the scheme is a reminder that well-armed people simmering with hatred are ever present and easily stoked to violence, that they're not easily typed by race or ethnicity, and that terrorism is sometimes homegrown.
>
> The group – which dubbed itself 'Hutaree', a word it said meant 'Christian warriors' – viewed local law enforcement as the 'foot soldiers' of the federal government, and according to prosecutors, it planned to attack a local officer, then detonate explosives to murder those gathered for that officer's funeral. Their hope was to incite an anti-government uprising.[80]

The *Daily News* in Bowling Green, Kentucky was also critical of Hutaree but refrained from using the words 'Christian terrorists'!

These people are just as bad as the terrorists we are fighting in Iraq and Afghanistan. What is even more twisted about this group is that its name, Hutaree, means 'Christian warrior.' The group quotes several Bible passages and declares: 'We believe that one day, as prophecy says, there will be an Antichrist . . . Jesus wanted us to be ready to defend ourselves using the sword and stay alive using equipment.' What Jesus says in the Bible can be subject to different interpretations, but to reach the conclusions these folks did defies belief. These suspects are, quite frankly, crazy and should provide a wake-up call to us all that people who wish to do us harm aren't just overseas. Some terrorists are homegrown and living among us.[81]

The *New York Post* was sympathetic towards the Christian militia. It compared the Hutaree militia with the 9/11 plotters and Fort Hood gunman, and declared that Hutaree was a lesser threat:

Alas, the Hutaree case is likely to boost the bogus narrative that such antigovernment militias represent fundamentally the same threat as Islamist terrorists . . . But one need only contrast the wild fantasies indulged by the Hutaree kooks with the lethal calculation of killers like the 9/11 plotters or the Fort Hood gunman (not to mention their respective body counts) to understand the radical difference between the two threats. One consists of the dedicated agents of a ruthless, religion-driven ideology. The other: a few guys in the woods with guns. The Obama administration – Attorney General Eric Holder and Homeland Security Secretary Janet Napolitano, in particular – needs to keep its eyes on the ball.[82]

Sympathetic tones towards Muslims

In the 753 Factiva American news items, I found three columnists (Omar Sacirbey of the *Houston Chronicle*, Leonard Pitts Jr of the *Virginian-Pilot & Ledger-Star* and an anonymous writer in *Christian Century* magazine) who were critical of the media or mainstream Americans' selective use of the word 'terrorism'. For example, in his piece 'Muslims see double standard in "terrorist" label' Sacirbey observed that after the Hutaree arrests some Muslim leaders pointed out the 'double standards' of some American media.[83] They observed that the 9/11 Twin Towers attack was labelled an act of 'Islamic terrorism'. With regard to Hutaree, the media avoided the words 'Christian terrorism'. Sacirbey cited Alejandro Buetel, the government liaison officer for the MPAC in Washington, who commented, 'In cases of violence committed by Muslims, when it's politically motivated, yes, call it Muslim terrorism. But when other faiths or ideologies commit violence, it has to be the same. We're calling for consistency.' Similarly, on the *Huffington Post* website, the Muslim commentator Yasmin Mogahed (cited by Sacirbey), pointed out that after the Hutaree arrests she did not see any expert on TV exploring whether Christian doctrine condones violence, yet after any Muslim-related incident the media rushes to bring in experts to search the Quran for verses condoning violence. Mogahed said, 'If there's news of a Muslim terrorist, Islam becomes complicit in the crime. Yet few people are going to accuse Christianity of motivating the terrorism of the Hutaree militia.' As discussed earlier, I found only 2 per cent of the 753 Factiva American news items (from 28 March 2010 to 27 January 2011) use the label 'Christian' or 'Christianity' in their headlines.

Similarly, Leonard Pitts Jr was critical of Americans who avoid the term 'terrorism' for Christian violence. He gave examples of 'Christian terrorism':

> From Eric Rudolph's bombing of the Atlanta Olympics, a gay nightclub and two abortion clinics; to the so-called Phineas Priests who bombed banks, a newspaper and a Planned Parenthood office in Spokane, Wash.; from Matt Hale soliciting the murder of a federal judge in Chicago; to Scott Roeder's assassination of abortion provider Dr. George Tiller; from brothers Matthew and Tyler Williams murdering a gay couple near Redding, Calif.; to Timothy McVeigh destroying a federal building and 168 lives in Oklahoma City, we have seen no shortage of 'Christians' who believe Jesus requires – or at least allows – them to commit murder.
>
> If federal officials are correct, we now have one more name to add to the dishonor roll. That name would be Hutaree.[84]

Pitts observed that many Americans accept that it would be unfair to tarnish all Christians as 'terrorists' for these acts. He said, 'We are conditioned [by the media] to think of terror wrought by Islamic fundamentalists as something strange and alien and other . . . we are pleased to believe, [there is] a hard, immutable line between us and Them.' Similarly, the anonymous writer in *Christian Century* commented:

> The Christian militia group known as the Hutaree, whose leaders were arrested by the FBI during Holy Week, is fond of quoting Christian scripture. Its Web site features this line from Jesus in the Gospel of John: 'Greater love hath no man than this, that he lay down his life for his friends.' The mission of the group is spelled out: 'Preparing for the end time battles to keep the testimony of Jesus Christ alive.' . . . To the vast majority of Christians, the Hutaree represent an appalling distortion of Christian beliefs . . . The discomfort is understandable – and educational, for it gives Christians a chance to experience the incongruity many Muslims feel when the media refer to Muslim terrorists.[85]

Embarrassed to be Christians

Like the mainstream Muslims who found themselves tarnished by the 9/11 Twin Towers attacks and after the failed terrorist plot by Faisal Shahzad,[86] some Christians felt the same about the Hutaree incident. For example, the

Reverend Rachel Hackenberg was critical of some Christians:

> I am frustrated and fed up with groups like Westboro Baptist Church that continue to call themselves 'Church' or people like those in the Hutaree Militia who call themselves 'Christians' ...
>
> I am embarrassed and appalled as a Christian to carry the same name as Pat Robertson, James Dobson, Diane Gramley (of 'Out in the Silence' fame, or is it infamy?), and the like. Hatred and violence and the politics of fear were never, never part of the ministry of Jesus, yet often in the public arena when someone mentions 'Christian,' people think of these persons first and foremost – before Mother Teresa, before Martin Luther King Jr., before their local churches that contribute to food banks and organize clothing drives and serve great spaghetti dinners.[87]

Likewise, in his opinion piece 'Giving Christians a bad name', J. C. Watts stated:

> Both groups – the Hutaree in Michigan and the Phelps-led Westboro Baptist Church in Kansas – bring to mind the Ku Klux Klan parading in masks and robes, terrorizing and murdering minority families across the nation on Saturday night, and praising the Lord on Sunday morning in their local church pews.
>
> Where do these people come off calling themselves Christians? ... Every Christian in America should be outraged at this 'Christian militia' group in Michigan, the KKK and the Phelps family.[88]

And in a letter to the *Commercial Appeal* in Memphis, Vaughn Denton wrote:

> The men who call themselves a Christian Militia Group who were arrested by the FBI in raids over the weekend of March 27 in Michigan, Indiana and Ohio were wicked men ... True believers in Christ are not 'white supremacists' and right wing extremists, nor are we Ku Klux Klan members.[89]

Not all media is bad

Table 4.1 shows that nineteen participants in my study held positive views about the American media. For example, Irfan (male, 25, overseas born of Pakistani background, national identity: Pakistani American) said, 'I don't watch Fox ... I don't watch CNN ... I love business so I watch CNBC all the time. I read the *Wall Street Journal* every day ... I read the business news' (interview, Massachusetts, November 2009). Benazir (female, 17, US born of Indian background, national identity: American Indian) said, 'I like watching MSNBC because I think they're better than ... But I think they're more open and accepting and I think Fox is very biased' (interview, Massachusetts, November 2009). Dina (female, 18, US born of Trinidadian background, national identity: Trinidadian Muslim) had a positive firsthand experience and she shared her favourable opinion of one particular newspaper:

> It was my 8th-grade year. I was president of student council for my 8th-grade year. And we worked with the city of . . . police department to collect school supplies to send to Afghanistan. And the *Sun-Sentinel* actually interviewed me and they posted up a story, 'Helping hands, kids helping kids'. And they had troops from Afghanistan send us pictures of when the kids actually got the school supplies. (Interview, Florida, March 2010)

Ameena (female, 20, US born of Egyptian background, national identity: Arab American Muslim) said, 'I watch Al Jazeera. I try to watch BBC the most. I don't watch CNN, I don't watch Fox News because it is so biased.' She added: 'But definitely, I appreciate some journalists who try to see both sides, try to listen to other people's opinions and get the full story, but for the most part, yeah, American media, I don't watch it' (interview, Florida, March 2010). Ameena implied that other outlets such as the British media and the Qatari media showed both sides of the story. Yet there were some participants who appreciated some CNN and Fox programs. For example, Ruhee (female, over 30, overseas born of Palestinian background, national identity: 'Muslim, first and foremost, then Arab American') spoke of the three-part CNN documentary *God's Warrior*, aired in August 2007. The documentary focused on the three Abrahamic religions (Judaism, Christianity and Islam) in the United States, Europe and the Middle East. Ruhee said:

> In their documentary they shed light on post-9/11 and the Muslims here. So they talked about a lot of people who converted to Islam weeks after 9/11 so you hear a lot of positive. You know in this society, you'll always hear of the positive and negative and for me I try to dwell on the positive. (Interview, Michigan, April 2010)

It is interesting to note that a few participants in the 20–30 age group spoke positively of Jon Stewart's *Daily Show* on Comedy Central. Sonia (female, 20, US born of Egyptian origin, national identity: Muslim) said:

> If you think of people like Jon Stewart, he's very positive and he's a liberal and he kind of shows both sides and sometimes it depends on what the topic is but, you know, compared to like five or six years ago, it's gotten better. (Interview, Florida, March 2010)

Conclusion

In this chapter, I have discussed how the participants felt about the US media. Since many respondents had negative views about some media outlets, I decided to examine the print media on pertinent topics. For news about Muslims, I investigated print media representation of the Fort Hood incident in detail. I briefly examined other incidents that involved both Muslim and non-Muslim perpetrators, such as the Times Square bombing attempt, the pipe bomb blast, the Arizona shooting and the Hutaree case. By comparing the non-Muslim/Christian incidents such as the pipe bomb blast, the Arizona shooting and the Hutaree case, I was able to test the validity of the participants' view that the media is biased, that it labels Islam/Muslims and so on. Of course, the Fort Hood shooting incident, the Arizona shooting, the Times Square bombing attempt and the pipe bombing in Florida were horrendous. The Hutaree Christian militia's alleged plot against the government was quite serious. Some print media sources on Hutaree included 'Christianity' in their headlines, but the news was not spread nationally as is commonplace with Muslim cases. (I only came to know about the Hutaree militia incident through a Muslim leader's interview in Michigan.)

Fifty-two participants mentioned that the media has positive or somewhat positive attitudes, and eight respondents expressed the opinion that Muslims should get involved in the media to give a better Muslim representation. I will explore this topic in the Conclusion.

Overall, the media involves a wide range of outlets. From my brief examination of the print media, I found that, when the perpetrator is a Muslim, there is a tendency for journalists to connect the incident to the 'Muslim other' and blow their news reporting up out of all proportion to the event.

Notes

1. Pew Research Center, 'Muslim Americans: No Signs of Growth in Alienation or Support for Extremism', Pew Research Center website, 30 August 2011, http://people-press.org/2011/08/30/muslim-americans-no-signs-of-growth-in-alienation-or-support-for-extremism/, accessed 22 May 2012. The percentages from 2011 (55 per cent unfair, 30 per cent fair, 25 per cent unsure/depends) add up to 110. This is how they appear on the Pew website.
2. Ibid.
3. *USA Today, New York Times, Boston Globe, Boston Herald, Daily News* and *New York Post.*
4. Edward Said, *Covering Islam: How the Media and the Experts Determine How We See the Rest of the World*, rev. edn (New York: Viking, 1997), pp. ix–xvi.
5. E. Ghareeb, 'The Middle East in the U.S. Media', *Middle East Annual: Issues and Events* 3 (1983), pp. 185–210.
6. Ahmadullah Siddiqi, 'Islam, Muslims and the American Media', in Amber Haque (ed.), *Muslims and Islamization in North America: Problems and Prospects* (Beltsville, MD: Amana, 1999), pp. 203–29, see p. 210.
7. Ibid. pp. 211–13.

8. Ibid. p. 212.
9. Jeremy Earp and Sut Jhally (dir.), *Reel Bad Arabs: How Hollywood Vilifies a People*, DVD (Northampton, MA: Media Education Foundation, 2006).
10. Saud Joseph, Benjamin D'Harlingue and Alvin Ka Hin Wong, 'Arab Americans and Muslim Americans in the *New York Times*, before and after 9/11', in Amaney Jamal and Nadine Naber (eds), *Race and Arab Americans before and after 9/11: From Invisible Citizens to Visible Subjects* (Syracuse, NY: Syracuse University Press, 2008), pp. 229–75, see pp. 234–5.
11. Ibid. pp. 236–7.
12. Laurie Goodstein, 'In U.S., echoes of rift of Muslims and Jews', *New York Times*, 12 September 2001, p. 12; see also Joseph, D'Harlingue and Wong, 'Arab Americans and Muslim Americans', pp. 240–1.
13. Goodstein, 'In U.S., echoes of rift of Muslims and Jews'.
14. Jane I. Smith, *Islam in America*, 2nd edn (New York: Columbia University Press, 2010), p. 190.
15. Ibid, p. 190; see also Wayne Kopping (dir.), *Obsession: Radical Islam's War against the West*, Pulsar Productions, Liberty Film Festival, October 2005.
16. Smith, *Islam in America*, p. 190.
17. Ibid. pp. 187–8.
18. Jennifer Steinhauer, 'Gunman kills 1 and wounds 5 at Florida office', *New York Times*, 7 November 2009, p. 9.
19. 'Tragedy at Fort Hood: rampage tears into soldiers' sanctuary', *USA Today*, 6–8 November 2009, p. 1.
20. 'Top brass warn against anti-Muslim backlash', *USA Today*, 9 November 2009, p. 1.
21. 'Red flags at Fort Hood', *USA Today*, 9 November 2009, p. 10.
22. 'FBI: Fort Hood suspect had ties to radical imam', *USA Today*, 10 November 2009, p. 2.
23. Lucinda Roy, 'Don't let the shooters win', *USA Today*, 10 November 2009, p. 11.
24. James Alan Fox and Jack Levin, 'Fort Hood tragedy: terror or typical workplace violence', *USA Today*, 11 November 2009, p. 21.
25. Debra Adkins, Roanoke, VA, 'Writing on the wall', Letters to the Editor, *USA Today*, 12 November 2009, p. 10.
26. James Dao, 'Told of war horror, gunman feared deployment', *New York Times*, 6 November 2009, pp. 1, 16.
27. Clifford Krauss and James Dao, 'Details trickle out as army tests sole-killer theory', *New York Times*, 7 November 2009, p. 1.
28. Ibid.
29. James C. McKinley Jr and James Dao, 'After years of growing tensions, 7 minutes of bloodshed', *New York Times*, 9 November 2009, p. 1.
30. Andrea Elliott, 'A hard time for Muslims to serve their country, especially after shootings', *New York Times*, 9 November 2009, p. 17.
31. Ibid.

32. Thomas M. Doran, Plymouth, MI, 'As the nation grieves over Fort Hood', Letters to the Editor, *New York Times*, 10 November 2009, p. 30.
33. David Brooks, 'The rush to therapy', *New York Times*, 10 November 2009, p. 31.
34. Ibid.
35. Abroo Shah, Westfield, NJ, 'The search for the "why" of Fort Hood', Letters to the Editor, *New York Times*, 12 November 2009, p. 30.
36. April Castro and Devlin Barrett, '12 killed in rampage at Fort Hood', *Boston Globe*, 6 November 2009, p. 6.
37. 'Suspect feared deployment, relative says', *Boston Globe*, 6 November 2009, p. 6.
38. Greg Jaffe and Dan Eggen, 'As shots rang out, she answered call', *Boston Globe*, 7 November 2009, p. 1.
39. Mike Baker and Brett J. Blackledge; 'Suspect a study in contrasts', *Boston Globe*, 7 November 2009, p. 6.
40. 'Muslim leader troubled by talks with suspect', *Boston Sunday Globe*, 8 November 2009, p. 6.
41. Devlin Barrett, 'Fort Hood suspect reached out to radical imam', *Boston Globe*, 10 November 2009, p. 2.
42. 'Vox Op', Letters, *Boston Globe*, 10 November 2009, p. 15.
43. 'Docs were wary of alleged shooter', *Boston Herald*, 12 November 2009, p. 19.
44. 'Face to face with evil', *Daily News*, 9 November 2009, p. 1.
45. 'Fanaticism hits home', *Daily News*, 10 November 2009, p. 22.
46. Ibid.
47. Charles Krauthammer, 'Medicalizing mass murder', *Daily News*, 13 November 2009, p. 27.
48. 'Fort Hood massacre, mosque of evil, killer's 9/11 terror link', *New York Post*, 9 November 2009, p. 1.
49. 'Officials admit shrugging off gunman's e-mails to al-Qaeda', *New York Post*, 10 November 2009, p. 5.
50. Ibid.
51. 'Eyes wide shut', *New York Post*, 10 November 2009, p. 28.
52. Ibid.
53. Peter Manasse, Monaco, 'When terror hits home, America's PC suicide', *New York Post*, 10 November 2009, p. 28.
54. Ralph Peters, 'Fudging the facts on Fort Hood', *New York Post*, 10 November 2009, p. 29.
55. Rich Lowry, 'Sorry, this killer's no victim', *New York Post*, 10 November 2009, p. 29.
56. Paul Sperry, 'Moderate terror pals', *New York Post*, 13 November 2009, p. 31.
57. Bill O'Reilly, 'Obama's problem with reality', *New York Post*, 13 November 2009, p. 31.
58. E.g. *Boston Globe*, *Daily News*, 9 November 2009.
59. 610 WIOD/CBS 4 news, cited in 'South Florida Muslims pray for peace', CAIR-FL

video, 6 November 2009, http://www.youtube.com/watch?v=iuGHJbpN8rs, accessed 22 May 2012.

60. Andrea Elliott, 'Complications grow for Muslims serving in the U.S. military', *New York Times* website, 8 November 2009, http://www.nytimes.com/2009/11/09/us/09muslim.html?pagewanted=all, accessed 28 May 2012.

61. Ibid.

62. 'CAIR not happy Hasan's Islamic faith is discussed; "so what" if he said "Allahu Akbar!"', CAIR video, 6 November 2009, http://www.youtube.com/watch?v=3cf saByxg9Q&feature=related, accessed 22 May 2012.

63. Howard Chua-Eoan, 'Broadway bomber', *Time*, 17 May 2010, pp. 15, 17.

64. Ibid. p. 18.

65. Ibid. pp. 14–21.

66. Kenneth Lee, Raytown, MO, Letters to the Editor, *Time*, 7 June 2010, p. 4.

67. Lynne Gaylor, Clearfield, PA, Letters to the Editor, *Time*, 7 June 2010, p. 4.

68. Reem Bakker, New York, NY, Letters to the Editor, *Time*, 7 June 2010, p. 4.

69. Zoya Mehmoud, Alexandria, VA, Letters to the Editor, *Time*, 7 June 2010, p. 4.

70. Syed Naheer Ameer, Karachi, Pakistan, Letters to the Editor, *Time*, 7 June 2010, p. 4.

71. Keith Olbermann, 'There is no "Ground Zero mosque"', MSNBC TV website, 16 August 2010, http://www.msnbc.msn.com/id/38730223/ns/msnbc_tv-count down_with_keith_olbermann/, accessed 22 May 2012.

72. Hesham A. Hassaballa, 'Terror double standard (pipe-bomb explosion @ Florida mosque vs. Times Square plot)', MuslimMatters website, 18 May 2010, http://muslimmatters.org/2010/05/18/terror-double-standard/, accessed 22 May 2012.

73. 'FBI: Fla. bombing suspect killed in Okla. was paranoid that cops were after him, hated Muslims', Associated Press Newswires, 6 May 2011.

74. Jim O'Sullivan, 'Arizona shooting rocks the political world', *National Journal*, 8 January 2011.

75. *Glenn Beck*, Fox News, 10 January 2011.

76. 'Texas pilot air attack on US office', BBC News website, 18 February 2010, http://news.bbc.co.uk/2/hi/8522746.stm, accessed 22 May 2012.

77. Mark Reiter and Christopher D. Kirkpatrick, '9 alleged militia members indicted for plotting to kill police', *The Blade* (Toledo, OH), 29 March 2010.

78 Ibid.

79. Retrieved through Factiva database, accessed 27 January 2011. These headlines with the label 'Christian' did not appear in the Factiva database: 'Feds: Christian militia needed to be "taken down"' (*Boston Globe*, 30 March 2010); 'Christian Militia members charged with plots to kill police officers' (*USA Today*, 29 March 2010); 'Hutaree Christian militia plotted to kill cops in name of "top general" Jesus Christ: FBI', (*Daily News* (New York), 29 March 2010).

80. 'Militia arrests show there's no stereotyping terrorism', *USA Today*, 31 March 2010, p. 10.

81. 'Terror plot shows it exists here as well', *Daily News* (Bowling Green, KY), 1 April 2010.

82. 'Gunmen in the woods', *New York Post*, 31 March 2010, p. 28. This was also cited on the Newscorpwatch website at http://newscorpwatch.org/blog/201003310003, accessed 22 May 2012.

83. Omar Sacirbey, 'Muslims see double standard in "terrorist" label', *Houston Chronicle*, 9 April 2010, p. 11.

84. Leonard Pitts Jr, 'Violence cloaked in Christianity', *Virginian-Pilot & Ledger Star*, 9 April 2010, p. B-9.

85. 'Christian terrorists?', *Christian Century*, 4 May 2010, p. 7.

86. See Bilal A. Rana, 'Bomber, a fanatic,' Letters to the Editor, *Detroit News*, 14 May 2010, p. 12.

87. Rev. Rachel Hackenberg, 'Christian bows out of hate-filled take on faith', *Sunday News* (Lancaster, PA), 25 April 2010, p. 1.

88. J. C. Watts, 'Giving Christians a bad name', *Las Vegas Review-Journal*, 11 April 2010, p. 5D.

89. Vaughn Denton, 'Hutaree militia is not Christian', Letters to the Editor, *Commercial Appeal* (Memphis, TN), 7 April 2010, p. A11.

CHAPTER

5

BARACK HUSSEIN OBAMA AND YOUNG MUSLIMS' POLITICAL AWARENESS

Oh, in the symbolic sense, absolutely, it is a big change to have a black president. I think there's a change of attitude more than there's a change of policy. And, above all the other promises that he made, I think – the promise that he's uniting a country, and to a further extent uniting the global community, I think he's really held true to that promise more than all the other promises that he's made. I think he's had outreach into the Muslim community a few times so far. First in Turkey, then in Cairo, in a more political way to the Islamic Republic of Iran, so his outreach efforts definitely helps . . . Well, US foreign policy doesn't change as drastically as we would like. (Faisal, male, 20, US born, Uzbek origin, interviewed in Massachusetts, November 2009)

Faisal identified himself as American Muslim and his opinions suggest that President Obama's election in 2008 was a 'big change in the symbolic sense'. Arguably, Faisal connected with the American half of his identity when he cited Obama's success in uniting the country, and then he linked the Muslim side of his identity with Obama's efforts to reach the Muslim world. In his interview Faisal also said that he was actively involved in Obama's campaign and that he 'was a fervent supporter of Obama'. Yet, despite his optimism, Faisal was sceptical of US foreign policy when he observed that it could not be radically changed. Half the participants in this study were in the age group 15–17 and had not yet reached voting age, but for the most part they were enthusiastic about Obama. The participants' views on Obama varied from admiration, inspiration and optimism through scepticism to criticism, but overwhelmingly they felt connected to Obama, and to American politics.

In this chapter I first examine the dynamics of Muslim identity in the American political context. Secondly, I sketch the responses of the partici-pants on the topic 'Barack Hussein Obama' and summarise them in Table

5.1. Thirdly, I analyse their responses and evaluate their political awareness. Finally, I examine some participants' views on the legitimacy of the Nobel Peace Prize awarded to Obama.

Identity still matters

Some researchers, such as Janelle Wong et al., James Avery and Atiya Stokes-Brown, have observed that identity plays an important part in the political views of most Americans who take an interest in politics or are keen voters. For white and black Americans race plays an important role, while for Asians and Latinos ethnicity is crucial.[1]

Studies on political behaviour among African Americans show that they have a high rate of political participation (when controlling for socioeconomic status), which is attributable to heightened levels of group consciousness. According to Avery, this implies that African Americans are aware of their shared status as victims of 'racial inequalities and discrimination'.[2] Before elections black churches work to raise the consciousness of their members and thereby increase individual levels of civic skills, political efficiency and political knowledge. These churches attempt to galvanise group identity and group consciousness by suggesting that some political parties could contribute to the betterment of their group.[3]

In their research in 2000–1 on 1,218 Asian American adults (Chinese, Korean, Filipino and south Asian) in the Los Angeles, New York, Honolulu, San Francisco and Chicago metropolitan areas, Wong et al. found that those with a strong sense of ethnic or pan-ethnic identity did not participate in national politics at a higher rate than those with a weak sense. Yet participants with a strong ethnic or pan-ethnic identity did participate in local community-level (or state-level) politics, presumably because this level had more impact on their ethnic groups or organisations.[4] In other words, their group consciousness made them aware of their 'shared status as an unjustly deprived and oppressed group', and in consequence their voice at the local level would make a difference.[5]

In another study, it was found that those who racially identify themselves as Latino are significantly more likely to choose a Latino candidate over a non-Latino one. Latinos, when stimulated by a sense of commonality and ethnic group consciousness, are more likely to participate in a wide range of political activities, including voting.[6]

Muslims are a politically diverse group. Amaney Jamal observed that in the US, Muslim organisations, such as CAIR and the MPAC, play an active role in mobilising voters. They carry out voter registration drives, encourage mosque members to vote, and appeal to a wider constituency through mosque outreach campaigns. Arab American groups are also effective in mobilising people during election campaigns.[7] Alexander Rose commented that Muslims' political activity and mobilisation depends mostly on the foreign policies of the political parties. For example, in the November 2000 US presidential election, many Muslims supported the Republican presidential candidate, George W. Bush. Traditionally, American Muslims have supported the Democrats, but on this occasion some analysts suggested an affinity with Bush because he was conservative on social issues such as abortion, women's rights and gay rights.[8] But others say the main reason why Muslim voters turned against the Democrats was that before the election, during the Al-Aqsa intifada in September 2000, the Clinton administration supported Israel against the Palestinians. Muslim (and Arab) voters were also disappointed at Al Gore's decision to appoint the Jewish Democrat Joe Lieberman as his vice-presidential running partner.[9]

Nevertheless, during the 2004 presidential election, when President Bush stood for his second term, he was generally unpopular among Muslims. In particular, MAPS data showed that many Muslims were displeased with the Bush administration's foreign policy. About 87 per cent of Muslims were against the Iraq war, 90 per cent said the US should reduce financial support for Israel, and 94 per cent believed that the US should support a Palestinian state. According to MAPS data in 2004, 7 per cent of Muslims voted for President Bush, 82 per cent voted for Democrat candidate John Kerry, and 10 per cent voted for the independent candidate Ralph Nader, who is a Lebanese American Christian.[10]

In 2011, a Pew Research Center survey found that Muslims strongly aligned with the Democratic Party and voted overwhelmingly for Barack Obama in the 2008 election.[11] The poll results indicate that the voters' collective identity or group consciousness is often reflected in their voting behaviour. Muslim leaders in this study, however, thought that the time when many Muslims are truly involved in the political process was still a long way off. For example, Yusef Ahmed (male, over 30, overseas born, national identity: Asian American) stated:

> What I'm concerned about is that the Muslim vote per se would become something that would be taken for granted just like the way the African American vote is taken for granted in this country, that they are just going to be Democrats. I think it was about 90 per cent Muslims voted for Obama. My issue is: how critically engaged are we? Are we going to vote for Obama or Democrats the next time? If so, we should look and see if it's in our interests. (Interview, Florida, March 2010)

Another leader, Zahed Omar (male, over 30, US born, national identity: African American, interviewed in Michigan, May 2010), pointed out that Muslims should learn to empower themselves so that they can address the issues impacting on them, such as deportation and racial profiling (discussed in previous chapters).

The Pew Research Center's 2011 report, however, found that Muslims overall are taking an interest in the Obama administration. Out of 1,033

American Muslims surveyed, three-quarters (76 per cent) approved of President Obama's job performance, while 14 per cent disapproved. The American public as a whole was divided: 46 per cent approved and 45 per cent disapproved of President Obama's performance.[12]

In the next section, I examine the participants' interest in American politics. I asked them, 'How do you view the change in American politics? Does the rise of the first black American president inspire you?' It generated several responses, as shown in Table 5.1.

In the first six rows (admiration, inspiration, personal connection, historical and global change, and optimism) of Table 5.1, a total of 208 participants (55 per cent) spoke highly of President Obama. For example, nineteen participants expressed their admiration for him, and sixty-six participants were inspired by his achievements. Nine participants explicitly spoke about the historical changes that came about with Obama's election. Thirteen participants spoke of a personal connection with Obama's African and Muslim background. Thirty-four participants observed the changes Obama had brought about nationally and internationally. And sixty-seven participants said that they were optimistic about Obama's performance. In rows 7 to 9, twenty-six (7 per cent) of participants were sceptical of Obama's performance, thirty-one participants (8 per cent) were thoroughly critical of him, and fourteen (4 per cent) gave a mixed appraisal (multiple views). In rows 10 to 13, the views of seventy-seven participants (20 per cent) varied from somewhat sceptical to sympathetic. And the remaining twenty-three participants(6 per cent) said that they did not have any interest in politics or were disappointed with politics. It should be noted that among the 379 participants, about fifty commented on the legitimacy of the Nobel Peace Prize awarded to President Obama. I did not engage all participants in this topic, partly because I had already conducted some interviews prior to the Nobel Peace Prize ceremony in December 2009, and partly because for one reason or another I did not raise the question, for example, I was distracted by other discussions. In the next section, I examine the views of the participants (as shown in Table 5.1). The subsequent discussion is on Obama's Nobel Peace Prize.

High opinion of Obama: admiration, inspiration, personal connection, and optimism

As I indicated in Table 5.1, about 55 per cent of the participants of this study held high opinions of President Obama. Their opinions ranged from 'I love him' and 'He is my hero', through 'He is a voice of reason' to 'He has Muslim connections' and 'He brought a change in history'. Nadira, of Bangladeshi background (female, 17, overseas born, national identity: Bangladeshi American), appreciated Obama's speaking skills: 'He's very charming and if you compare him to the other presidents he feels friendlier. Like Bush, you know, he was

Table 5.1 Responses on the topic of President Barack Hussein Obama

	Number of participants	Responses	Key points
1	5 m, 14 f	Admiration	I love him. He is my hero. He is charismatic. He is honest, a great speaker, a voice of reason.
2	24 m, 42 f	Inspiration	Muslim, American dream, good role model in the world, connects the youth.
3	1 m, 12 f	Personal connection	African; Muslim.
4	9 m, 0 f	Change, historical	It is a step forward. Forty years ago, a black American president was unthinkable.
.5	18 m, 16 f	Change, global	Political awareness, young voters, Cairo speech.
6	26 m, 41 f	Optimism	Foreign policy, health, youth, family support.
7	16 m, 10 f	Sceptical	*La politique c'est l'art du mensonge*: politics is the art of lying.
8	15 m, 16 f	Critical	Domestic and foreign polices.
9	5 m, 9 f	Multiple views	Expressed bits of all views: change, scepticism and optimism.
10	10 m, 7 f	Change but somewhat sceptical	Obama's rise is itself a change but can he deliver?
11	13 m, 24 f	Change but too early to judge	Change is a long process. It is too early to evaluate his presidency.
12	2 m, 6 f	Obama should be more aggressive	We need more change, e.g. education and economy.
13	9 m, 6 f	Sympathetic	Obama inherited most of President Bush's wrongdoings, and he has to change a bunch of them. He is trying, and he is doing well.
14	2 m, 0 f	No difference	Obama is like any other president.
15	1 m, 0 f	Not in my religion	Voting is against my religion (discussed in the national identity chapter).
16	3 m, 2 f	Did not vote	Not Obama's fan.
17	2 m, 1 f	Disappointed	President Obama is too shy to reveal his Muslim connection.
18	3 m, 4 f	Not interested in politics	War is disturbing.
19	3 m, 2 f	No comment, not sure	I don't watch the media, so I don't keep up with politics.

different, but Obama seems nice; he seems like he speaks to the people' (interview, New York, January 2010).

Fahad, of Egyptian origin (male, 16, US born, national identity: Egyptian American), thought that Obama was better than the former president, George

W. Bush: 'I think he's very inspirational; I think he's a better leader than Bush. I reckon Bush messed up everything and just walked away; I think Obama's going to do a lot of good stuff' (interview, New York, January 2010). Sumaiya, of Algerian background (female, 16, US born, national identity: Algerian American), also spoke enthusiastically about Obama:

> During his campaign, I watched every single election night, every single thing that had primaries, I'd be watching. I didn't agree with some of his ideas, but in comparison to any other politician, he's really, really good. And the way he connects the youth, I think it's a great key that McCain didn't have. I went to the inauguration, and I was so impressed. (Interview, Michigan, April 2010)

Seerat, of Palestinian background (female, 17, US born, national identity: 'an Arab for Palestine'), said that Obama proved that one can achieve success even if one is a non-white person:

> Yes, I admire him a lot. Not only because he is the first black president, but because he proved so many people wrong. It doesn't matter who you are, you can become president. If you strive to do what you want, you will become it. If there's a will, there's a way. If you want something, go after it and get it. (Interview, Florida, March 2010)

Similarly, Habib, of Libyan background (male, 16, overseas born, national identity: Arab American) thought that race was no longer an issue: 'Yeah, I mean he's the first black president, he's done something really different than anyone else could do. It just shows that our country's changing and people are more accepted everywhere' (interview, Florida, April 2010). Rabab, of west African background (female, 15, US born, national identity: 'Muslim first, then African American'), connected her African American identity with Obama:

> My dad, he loves Barack Obama. Me, too. Oh, my God, because Barack Obama, his father's from Kenya, it makes me happy because he's [an] awesome African American to me. The world is seeing change. I honestly thought like, 'Okay, he's going to win. No, he's going to lose. He's going to win. He's going to lose.' And when he won, it made me confident like the world can have change. The world is ready for change. We don't have a different coloured man in the house, or whatever. That makes me hold me up, me a Muslim, to think I can be anything. (Interview, Michigan, May 2010)

Some interviewees believed Obama's Muslim connection would be helpful, as Faeezah, of Palestinian origin (female, 15, US born, national identity: Palestinian Muslim), commented: 'Because his father was a Muslim so he's part Muslim so we feel he could help us, help the Muslims and Muslim countries; he can make a change' (interview, New York, January 2010). Samer, of Pakistani background (male, 17, overseas born, national identity: 'I'm more Pakistani'), was optimistic that since Obama as a 'black' person had succeeded, Samer could now succeed despite his Islamic visibility:

> Yeah, he is an inspiration to young people, because he showed that times have changed and that people of colour can do great things. Say, when I was little, I used to want to get [work] in government . . . everybody used to tell me, 'No, you can't do it, because you're Pakistani.' Then I started to grow a beard and people said, 'Oh, you can't do it, you have a beard. You're going to have to cut that off if you become president.' But I was like, 'Barack Obama made it, so why can't I?' (Interview, Florida, May 2010)

It is interesting to note that the above participants, aged fifteen to seventeen, belonged to diverse backgrounds: Algerian, Bangladeshi, Egyptian, Indian, Libyan, Pakistani, Palestinian and west African, and also lived in different states, but they found a connecting factor in Obama. They appeared to be taking an interest in American politics even though they had not yet reached voting age. And most of them thought Obama was a better president than George W. Bush.

Historical change

Abdallah, of Palestinian origin (male, 17, US born, national identity: Arab American), spoke of the historical change symbolised by Obama's election as president:

> Twenty years ago, if you told someone 'Oh, there'll be a black president', he'd start laughing at you. They'd say 'No, that's impossible'. You look at our presidents so far, white, white, white, white, and then you have Barack Obama, the president of 2008, right, Barack Obama, African American president. That's a huge inspiration. That just proves that you can do anything, history can be changed, it's not repetitive like everyone says. You can alter history, it could be changed. So I mean that just, yeah, it does inspire you. It gives you hope; like you know what, I could do whatever I want. (Interview, New York, January 2010)

Ali, of Egyptian background (male, 17, US born, national identity: 'an Arab American but sort of Egyptian'), concurred with Abdallah's viewpoint:

> Obama became the first African American president, and in the past 200–300 years they've been persecuted and segregated, but now he's a president. He is trying to bring a change and I think he's doing a pretty good job at it. (Interview, New York, January 2010)

Qamar, of Indian background (female, 21, US born, national identity: American Muslim), commented:

> I know a lot of older people thought they would die before they would ever see an African American president, like that song by Tupac Shakur, 'We ain't ready to see a black president.' No one thought it would happen, so it's pretty cool . . . that gave us hope that maybe one day we could see a Muslim as president, *insh'Allah*. (Interview, Florida, May 2010)

The interviewees noted the remarkable change in American race relations. Qamar recalled the lyrics of Tupac Shakur's song 'Changes'.[13] Tupac Amaru Shakur was an American hip-hop singer who died in 1996 but who remains popular among young people. Most of Shakur's songs are about the hardships of growing up around violence in United States ghettos, poverty and racism, and sometimes his feuds with fellow rappers. Messages of political, economic and racial equality pervade his work.

Of course, Obama's election in November 2008 was seen as a historic cultural shift in American politics, and the culmination of the changes that began with the Civil Rights struggle in 1964. His remarkable rise touched not only black voters but also white voters and other non-white voters (including Muslims of diverse racial backgrounds). Jerry Harris and Carl Davidson proposed that perhaps Obama can connect with young Americans because of his mixed racial background. Obama's personal history is 'grounded in the multi-cultural and global reality of today's world'. He was born in Hawaii, which is often considered 'as the most Third World of all US states', and spent his early years in Indonesia. This added to 'Obama's universal appeal as an important symbol of multicultural globalization'. Through his exposure to a wide range of cultural influences, President Obama reflects 'the sensibilities of today's youth and the first glimpse of US society in a new century'.[14]

Enhancing the US's global image

President Obama took a new approach to international diplomacy to connect with the Muslim world. In his first year in office, he gave his first interview on the Arab satellite channel Al Arabiya on 27 January 2009. In a reconciliatory gesture in his interview, President Obama offered the Arab and the Muslim worlds 'a new partnership based on mutual respect and mutual interest'.[15] Later, on relevant occasions, Obama sent greetings to the Muslim world. His effort to reach the Muslim world was praised by thirty-four participants in this study (see Table 5.1). On 21 March 2009, on the occasion of the Persian New Year, *Nowruz*, Obama delivered a special holiday message to the Iranian people and the leaders of Iran through Voice of America. In his speech at *Nowruz* he told Iran that the United States was committed to diplomacy and 'this process will not be advanced by threats. We seek instead engagement that is honest and grounded in mutual respect.' President Mahmoud Ahmadinejad's media advisor, Ali Akbar Javanfekr, appreciated the US government's friendly gesture and said, 'We welcome the interest of the American government to settle differences.'[16] Obama's *Nowruz* greetings were also appreciated by some participants in this study. An overseas-born woman of Afghan origin, Rehana, aged twenty-five (national identity: Afghan), commented:

> I think it's not only me, I think the whole world believes that it was a great change for the US, and I do admire him for his being very respectful to all religion, not only Islam. I loved his speech for *Nowruz*. (Interview, Massachusetts, October 2009)

Though *Nowruz* is widely referred to as the Persian New Year, it is also celebrated in Iran's neighbouring countries, such as Afghanistan, Azerbaijan, India, Kyrgyzstan, Pakistan, Turkey and Uzbekistan. *Nowruz* promotes the values of peace and solidarity between generations and within families, as well as reconciliation and neighbourliness, thus contributing to cultural diversity and friendship among peoples and various communities. In 2009, UNESCO recognised the international day of *Nowruz* as a spring festival of Persian origin and inscribed it on the Representative List of the Intangible Cultural Heritage of Humanity.

In April 2009, Obama visited Turkey and said the United States and the Islamic world were not at war. In June 2009, he delivered a major speech in Cairo to call for reconciliation with Muslims. It is generally accepted that relations between the United States and the world's Muslims had been damaged during the term of the previous president, George W. Bush, mostly because of the invasion of Iraq. So Obama's outreach effort was appreciated by many people, including most of the participants in this study. For example, Hameed, of Egyptian origin (male, 15, US born, national identity: Arab), said, 'His Cairo speech was very inspiring . . . the first thing he said [was] *Assalamu alaikum* [peace be upon you]' (interview, New York, January 2010). Illyas, of Pakistani origin (male, 15, US born, national identity: Pakistani-German and American), was also impressed: 'Yeah, the Cairo speech was really good and when he gave the *salaam*, it really touched my heart' (interview, Maryland, February 2010). In Florida, Haneef, of Egyptian background (male, 17, US born, national identity: Arab American), commented: 'His Cairo speech was praised because you haven't found in history a lot of presidents who talk about Islam openly or at least in a non-violent way' (interview, Florida, March 2010).

In his book *The Promise: President Obama, Year One*, Jonathan Alter observed that Obama's Cairo speech was intended to win the 'hearts and minds' of average Muslims. It was significant that in this speech Obama never mentioned the words 'terrorism, terrorist, or war on terror'.[17] Alter gave a historian's summing up of Obama's Cairo speech, claiming it aimed at confronting violent extremists, devising a two-nation state solution for Israelis and Palestinians, preventing a nuclear arms race in the Middle East, promoting democracy, respecting religious freedom, securing women's rights, and promoting economic development.[18]

Obama's Cairo speech was hailed both nationally and internationally. In Europe, polls showed Obama to be more popular than the German Chancellor, Angela Merkel, and the French president, Nicolas Sarkozy. In the outskirts of Paris, young Muslims from the marginalised suburbs wore T-shirts emblazoned with Obama's image. His approval rating in Britain surged to 86 per cent, compared to 16 per cent in 2008 for President Bush. Alter notes that the approval rate was over 60 per cent in most countries – except in Israel, where his approval rate dropped after the Cairo speech.[19]

In this study, four participants referred to Obama's international profile. Ameena, of Egyptian background (female, 20, US born, national identity: Arab American), said:

> My aunt called me [from Cairo] and my uncle was there in the first row; he's a journalist in Cairo. Yeah, so he really commended Obama for really taking that time to go and speak to the Arabs and show his support for them, and so I think that was a good gesture foreign policy-wise. (Interview, Florida, March 2010)

Parvez, of Pakistani American background (male, 22, US born, national identity: 'human'), said:

> When Bush was president, and people associated America with the Iraq war, I did not feel proud to represent the American government. But now, you know, in Honduras people talk about Obama and I feel happy to represent this guy. (Interview, Massachusetts, November 2009)

Cynthia, a white American Muslim convert (female, 28, US born, national identity: American), commented, 'I see the president as the face of America. I think anything would have been better than George Bush. For instance, you can go anywhere in Africa and say Barack Obama and everyone's like, "Oh, Barack Obama!"' (interview, Florida, March 2010). Najeeb, an Egyptian studying in the US (male, 25, overseas born, national identity: Egyptian), said:

> Actually, we were very optimistic when we saw his [Cairo] speech. And everyone in Egypt was saying 'This is the chance of a lifetime to communicate with the Obama administration'. So we [the Egyptians] have to communicate with him, and we have to cooperate. We see [Israeli] settlements every day in Palestine. (Interview, Florida, March 2010)

I discuss the Palestinian issue in the next chapter. However, people in the Muslim world recognised the merits of Obama's reconciliatory gesture. As mentioned above, Parvez and Cynthia, when they visited Honduras and Africa respectively, saw the difference in people's attitude towards the USA after Obama became president. Analysts say that, even before the election, images of Barack Obama were circulated around the world. For example, in Tanzania, hawkers had images of Obama and his family in their carts (in an advertisement) as they sold items to tourists. Similarly, some business corporations in the USA endorsed the 'Obama logo' in their items for transnational circulation, thereby aiming to restore the US's waning reputation around the world. Even controversial images, such as the photograph of Obama in Kenya wearing a traditional African headdress, incorrectly dubbed a 'turban' by Republicans, have contributed to the globalisation of the Obama logo.[20]

The next step towards reconciliation was Obama's *Ramadan* greeting to the Muslim world. In August 2009, Obama said, 'On behalf of the American people – including Muslim communities in all fifty states – I want to extend best wishes to Muslims in America and around the world. *Ramadan kareem.*'[21]

Obama's subsequent efforts to engage in dialogue with the Muslim world were appreciated by the participants in this study. Some were initially sceptical of Obama's motives before the election, as Sohaib, of Pakistani origin (male, 26, national identity: multiple identities), remarked:

> I was a bit upset in the beginning because before his election he really just did not talk about the Muslim issue much and I think it was because of politics. He definitely wanted the votes and he felt if he would talk about the issue then he wouldn't be able to get the votes. But it was a good sign, I think it was in June [2009], when he came out with the Cairo speech, and even recently during *Ramadan* he had an address to Muslims and it shows that he's taking more of this diplomatic approach, which America should be doing. (Interview, Massachusetts, November 2009)

As Sohaib noted, in his pre-election campaign Obama was not explicit about the 'Muslim issue'. This may have been because the media and other politicians aimed to undermine Obama through his Muslim connection (his father was a Muslim). For example, on 24 February 2008, the leader of the Nation of Islam, Louis Farrakhan, is said to have endorsed Obama's nomination.[22] At the same time, a photo of Obama dressed in traditional Somali robes was circulated on the internet along with rumours that he was a Muslim. Conservative talk show hosts and some Republican officials used Obama's middle name (Hussein) when referring to the candidate, and some referred (incorrectly) to the Somali robes as 'Muslim' dress.[23]

On the cover of the *New Yorker* magazine on 21 July 2008 was a cartoon that depicted Obama fist-bumping his wife Michelle. He is shown in a one-piece Muslim garment and *topi*, while she, Afro-haired, is wearing boots and camouflage clothes with an AK-47 and ammunition belt slung over her shoulder. Also in the cartoon, beneath a portrait of Osama bin Laden, the American flag burns in the fireplace in the presidential Oval Office.[24] Of course, cartoons are typically designed to be humorous but at the time of the presidential campaign, when race and religion were sensitive issues, this image was offensive, and it certainly showed the *New Yorker*'s political leaning.

Scepticism: *'la politique, c'est l'art du mensonge'*

Voices of scepticism from the participants in this study varied from doubts about whether Obama represents African American people to the suggestion that he is a politician like any other and therefore we cannot trust him. For example, Haider, of Lebanese origin (male, 16, US born, national identity: American Lebanese Muslim), felt that Obama would be a more likely person to inspire African Americans: 'Not really to young people, but I guess mostly to African Americans, because what most Americans would consider a minority has become president, the highest job you can ever get in America' (interview, Florida, May 2010). On the other hand, Manzur, of Moroccan origin (male, 20, overseas born, national identity: Moroccan), felt offended during his visit to Belgium in 2008 when he found some Belgian-Moroccan people 'insulting America'. Yet he was sceptical about politics:

> It's like blaming the whole country 'bad' for a president [Bush]. They had the idea that 'Well then, this is an African American with a Muslim background so when he's elected overnight it's going to get better', but it doesn't work that way. By nature I don't believe in politics. In French we say *'La politique, c'est l'art du mensonge'* [politics is the art of lying]. (Interview, Massachusetts, November 2009)

While Manzur believed politics is the art of lying, Saiful, of Pakistani background (male, 30, overseas born, national identity: 'more American') noted that politicians are 'mere puppets':

> But again I honestly think that presidents are puppets. You know there's a driving force behind them that tells them what to do, what to say, what speeches to make. I used to work with the county government and dealing with a lot of the commissioners of the city and state and the country, I know that they do things for certain reasons only to be favoured by their constituents so they can get re-elected. So with that in my mind, when I look at the president I just think of him as someone that's a puppet. That's what the bottom line is for me at least. (Interview, Florida, March 2010)

The view that politicians are 'mere puppets' was shared by fifteen more participants in this study. Bakr, of Syrian origin (male, 18, US born, national identity:

Arab American), said: 'Other than the fact that he's the first black president, I hear my dad talk about politics and I think I heard my dad say that he is like any other president' (interview, Michigan, April 2010). Daniel, of Palestinian origin (male, 19, US born, national identity: American), decided to vote for everything else but not for the presidency:

> I voted last year. I didn't register a vote for the president. I voted for everything else, all congressional and local laws, and left the president section blank. I didn't vote for a president because I felt that both candidates were disingenuous.
>
> So this is my first election, I took it as a learning experience. I didn't want to be rash and I know a lot of people who just say 'It's one vote', but at the same time I would be culpable in the case of, on my part I didn't feel that I was well read or well researched enough to actually give my full trust in that candidate, so . . . (Interview, Florida, May 2010)

Of course, the issue of political mistrust is not confined to Muslims. In the context of Latino Americans, some scholars such as Marisa Abrajano and Michael Alvarez have observed that trust in a government may suggest a belief that the government or an elected official possesses the ability to perform well.[25] But there have been occasions in US history when American voters have lost trust in politicians, such as during the Vietnam War and the Watergate scandal. The distrust remained even when the administrations responsible for these events changed.[26]

Obama's Cairo speech

Hameed, of Egyptian background (male, 15, US born, national identity: Arab), commented:

> President Obama's Cairo speech was very inspiring . . . The first thing he said, '*Assalamu alaikum*'. But I think the only change he brought was that he is the first African American president . . . He also has to learn how to say *hijab* instead of *hajib* . . . Oh! at least he had the guts to say it. (Interview, New York, January 2010)

Hameed appreciated President's Obama's respect for Muslim woman though he could not pronounce the word *hijab*. Yet Rasheed, of Pakistani background (male, 19, US born, national identity: Muslim American) thought that Obama's Cairo speech was nothing new, and that he was simply carrying on the Bush legacy:

> One of my graduate student friends from Pakistan posted a link on his Facebook wall about the speech and, at the very end of the speech that he had posted, it said 'These were the words delivered by President George W. Bush after 9/11'.

So he was pointing out that, although things have changed, all the people have changed, the speeches haven't. But people are just seeing it differently because they want to see it differently. (Interview, Massachusetts, October 2009)

Of course, there were similarities between President Obama's speeches and those of George W. Bush but there were differences as well. President Bush delivered his speech on 24 June 2002 from the White House but in June 2009 President Obama went to Cairo to deliver his speech. The Bush speech was a reconciliatory offer to the Muslim world, particularly to the Middle East, and the main focus of his speech was advocating a reformed Palestinian state. Though Bush appeared sympathetic to the Palestinian cause, he uttered the words 'terror', 'terrorist' and 'terrorism' several times. For example, he said, 'If Palestinians embrace democracy, confront corruption and firmly reject terror, they can count on American support for the creation of a provisional state of Palestine.'[27] On the other hand, Obama refrained from using those words and focused on other issues, such as women's rights, education, US trade with Muslim countries and so on.[28] But the most appealing part of Obama's speech was his respect for Islamic heritage; he referred to the Quran four times, whereas Bush never mentioned the Quran, but quoted from the Bible instead. So most Muslims saw the difference in attitude of the two US presidents, and were more impressed with Obama's approach.

Critical views: domestic and foreign policies

Thirty-one participants in this study made critical remarks about the Obama administration. A few spoke about domestic issues, but the majority concentrated on US foreign policy. The comments about domestic issues mainly concerned health care reform, education, unemployment and small businesses.

Domestic policy: Health reform

When I started my survey in October 2009, the Obama health care debate was in full swing in the US media. Ifrah, of Somali background (female, 22, overseas born, national identity: Somali), commented: 'Health care in the US is not good. People are trying to move to different countries, like the UK, for free health care' (interview, Massachusetts, October 2009). Kishwar, of Pakistani-Indian background (female, 15, US born, national identity: 'one-third American, one-third Pakistani, one-third Indian'), said:

Obama said that he was going to do universal health care, but then universal health care has its pros and cons. People can't get health care right away, they have got to wait three months, but within the three months someone can have serious illness, and they can be dead. (Interview, Florida, March 2010)

Bushra, of Bangladeshi background (female, 20, US born, national identity: Muslim), offered her perspective:

> Growing up, most of our life, we did not have health insurance. And my parents struggled extremely to provide medical care. When we go to the hospital, we have to be concerned about the bill and not our health ... Now that it has passed, a lot of people are going to get free health care. But the problem is, the system is going to be backed up, because for people that have already had health care, they're probably going to have a longer wait list now that everyone has health care. So everyone has the same opportunity. So when they make a doctor's appointment, they may have to wait longer. (Interview, Michigan, April 2010)

On 21 March 2010, Obama's health care bill was passed by the Congress by 219 votes to 212. *The Guardian* reported that the new US health care provisions will cost an estimated $940 billion (£627 billion) over ten years, expanding care to thirty-two million more people, predominantly the poorest, and giving the country 95 per cent coverage.[29]

Education

On the subject of employment and education, in Florida a self-employed participant of Pakistani background, Saeed (male, 26, overseas born, national identity: 'just Muslim'), was concerned about the student debt he still carried:

> You go to school and you're working to pay off school. And I believe I read somewhere in an article that the American system is designed to put everybody in debt by the age of twenty-five.
> Yeah. So that's the American system. So if you're in America, you're living off of credit cards or other loans you've taken, and you're in debt ... So, I worked and I did take a loan. [Now I'm] paying it off. It takes a long time to pay those off. (Interview, Florida, March 2010)

Mariyam, an African American Muslim woman (female, 22, US born, national identity: African Muslim American), spoke of the financial constraints on her education:

> Yes, I went to XXX Tech Institute. No, I didn't finish. I have to start back next year to renew my financial aid. Oh, it's too much money. Oh my goodness, for financial aid it's maybe like ... I have to tell you the truth, maybe over $27,000 a year. But if I went to a community college it would have been cheaper, only $4,000. But ... you gotta pay! Yeah, so you took a loan and then you will repay later on? But even though they say, like I have to be careful of some things *harram*, like interest and stuff. (Interview, Massachusetts, December 2009)

Salman, of Moroccan background, employed in an Islamic institution (male, 26, overseas born, national identity: French, American, Arab and Muslim), also spoke of the financial burden one faces at the college/university level. He did not get admission to a university, the cost of which would have been about $40,000 per year. He said, 'The other option, if you are lacking funds, is to start with the community college and take courses as you go – courses that you may transfer later.' Salman received his degree from a community college. He worked part time and managed to pay his fees. He said, 'I was just against getting a loan so I was mostly working' (interview, Massachusetts, December 2009). Another interviewee, an engineering student of Guyanese background, Saif (male, 20, US born, national identity: 'Muslim only'), was frustrated with the current US economy when he said, 'Heaps of students are graduating but there are no jobs' (interview, Florida, March 2010).

The Obama administration did not create the American education system. But the point is that because of the debt they would carry after their graduation such a system restricts students' choices to go to a renowned university. Also, due to the economic downturn, new college/university graduates may remain unemployed.

Unemployment

It is generally believed that before the election Obama gave the impression that he would 'transform the nation'. So Americans expected change in every field. But in the economic sector, things did not move as expected. In 2001 Bill Clinton left office with a $236 billion budget surplus, whereas eight years later George W. Bush left a $1.3 trillion deficit. Moreover, the economy has not improved much during the Obama administration. In 2009, about 700,000 Americans were losing jobs every month. Some economists speculated that if job losses continued at this rate, then about 8.5 million more Americans would lose their jobs in 2009, and this might lead to a depression.[30] Many institutions such as banks, manufacturing and automobile companies have gone bankrupt. So in 2009, the Democrats passed a stimulus package of $787 billion to promote a speedy economic recovery;[31] yet by the mid-term congressional election in November 2010 the unemployment rate was still high at 9.6 per cent.[32] As a consequence, Obama's Democratic Party lost more than sixty seats in the 435-member House of Representatives. Obama believed that the economy was the main concern of voters, and said, 'What they were expressing great frustration about is the fact that we haven't made enough progress on the economy.' Obama admitted, 'I've got to take direct responsibility for the fact that we have not made as much progress as we need to make.'[33]

In my survey, which was conducted before the mid-term elections, some young Muslims registered a concern about the president. For example, Arpeeta, of Bangladeshi origin, father unemployed (female, 15, overseas born, national identity: 'mostly Bangladeshi'), said, 'Yeah, as a black person he's great and I kind of like him . . . I expected the economy would be better but it's still the same; people don't have jobs, they don't have health care' (interview, New York, January 2010). Saif, of Guyanese background (male, 20, US born, national identity, 'Muslim only'), commented:

> I think it all started with Bush: the economy went bad when he was in office, so it's getting better, like, Barack Obama's taking steps towards making the economy better and that's good, but it's still on the down trend, it's still pretty bad out there. Because a lot of educated people coming out of university can't find jobs and that's ridiculous. (Interview, Florida, May 2010)

Rafiq, of Palestinian origin (male, 17, US born, national identity: Palestinian American), remarked:

> It's too early to evaluate his presidency. We have to see how all his stimulus packages and everything he's been doing plays out in the next ten – it might not even be in his term – ten to fifteen years. Then we can evaluate him as a president, but I believe his path from where he was to where he is is very inspirational. (Interview, Michigan, April 2010)

Small businesses

Kabeer, of Palestinian background (male, 16, US born, national identity: Arab American), said that his family's restaurants were affected by some of the Obama administration's laws:

> He is an inspiration to young people and he's showing change and that anything's possible but I don't agree with some of his policies. Because you're not allowed to smoke in public places no more, like in restaurants and at the bar, you're not allowed to smoke there any more. This was about a month ago that he started saying that and the law is going to apply May 1st. There's a smoking section in restaurants. So this will be banned. So I mean this can also hurt their economy too because people go to these places to smoke and relax . . . I don't smoke so I don't care – but that's taking away someone's freedom. (Interview, Michigan, April 2010)

From 1 May 2010, a new anti-smoking law came into effect in Michigan. In this context, Kabeer (being a minor) could not comprehend that the anti-smoking law was a state law, and that President Obama should not take responsibility for it. The law is designed to protect people from the harmful effects of secondhand smoke. It does not apply in private homes or home offices, and for the most part it does not apply outdoors. The only other exceptions are in cigar bars, speciality tobacco shops and some areas of casinos. Some *hookah* café and lounge owners in Michigan said that they have been unfairly targeted by the new anti-smoking law; it was pushing them to the brink of closure, and they were looking at ways to change the law.[34]

In 2010, Michigan had the country's highest unemployment rate at 14.1 per cent. Fay Beydoun, executive director of the Michigan-based American Arab Chamber of Commerce, said that, although her organisation had no official position on the smoking ban, it advocated support of small businesses. Beydoun said: 'The economy being so bad the way that it is in Michigan, you are putting a lot of these small businesses out of business. In return, it is a loss of jobs for the state of Michigan.' Mike Berry, a spokesman for the *hookah* café owners, argued that the government was saying that if you smoke 'a Cohiba [cigar] and drink Grey Goose [vodka], then that is healthier than if you are smoking a strawberry *hookah* and drinking a mango smoothie'.[35] Regarding the high unemployment rate in Michigan, in my survey of 379 participants from six states, I found that out of seventeen unemployed fathers, eleven were from Michigan. Michigan has also the highest concentration of Arabs, and *hookah* smoking in gatherings is their cultural practice, so the ban would obviously affect small businesses such as Arab cafés.

Foreign policy: Involvement in war

It appears that on foreign policy issues President Obama faces a complex situation. George W. Bush started the war on Afghanistan, then diverted his attention to Iraq. In his Cairo speech, Obama pledged to pull out troops first from Iraq and later from Afghanistan, and to deal with the Israeli–Palestinian issue.

Some participants in this study were critical of US involvement in the wars in Iraq and Afghanistan. For example, Irfan, of Pakistani origin (male, 26, overseas born, national identity: Pakistani American), commented:

> If you ask me 'Are you satisfied?', I think that I will be satisfied when I see the results. When I can see the American troops coming back home, and I can see the Iraqi people having their own government, and I can see the Palestine people having their own government, that's when you can say that Obama did a good job. I think his strategies are fine. But I'm afraid his people who are advising him, I feel that they're being disconnected. You know they, he should be going to a local guy in Pakistan and saying 'What do you want?'
>
> I think the point that I'm trying to bring up is that we're ... we're fighting a war that I'm afraid will never have an end. (Interview, Massachusetts, January 2010)

Azeez, of Pakistani background (male, 24, US born, national identity: Muslim Pakistani American), was critical of the presence of American troops in Iraq and Afghanistan. He said, 'Even if you think that many Muslims are happy because Obama's [middle] name is Hussein, big deal, his name is Hussein.

There's still Muslims dying every single day, you know' (interview, Florida, March 2010). Sonia, of Indian background (female, 47, overseas born, national identity: Indian Muslim), commented, 'I'm just hoping the war ends ... Iraq, Afghanistan ... Yeah, it's Iran, now ... Pakistan, it's together all' (interview, New York, January 2010). And Fatima, a mainstream American (female, 50, US born, national identity: American), expressed her frustrations:

> Iraq. The one that's costing us $700 billion a year, some outrageous amount of money, which is why the country's in the financial state it's in. You can't sustain an unwinnable war ... pointless war in Afghanistan. They [the Afghans] don't even have a speck of oil. What is the point? No one talks about the anti-war movement any more, have you noticed? No one talks about stopping the war even at all ... Yes, another very important issue, the Israel–Palestine issue. (Interview, Massachusetts, October 2010)

Aasia, of Indian-Kashmiri origin (female, 18, US born, national identity: south Asian Kashmiri), has similar views:

> And Obama has not accomplished anything. The global economy and the wars and everything, but still people are putting him on this high place and he's not that high. He's just a regular person trying to cope with stuff. He's not our saviour. (Interview, Maryland, February 2010)

There were also those who regretted voting for Obama. For example, Nargis, of Pakistani origin (female, 15, US born, national identity: Pakistani American) said, 'My older brother who voted for Obama is now frustrated and said that he has wasted his vote' (interview, Michigan, April 2010). These interviews were conducted before the Obama administration reduced the number of US troops in Iraq in 2010. It is reported that from a peak of 170,000 troops in Iraq in 2007, US troops in Iraq were reduced to 50,000 in 2010. The last US soldier exited Iraq in December 2011.[36]

In 2004 the Iraq war was declared by the then UN secretary general, Kofi Annan, to be 'illegal'. It has resulted in many civilian casualties. It is said that the number of civilian casualties in Iraq runs into hundreds of thousands, and far exceeds the number allegedly killed by the ousted and executed President Saddam Hussein during his presidency.[37] Britain and the US have always claimed that they kept no record of civilian casualties in Iraq but, according to US statistics, of the 109,032 violent deaths between 2004 and the end of 2009, 66,081 were civilians, 23,984 were classed as 'enemy' (insurgents etc.) and 15,196 were members of the Iraqi security forces. The remaining 3,771 were coalition military.[38] There were also concerns raised by some participants about the unresolved Palestinian issue, which is discussed in the next chapter.

Drone attacks

Aalia (female, 18, US born, national identity: Muslim Egyptian) was critical of US drone attacks in Pakistan and the Obama administration's handling of the Israeli–Palestinian issue:

> The fact that Obama is a young president and not a white president doesn't mean anything. People say that, oh, just the fact that he's in office means something. I mean that's not good enough, to come into office and be like, 'Look, you guys, I'm black' or 'Look, you guys, I'm not white, I'm going to bring hope'. I don't think that's good enough. You actually have to do something and the fact [is] that he's escalated the war, he's sent those drones into Pakistan and he's shown his support for Israel. (Interview, Maryland, February 2010)

Between 2004 and 2007, the US carried out nine drone strikes in border areas of Pakistan and Afghanistan. In 2008, the number rose to thirty-four, continuing to rise to fifty-three in 2009, and eighty by mid-2010.[39] SBS News (Australia) reported that by the end of 2010 there had been 110 US drone attacks on Pakistan. And night raids in some parts of Afghanistan have risen from 100 to 1,000 per month.[40] As I discussed in Chapter 1, the United States is not immune to terrorism. On 26 May 2009, through a secret presidential briefing headlined 'North American al-Qaeda trainees may influence targets and tactics in the United States and Canada', it was announced that at least twenty al-Qaeda converts with western passports were training in Pakistani safe havens in order to return to the West for high-profile action.[41] On the one hand, the US is justifying the drone attacks on the grounds of security but on the other hand, they are costing innocent lives.

Yet the other al-Qaeda operations, in Sudan, Somalia and Yemen, on the north-western frontier of Pakistan and in the Taliban-controlled areas of Afghanistan, remain a concern for the Obama administration. In the first year of his presidency, Obama focused on attacking al-Qaeda's 'high-value targets'. For example, CIA-run Predator drones attacked the Yemeni-based AQAP, which claimed responsibility for the failed ' underwear bomb' attempt on Christmas Day 2009. The would-be bomber, Umar Abdulmutallab, was trained by AQAP in Yemen.[42] In October 2010, al-Qaeda operatives in Yemen sent two packages in cargo planes addressed to synagogues in Chicago containing the hard-to-detect explosive PETN hidden in printer ink cartridges. These packages were uncovered in Dubai and at Britain's East Midlands airport. AQAP also claimed responsibility.[43]

One of the interviewees in this study was critical of the way the Obama administration dealt with the terrorist threat posed by Abdulmutallab.[44] Fariha, of Palestinian background (female, 17, US born, national identity:

'mostly American and half Arab and half Muslim'), thought that the US security services were not efficient enough to detain the alleged bomber earlier:

> I think he [Obama] was definitely inspiring when he was first elected. Now I think that some of the dazzle has worn off. I don't like the way the Christmas Day bomber was handled.
>
> Oh well, the Feds, they put twenty-five countries on their [watch] list, so they ought to go through extra security . . . First of all the guy was on the no-fly list and second of all, his dad had contacted the CIA warning them that he was about to go on board. Then all of a sudden, they had to be showing that they were proactive and doing something . . . And I was reading this piece on NPROs and one lady was really upset about it because it was the first time that anything had happened from Nigeria and then all of a sudden it felt they were being typecast. (Interview, Michigan, April 2010)

On 25 December 2009, Abdulmutallab, a 23-year-old Nigerian, who was on a terrorist watch list, managed to get on a Northwest Airlines flight headed from Amsterdam to Detroit with an explosive hidden on his body. Fellow passengers and crew members subdued him as he was trying to ignite the device. US Homeland Security Secretary Janet Napolitano initially said that the '[security] system worked'. After being heavily criticised by some mainstream Americans, Napolitano admitted that the aviation security system has failed miserably in the foiled Christmas bombing. Obama stepped in and admitted that allowing the Christmas Day terror suspect to board an airliner reflected 'systemic failure'.[45]

Guantánamo Bay detention centre

Four participants in this study emphasised the shutting down of the Guantánamo Bay prison camp. For example, Ata (male, 16, US born, national identity: African American) said, 'There are some things I expect from him [President Obama] . . . Health care, they are doing that now . . . Close up the Guantánamo Bay. And withdrawal of the troops' (interview, Michigan, April 2010). Another participant, Ameena (female, 20, US born, national identity: multiple identities) commented:

> Regarding Guantánamo Bay, President Obama said that he would close it, but even if he closes it, there are talks that they are going to open another place to transfer those people to. So I guess we will see what transpires in the next few years. (Interview, Florida, March 2010)

The Bush administration held hundreds of innocent men at the Guantánamo Bay prison camp because it was feared that releasing them would harm the push for war in Iraq, the broader war on terror and the security of the wider community. Among the detainees were children as young as twelve and men as old as ninety-three, many of whom were handed over by Afghans and

Pakistanis for payments of up to $5,000. Most of the detainees were subjected to intolerable torture (beatings, sexual assaults, waterboarding and mock executions, sleep deprivation, exposure to extreme hot and cold temperatures, being forced to stay in uncomfortable positions and strip-searches).[46] Before President Bush left office, more than 530 detainees were freed, but 180 remained in the facility.[47]

As one of his November 2008 presidential election pledges, Obama promised to shut down Guantánamo Bay, but his administration faced resistance. Many Americans were not keen to have the detainees settled in mainland America. For example, in December 2008 a federal judge found that seventeen Chinese Muslim Uighur prisoners at Guantánamo Bay detention centre did not have any links to terrorism, and ordered their release. But they did not want to be returned to China because there they were likely to be tortured or executed. The Obama administration attempted to move the Uighurs to Virginia. But this suggestion met with fierce resistance from congressional Republicans. In May 2009, the Senate voted 90:6 to prevent any foreign Guantánamo detainees from being located in the United States.[48] By April 2010 four Uighurs had been resettled in Bermuda, Albania took five, six went to the Pacific island of Palau, and Switzerland took two. At this time there still remained 183 detainees at the controversial Guantánamo prison, although President Obama had pledged to close it by January 2010.[49]

Was Obama worthy of the Nobel Peace Prize?

On 9 October 2009, it was announced that President Obama had been awarded the Nobel Peace Prize 'for his extraordinary efforts to strengthen international diplomacy and cooperation between peoples'. Two months later, on 10 December, Obama received the prize medal in Oslo. But in early December 2009, he announced that by June 2010 he would deploy 30,000 more troops in Afghanistan to target insurgencies and secure key population centres, and support a smooth upcoming election in Afghanistan.[50] At the same time Obama said that American forces would be withdrawn from Afghanistan by July 2011. The president spoke at a time when Americans' support for the war continued to weaken. A survey by the Gallup organisation showed that only 35 per cent of Americans surveyed approved of Obama's handling of the war and 55 per cent disapproved.[51] The commitment to send more troops to Afghanistan generated controversy among some Americans, who asked, 'How can a Nobel Peace Prize winner engage in a war?' At his award-giving ceremony, Obama admitted that the Nobel Peace Prize decision had generated controversy but he emphasised the need for a 'just war' and that the use of force in Afghanistan could bring a lasting peace.[52]

Just as Americans generally were divided about Obama's handling of the war in Afghanistan, the participants in this study were divided on the legitimacy of his Nobel Prize. Fifty-three participants in this study spoke on this issue. Thirty-five said that President Obama deserved the prize, but eighteen participants questioned its legitimacy. In support of Obama, Ferdousi, a sixteen-year-old girl of Bangladeshi background (US born, national identity: Bengali), commented, 'I think he worked hard, coming from where he came from, and I think he definitely got what he deserved' (interview, New York, January 2010). Ameena, of Egyptian background (female, 20, US born, national identity: Arab American Muslim), observed, 'I think it [the Nobel Peace Prize] will motivate him to do more things to hold up to that title, and I think people were too harsh on him' (interview, Florida, March 2010). But Omar, of Bangladeshi background (male, 26, overseas born, national identity: Bengali Muslim), wondered about the validity of the Nobel Peace Prize:

> I've been a physics major; you know, someone gets a Nobel Prize who studies physics and makes the highest achievement, so I was obviously disappointed when I heard of Obama's winning the Nobel Peace Prize. But I believe there is some explanation to it, though I don't know if it is accurate. It is the world rejoicing for Bush stepping down, not for Obama coming into place, I believe. (Interview, Maryland, January 2010)

Some considered it a little premature. Nargis, of Afghan origin (female, 15, US born, national identity: Afghan American) commented:

> I think that it was a little too early and I think they were giving it to him just because he changed everything, like he was the first black president, and I think that they should have waited for him to actually do something amazing. (Interview, Virginia, January 2010)

Siddique, of Pakistani origin (male, 23, overseas born, national identity: Pakistani American), noted:

> I really share President Obama's views on nuclear non-proliferation. I feel like he has very good ideas. But I do think that maybe it was a bit premature because this was his first year in office and he is sending 30 or 40,000 troops to Afghanistan while at the same time he's saying 'We're going to end the war in Iraq'. I feel his ideas may be worthy of a Nobel Peace Prize, but I feel like he has to go through with those ideas before he gets serious consideration for that. (Interview, Virginia, January 2010)

To sum up, of the thirty-five participants who thought President Obama deserved the prize, twenty-three said it would motivate him to do good work (and the world was rejoicing at the departure of Bush), and twelve associated the prize with Obama's 'blackness' and his 'minority status'. Of the eighteen participants who questioned President Obama's peace prize, five thought that it was a hasty decision. However, the remaining thirteen participants were puzzled as to how a warmonger could be awarded a peace prize. For example, Zeenat, of Bangladeshi origin (female, 16, US born, national identity: Bengali), said:

> We had a debate about this in social studies [class] . . . a lot of students said that by him sending troops to Afghanistan it would have been a good thing 'cos he's enforcing education and all that stuff. [But] I feel that was completely unnecessary. He really made no changes in the world and Nobel Peace Prizes are for people who work against violence, but at the same time he's sending 30,000 troops to Afghanistan – that's ridiculous. (Interview, New York, January 2010)

Similarly, Naveed, of Palestinian background (male, 17, US born, national identity: American), said: 'You would give it to a guy who invented something that would be beneficial to the world, not to a guy who's not even for peace, he's given war to people' (interview, Florida, March 2010). Osman, of Pakistani background (male, 17, national identity: 'American 99 per cent, Pakistani 1 per cent'), commented: 'The Nobel Peace Prize really holds no meaning . . . it doesn't tell you anything. Actions speak louder than awards' (interview, New York, January 2010).

Afghanistan: is it a 'just war'?

By August 2010, there were more than 140,000 NATO forces, including 120,000 Americans, in Afghanistan. President Obama himself is not a proponent of war. In an interview with Bob Woodward (author of the book *Obama's Wars*, 2010) he said: 'To quote a famous American "War is hell". And once the dogs of war are unleashed, you don't know where it is going to lead.'[53] However, the situation in Afghanistan appeared to be far more complex than one could comprehend. When Obama came to power in 2008, the war in Afghanistan was not going well and Hamid Karzai's government in Kabul was regarded as corrupt. The Taliban were intimidating the villagers and often made inhuman demands. Yet they had secured a safe haven along the Pakistan–Afghanistan border, and Pakistan's nuclear arsenal was unsecured. In 2010, Obama sent 32,000 new troops to Afghanistan, including 17,000 with an emphasis on protecting the integrity of a fair election, which was due in September 2010, and 4,000 to train the Afghan security forces, although he planned to withdraw troops from Afghanistan gradually by the end of 2012.[54] According to Jonathan Alter, apart from securing the Afghan election, President Obama's decision to send more troops to the region was important for regional stability.[55]

Surprisingly, whereas US forces were trying to help the Karzai government in 2010, President Karzai himself was outspoken in his criticism of the US-led war effort and told people that the American counter-insurgency was flawed.[56] He also believed that Afghan forces should take the lead in the war effort so that they could win support from deeply conservative Afghan villagers who harboured suspicion of foreigners. But the Karzai strategy does not gel with the one pursued by the top NATO commander, General David Petraeus, who called for US troops to live closer to villagers so as to win their trust and protect them from the Taliban.[57] Regarding the mistrust or miscommunication prevailing between Afghans and Americans in Afghanistan, one Bangladeshi respondent, Shahnaz (female, over 30, national identity: 'I'm Muslim'), said:

> They are two different things. I mean we [the Americans] hear one side of the story, we don't see the other side of the story. Looking from our side of it, we are sending troops to stop the war over there, we are not fighting them, we are trying to establish schools, we are trying to give them education, you know, that's what we are trying to do. But the people over there have mistrust of us because they think that we are doing it for our national interest and not for the local [Afghan] interest. (Interview, Maryland, February 2010)

The controversial Wikileaks 'war logs' indicated that there have been civilian casualties in Afghanistan, such as in an operation by US Marines near the city of Jalalabad in March 2007, when nineteen unarmed civilians were said to have died and up to fifty were injured. The 'war logs' also mentioned that the US special forces arranged for six 2,000lb bombs to be dropped on a compound in Helmand province in Afghanistan in August 2007. Later it was claimed that up to 300 civilians were killed in this incident.[58]

In the whole complexity of the situation, however, only eight female participants in this study saw the benefit of the presence of American and coalition troops in Afghanistan to secure women's protection. Among them, for example, Nazneen, of Afghan origin (female, 18, US born, national identity: Afghan), observed:

> Obama deserved the Nobel Peace Prize. He doesn't hate Muslims and whenever I saw George Bush talk, whenever he would say the word 'Muslim', I thought that he was going to like throw up or something . . . Obama, he's accepting and he's tolerant of everyone. (Interview, Maryland, January 2010)

Nazneen then pointed out the justification of US involvement in Afghanistan:

> Well, I'm just glad that the US soldiers are out of Iraq because I didn't think that we belonged there in the first place. I really think that Afghanistan needs the Americans' help because of the Taliban; if they [Americans] leave, the Taliban are just going to come right back.

Nazneen was concerned that if the Taliban returned they would impose their interpretation of the Quran. She said, 'The Taliban, when they come, they say "Oh, this is what Islam says", and Afghans are so religious, we love Islam a lot, we're like "Oh, okay, then we'll do it".' However, she observed that though the American forces were in Afghanistan they could do more good for its people if they understood the Afghan culture:

> A good thing by being there, but they could do a better job by not bombing weddings; they really need to understand the culture.
>
> It's very important and they need to understand how to treat the women, 'cos if you look at an Afghan lady in the eyes, the husband's going to kill you. They are very serious, especially in the villages and rural areas, yeah.

Nazneen's comment on bombing weddings was perhaps based on an incident in July 2002 when US helicopter gunships and jets fired on an Afghan wedding, killing about forty people and injuring about seventy. The attack occurred in the village of Kakarak in Uruzgan province, in the south of the country, where special forces and other coalition troops were searching for the remaining al-Qaeda and Taliban fighters.[59] Also, Nazneen's note on understanding the cultural complexities relating to women in rural Afghanistan was important.

Mahinoor, of Pakistani origin (female, over 30, overseas born, national identity: Pakistani American), said that she had heard stories from an Afghan relative about the condition of women in Afghanistan. Mahinoor thought Obama's Nobel Peace Prize, and the US involvement in Afghanistan, were both justified:

> I understand there are troops in Afghanistan but do you know what was happening to the women over there? These women were being tortured. My [Afghan] relative's sister was bombed in the school. And that I think is devastating. My relative used to tell me stories about how when, he was a teenager, the women used to be raped and everything over there. But now at least that's not what is happening.
>
> Did you see the movie *Osama*? It was about this young little girl, her mother cuts her hair because they didn't have a man to walk with, so they cut her hair. The mother had to work somewhere, so she had to walk with her daughter dressed as a man . . .
>
> I personally think, and a lot of Afghans think, that American troops do help. (Interview, Maryland, February 2010)

Bilqis, of Afghan origin (female, 18, US born, national identity: American), concluded:

> *Alhamdulillah*, we're known for fighting off things, but sometimes it's necessary. I think the troops in Iraq should be called back because they are there for no reason, but in Afghanistan we need them. The Taliban are down low right now but they're still there. (Interview, Virginia, January 2010)

Despite their different national identities, the respondents in this section recognised that if the Taliban came to power the position of women would once
again become vulnerable. Islam would be used to serve the Taliban's purpose,
and the Quran would be interpreted as they wished.

Conclusion

The discussions and analysis in this chapter reveal that Muslims, particularly
young Muslims aged between fifteen and thirty, felt connected to American
politics. It appeared that they envisaged Obama as one of 'us'. His minority
status (non-white), Muslim middle name (Hussein), and the colour of his skin
(black) were the binding factors in the participants' connection. Nevertheless,
some were sceptical of Obama as they viewed him as a typical politician, and
some were critical of his domestic and foreign policies (see Chapter 6). About
his Nobel Peace Prize, participants in this study remained divided, though
some of the women saw the merit of it from a feminist perspective. Overall,
many participants held a high opinion of Obama and noted that his election
had brought about a historic change in American race relations. This chapter
displayed the maturity and fair-mindedness of young Muslims who envisaged
themselves as a minority but believed that their voice would be important for
a better national and global future.

Notes

1. Janelle S. Wong, Pei-Te Lien and M. Margaret Conway, 'Group-based Resources
   and Political Participation among Asian Americans', *American Politics Research*
   33:4 (2005), pp. 545–76; James A. Avery, 'The Sources and Consequences of
   Political Mistrust among African Americans', *American Politics Research* 34:5
   (2006), pp. 653–82; Atiya Kai Stokes-Brown, 'Racial Identity and Latino Vote
   Choice', *American Politics Research* 34:5 (2006), pp. 627–52.
2. Avery, 'The Sources and Consequences of Political Mistrust among African
   Americans', p. 657.
3. See Amaney Jamal, 'The Political Participation and Engagement of Muslim
   Americans: Mosque Involvement and Group Consciousness', *American Politics
   Research* 33:4 (2005), pp. 521–44, see p. 522.
4. Wong, Lien and Conway, 'Group-based Resources and Political Participation
   among Asian Americans'.
5. Ibid., p. 546.
6. Stokes-Brown, 'Racial Identity and Latino Vote Choice', pp. 628–9.
7. Jamal, 'The Political Participation and Engagement of Muslim Americans', p. 526.
8. Alexander Rose, 'How Did Muslims Vote in 2000?', *Middle East Quarterly*,
   Summer 2001, pp. 13–27.
9. Paul A. Djupe, Eric McDaniel and Jacob R. Neiheisel, 'The Politics of the Religious

Minorities Vote in the 2004 Elections', in Mark J. Rozell and Gleaves Whitney (eds), *Religion and the Bush Presidency* (New York: Palgrave Macmillan), pp. 95–125, see p. 116.

10. MAPS data from 2004, cited in Djupe, McDaniel and Neiheisel, 'The Politics of the Religious Minorities Vote in the 2004 Elections', p. 114.

11. *Muslim Americans: No Signs of Growth in Alienation or Support for Extremism* (Washington, DC: Pew Research Center, 2011), pp. 11, 51, 75, 106.

12. Ibid., pp. 2, 54.

13. Tupac Shakur, 'Changes', 1992, available at http://www.azlyrics.com/lyrics/2pac/changes.html, accessed 23 May 2012.

14. Jerry Harris and Carl Davidson, 'Obama: The New Contours of Power', *Race and Class* 50:4 (2009), pp. 1–19, see p. 2.

15. Jonathan Alter, *The Promise: President Obama, Year One* (New York: Simon and Schuster, 2010), p. 113.

16. Ewen MacAskill and Robert Tait, 'Obama's video message to the Iranians: "Let's start again" ', *The Guardian*, 21 March 2009, p. 20.

17. Alter, *The Promise*, p. 350.

18. Ibid.

19. Ibid. p. 351.

20. John Carlos Rowe, 'Visualizing Barack Obama', *Journal of Visual Culture* 8:2 (2009), pp. 207–11, see pp. 207–9.

21. Andrew Malcolm, 'Obama's special Ramadan message to Muslim world', *Los Angeles Times* website, 21 August 2009, http://latimesblogs.latimes.com/washington/2009/08/obama-ramadan-greeting-to-muslim-world.html, 23 May 2012.

22. Todd Donovan, 'Obama and the White Vote', *Political Research Quarterly* 63:4 (2010), pp. 863–74, see p. 865.

23. James Joyner, 'Obama in Muslim garb', Outside the Beltway website, 25 February 2008, http://www.outsidethebeltway.com/obama_in_muslim_garb/, accessed 23 May 2012.

24. Andrew Malcolm, 'Is the *New Yorker*'s Muslim Obama cover incendiary or satire?', *Los Angeles Times* website, 13 July 2008, http://latimesblogs.latimes.com/washington/2008/07/obama-muslim.html, accessed 23 May 2012.

25. Marisa A. Abrajano and Michael R. Alvarez, 'Accessing the Causes and Effects of Political Trust among U.S. Latinos', *American Politics Research* 38:1 (2010), pp. 110–41, see pp. 113–15.

26. Ibid.

27. 'Full text of George Bush's speech', *Guardian* website, 24 June 2002, http://www.guardian.co.uk/world/2002/jun/25/israel.usa, accessed 23 May 2012.

28. 'Text: Obama's speech in Cairo', *New York Times* website, 4 June 2009, http://www.nytimes.com/2009/06/04/us/politics/04obama.text.html, accessed 23 May 2012.

29. Ewen MacAskill, 'Barack Obama's healthcare bill passed by Congress,' *Guardian*

website, 22 March 2010, http://www.guardian.co.uk/world/2010/mar/22/us-healthcare-bill-passes-congress, accessed 23 May 2012.

30. Alter, *The Promise*, pp. 88, 98.
31. 'Obama's remarks on signing the stimulus plan', CNN Politics website, 17 February 2009, http://articles.cnn.com/2009-02-17/politics/obama.stimulus.remarks_1_economic-stimulus-bill-sign-today-speaker-pelosi?_s=PM:POLITICS, accessed 28 May 2012.
32 Brad Norington, 'I've been inside a bubble: Obama', *The Australian*, 5 November 2010, p. 1.
33. Ibid.
34. M. Scott Bortot, 'Anti-smoking legislation unites Michigan's hookah café owners', America.gov website, 14 May 2010, http://www.america.gov/st/peopleplace-english/2010/May/20100514165615smtotrob0.7858698.html, accessed 23 May 2012; see also 'Hookah lounge owners unify, weigh options for May 1 smoking ban', *Arab American News*, 1–7 May 2010, p. 14.
35. Ibid.
36. 'Last American troops leave Iraq marking end of war', Fox News website, 18 December 2011, http://www.foxnews.com/world/2011/12/17/last-american-troops-leave-iraq-marking-end-war/, accessed 28 May 2012.
37. 'The dream comes true', *Kathmandu Post*, 19 January 2009.
38. Nick Davies, Jonathan Steele and David Leigh, 'Iraq war logs: secret files show how US ignored torture', *The Guardian*, 22 October 2010.
39. Tom Heyden, '"Obama's Wars" reveals the US is living "on borrowed time"', *The Nation*, 11 October 2010; Bob Woodward, *Obama's Wars* (New York: Simon & Schuster, 2010), pp. 110–11.
40 'Obama under pressure', *World News Australia*, SBS One, 19 October 2010, 6.30 p.m.
41. Woodward, *Obama's Wars*, pp. 120–1.
42. Alter, *The Promise*, pp. 342, 347, 375.
43. Justin Elliott, 'Obama set to escalate secret war in Yemen', Salon website, 11 November 2010, http://www.salon.com/2010/11/11/american_airstrikes_yemen/, accessed 23 May 2012.
44. In October 2011 Abdulmutallab pleaded guilty. See 'Underwear bomb trial: Umar Farouk Abdulmutallab pleads guilty', *The Guardian*, 12 October 2011.
45. Alter, *The Promise*, p. 336.
46. See also Woodward, *Obama's Wars*, p. 54.
47. Tim Reid, 'Bush Guantánamo "cover-up"', *The Times*, 9 April 2010, p. 1; Aidan Radnedge, 'US doctors involved in torture', *Metro* (London), 27 April 2011, p. 29.
48. Alter, *The Promise*, p. 342.
49. Jeremy Pelofsky, 'U.S. sends two Uighur detainees to Switzerland', Reuters website, 24 March 2010, http://www.reuters.com/article/idUSTRE62N38020100324, accessed 23 May 2012.
50. 'Obama: 30,000 more US troops to Afghanistan by mid-2010', Voice of America

website, 1 December 2009, http://www.voanews.com/english/news/Obama_
Troops_Afghanistan_strategy_announcement-78273987.html, accessed 23 May
2012.

51. Ibid.

52. 'Obama defends war as he picks up Nobel Peace Prize', BBC News website, 10
December 2009, http://news.bbc.co.uk/2/hi/americas/8405033.stm, accessed 17
August 2012.

53. Woodward, *Obama's Wars*, p. 110.

54. 'Obama to announce plan to pull 30,000 troops out of Afghanistan,' CNN
Politics website, 21 June 2011, http://articles.cnn.com/2011-06-21/politics/
obama.afghanistan.troops_1_troop-reductions-support-troops-afghan-security?_
s=PM:POLITICS, accessed 23 May 2012.

55. Alter, *The Promise*, pp. 133–4.

56. Christopher Bodeen, 'Blasts kill at least 7 US troops in Afghanistan', 30 August
2010, Bloomberg Businessweek website, http://www.businessweek.com/ap/finan-
cialnews/D9HU2RS01.htm, accessed 28 May 2012.

57. Ibid.

58. John Bingham, 'Wikileaks Afghanistan: suggestions US tried to cover up civilian
casualties', *Telegraph* website, 27 July 2010, http://www.telegraph.co.uk/news/
worldnews/asia/afghanistan/7913088/Wikileaks-Afghanistan-suggestions-US-
tried-to-cover-up-civilian-casualties.html, accessed 23 May 2012.

59. 'Civilian catastrophe as US bombs Afghan wedding', Rawa News website, http://
www.rawa.org/s-wedding.htm, accessed 23 May 2012.

THE PALESTINIAN QUESTION

Though I have not been to Palestine yet, I feel very passionate about the issue. Not simply because I'm Muslim, or because I'm Arab, but because it's a human issue, and I think it's central to a lot of the problems that we face . . . I do believe it's very important for the American population to understand and address, because we're so implicit in the actions of our government, Israeli government, whether we realise it or not, it's our tax dollars that are funding a lot of what's going on, and it's our support, our moral support, our spoken support . . . Even though there are verbal condemnations perhaps, but the real . . . I mean if your friend does something bad and you give them a condemnation and you keep slipping them $20, it's not going to really send the right message though. I just think that we have to, as a nation, wake up to all the issues around us and that's just one of the main ones. (Daniel, male, 22, US born, of Palestinian background, national identity: Muslim American, interviewed in Florida, March 2010.)

In my interview with Daniel in 2010, he pointed out that, although at certain times the United States condemned the Israeli government's excessive aggression against the Palestinians, its blind support for Israel morally and financially was not leading to reconciliation. Daniel's observation appears to be reasonable. In September 2011, Palestinian leaders proclaimed that they would request the United Nations to approve 'the recognition of a full membership of the state of Palestine established on the territories occupied by Israel in 1967, with East Jerusalem as its capital'.[1] Yet President Barack Obama said that his administration would veto such a ruling.[2] On 1 November 2011, the member states of UNESCO recognised Palestine. Nearly two-thirds of UNESCO nations defied warnings from Israel and the US to support Palestinian membership. Fourteen members voted against – among them were Australia, the US and Canada – and more than fifty countries abstained, including Britain.[3] The United States cut its fund to UNESCO.[4]

The most contentious issue impacting on the Palestinians is Israel's expansion of its settlement into the Palestinian occupied territories (for example, Gaza). International humanitarian law 'prohibits [an] occupying power [from transferring] citizens from its own territory to the occupied territory' (Article 49, Fourth Geneva Convention of 1949), but Israel contests this law. In addition some scholars have been critical of Israel's practice of zero tolerance towards Palestinians, for example Israel's control of water, its reluctance to grant permission to Palestinians to build homes, the construction of a huge apartheid wall, and Israeli soldiers' aggressive attitudes at checkpoints.[5]

The Palestinian question brings the issue of identity politics to the fore. Kwame Appiah wrote about seven ways that people might talk about identity politics:[6]

- political conflicts may be about who is in and who is out;
- politicians can mobilise identities;
- states can treat people of distinct identities differently;
- people can pursue a politics of recognition;
- there can be social micro-politics enforcing norms of identifications;
- there are inherently political identities like party identifications;
- social groups can mobilise to respond collectively to all of the above.

It occurs to me that what Appiah meant was that most political conflict is about power and entitlement – who gets to govern and why. Richard Jenkins also observed that when 'categories' are imposed and the issue is resources and power (and national identity), the more powerful impose boundaries on the less powerful.[7] Arguably, in the Israeli–Palestinian conflict, and in the already stratified and categorised structure of Israeli society, Palestinians are positioned as an orientalised 'other'.

So what exactly is the orientalised 'other'? In his book *Orientalism*[8] Edward Said observed that the West perceives itself to be powerful and aims to control the East. According to orientalists the West will always remain 'superior' to the 'inferior' East. Said observed that in contemporary world politics people are forced almost on a daily basis 'to declare themselves to be either westerners or easterners. No one seemed to be free from opposition between "us" and "them," resulting in a sense of reinforced, deepened, hardened identity that has not been particularly edifying.'[9] Said was a Palestinian Christian who strongly opposed the Israeli occupation of Palestine. He noted that in discussions about the 'Occupied Territories' of Palestine, and the 'continued support of Israel', the world is divided into two: the West (and its allies) and the Muslim/Arab world. The notion of 'westerners' and 'easterners' once again becomes clearer.

But how does the Palestinian question impact on young Muslims of

Palestinian heritage living in the United States? The fifty-three participants of Palestinian heritage quoted in this chapter defined their identities variously as Palestinian, Palestinian American, Arab American, Muslim American and Muslim Palestinian American. When they spoke about various issues, their comments connected to their identity (discussed later). In this context, it appears that, like Palestinians living in Palestine, the interviewees' identity was neither socially nor politically constructed. It was either based on their observations while residing in the United States or on firsthand experience of their visits to Palestine.

In this chapter, firstly, I briefly discuss the contemporary situation in Palestine. Secondly, I examine the responses of the participants of Palestinian heritage on the question of Palestine (summarised in Table 6.1). Whereas some participants of other ethnic backgrounds also expressed views on the Israeli–Palestinian conflict, I have included here only the opinions of the Palestinian Americans. I think it is important to discuss their views because the 'Palestine question' directly impacts on their identity/identities.

The Palestinian situation

The people of Palestine have experienced ordeals such as the 1948 war, the 1967 war, the first intifada of 1987 (uprising against Israeli oppression), the Oslo accords, the expansion of Israeli settlement, the Camp David summit, the second intifada of 2000, the separation barrier and the Israeli withdrawal from Gaza, and numerous United Nations resolutions for Israel. Yet the Palestinian question remains unresolved. There has been ongoing violence between Palestinians and Israelis. Since 1967, the pressing issues confronting Palestinians can be divided into the following issues: segregation, economic issues, political issues and military occupation. I now elaborate on each in turn.

Segregation

Over the years about 420,000 Israelis have settled inside the West Bank and East Jerusalem, and Israel plans to expand this number by several thousand. There are two kinds of settlers: ideological and ordinary (majority) settlers. Ideological settlers have an emotional and religious attachment to the land. They believe that the territory was given to the Jewish people by God, so it is their sacred duty to live there even if it means forcibly removing Palestinians from the land. But the majority of the Israelis are ordinary settlers who take houses offered by the government on cheap ten-year mortgages. One way that Israel extends its occupation is by demolishing Palestinians' homes: bulldozers are used by the Israeli soldiers to force Palestinians out of their valleys, which are the best agricultural lands. Every time Palestinian homes are bulldozed, a new town is built for Israeli settlers. By 2007, there were about 190 settlements all over the West Bank.[10]

The settlements are well connected by a network of roads that separate the Palestinian communities. This sort of arrangement enables the settlements to expand. The settlers' homes are often constructed near the best agricultural lands and water resources. These properties are protected by barbed wire, and the settlers are armed inside their area – with further protection by the Israeli military from the outside. According to a commentator, 'The bottom line of this occupation is to make the Palestinians leave the country . . . It is a kind of "ethnic cleansing".' The policy makers in Gaza and the West Bank are not Palestinians; they are Israelis and their policies are drafted in a manner that ensures the Palestinians remain confined in small spaces.[11]

Speaking of disparity, Saree Makdisi observed that one of Israel's several policies of control is to contain Palestinian growth and development in East Jerusalem. Makdisi noted that since 1967 many Palestinians have built their houses without official permission. But they have done it at considerable risk. Israeli construction in the occupied territories is state funded, but Palestinians build their housing with their own funds. The owners of illegally built properties are often punished and fined, and their constructions may be demolished. For example, a Palestinian resident, Daoud Abu Kaf, wished to move out of his parents' crowded apartment (ten people were sharing two rooms) in Ras al-Amud, in East Jerusalem. Starting in 1982, he lodged several applications for building permits to build a house next door to his parents. All his applications were denied, so in 1987 he built two apartments without a permit. As soon as he completed the building, officials from the Ministry of the Interior showed up and ordered the demolition of the entire structure within twenty-four hours.[12]

Tobias Kelly identified the Israeli–Palestinian conflict as a 'conflict over legal rights', in which issues of sovereignty, identity and territory are tied to the distinction between those who are entitled to rights and those who are not.[13] Under the Israeli arrangement an Israeli citizen will always be a citizen whether or not he or she lives in the occupied territories, whereas a Palestinian remains a subject under different authorities. Since 1967, Israeli occupation has allowed a form of 'legal pluralism' to coexist in the occupied territories. Several legal codes, such as Israeli military laws, pre-1967 Jordanian laws, Palestinian Authority laws and Israeli civilian laws, determine the rights of the people of the land. For example, in their everyday lives Palestinian workers have to negotiate with various intermediaries: Palestinian subcontractors, Israeli employers, Palestinian courts, Israeli courts, Israeli soldiers at checkpoints, Palestinian National Authority officials transporting the pass permits issued by the Israeli military authorities, and the NGOs helping Palestinians understand Israeli procedures and dealings with local Palestinian institutions.[14]

In 2005 Israel dismantled its settlements and military posts in Gaza and relocated its settlers. Although Israelis are not visibly present in the Gaza Strip,

Israel still retains ultimate control over the Gaza border, coastal water and air space, thus creating a virtual prison. After the eviction of the Israeli settlers from the Gaza Strip, Israel built a wall (the Bil'in Wall), twice the height of the Berlin Wall and, at 456 miles (730 kilometres) in length, four times as long, which runs through several villages and disrupts Palestinians' travel for work, education and health care purposes. The wall also separates farmers from their work. An Israeli study found that the wall was erected for confiscation of land and not, as publicised by the government, for security reasons.[15]

The Israeli military said that the Bil'in wall was needed for security and attributed to it a sharp reduction in suicide bombings in Israel. The barrier's opponents say it is primarily an Israeli tool to annex Palestinian land in the absence of a peace agreement. The route, as drawn, confiscates 10 per cent of the West Bank onto the Israeli side of the barrier, including more than half the territory of Bil'in. Due to this barrier, many Palestinians have to reroute their travel arrangements, which has made their lives more difficult.[16]

Israel has set up checkpoints within the West Bank causing the Palestinians to wait many hours in order to travel short distances; thus freedom of movement is denied to Palestinians on a daily basis, such as access to Jerusalem, and to hospitals, clinics and schools. Human rights activists observe that in Palestine about three million civilians are denied freedom of movement and that is a violation of international law (freedom of movement is a fundamental right in the UN Declaration of Human Rights).[17]

Economics

In 2007, the documentary *Occupation 101*, directed by Abdallah and Sufyan Omeish, reported on the disproportionate allocation of resources in Palestine: only 10 per cent of the West Bank is populated by Jewish settlers, yet they enjoy special privileges. Whereas Palestinians face water restrictions (for example only two hours' running water a week), the settlers enjoy swimming pools, water, electricity, gas and refuse collection. These services are all denied to the Palestinian people.

Hebron is an Arab city with about 100,000 Arabs and a couple of hundred Jewish settlers. The Jewish settlers in Hebron are allowed to carry rifles, and they have built roads for use as bypasses which Palestinians are not allowed to use. Therefore, Israeli settlers can walk about carrying rifles, intimidate and attack Palestinians, and occupy the Palestinians' houses. Some of the Jewish settlers are politically connected so they can get away with such behaviour. If settlers are accused of murder, very few are tried and even if they are the president gives them an amnesty, they are set free, or their term of imprisonment is shortened.[18]

According to World Bank estimates in 2007, nearly 53 per cent of the Palestinian population was unemployed, with 75 per cent of Palestinians living in poverty (on less than $20 a day).[19] In 2008, Saree Makdisi pointed out that

48 per cent of the Palestinian population in Israel was living in poverty compared to 15 per cent of the Jewish population. The infant mortality rate among Palestinians in Israel was 8.4 per thousand compared to 3.6 per thousand among Jews. The number of Jewish religious sites in Israel granted state protection and funding was 135, while the number of non-Jewish sites was zero.[20] Furthermore, it has been observed that the refugee camps in Palestine were overcrowded, with up to twenty-five people living in small spaces; there was no place for children to play, no streets but just little alleys. The British journalist Richard Falk and Archbishop Desmond Tutu compared the situation for the general population in Palestine to apartheid in South Africa. Yet even this, Falk thought, was much better than the refugee camps in Palestine.[21]

Politics

In January 2006 elections were held. The Palestinians voted the PLO-led government out of office and Hamas won a majority of seats. But Hamas could not form a government because it was regarded by the United States and Israel as a terrorist organisation. Hamas's demand for a genuinely independent Palestinian state (which the Oslo accords promised but never delivered) and an Israeli withdrawal to the 1949–67 borders was not acceptable to the US and Israel.[22] It is interesting to note that the United States advocates democracy worldwide (for example in Iraq) but not in Palestine. The academic S. Sayyid observes that the term 'democracy' can be interpreted variously both in the West and the Orient. In some contexts, pro-democratic western countries deny a genuinely elected democratic government (for example, Hamas in Palestine), and in other contexts Muslim countries justify their military intervention against an elected government, stating that it possesses the 'anti-western nature of Islamism', which 'is a threat to "democracy"' (for example, the military coup against the victory of the FIS in the Algerian elections).[23]

Military occupation

The world has been shocked by Palestinian suicide bombings; for example, on 9 August 2001 a horrendous attack on a pizzeria in central Jerusalem killed fifteen civilians and wounded 130 people. But critics argue that the Israeli occupation is far more brutal. American media such as Fox News, CNN, CBS, ABC News, the *New York Times* and the *New York Post* play a major role in manipulating stories and thereby keeping the American public uninformed of the facts.[24] In the process, major stories go unreported and news reporting is censored. In *Occupation 101*, some commentators (including Jewish-Israeli people) said that Palestinians live in constant fear, with high levels of anxiety, loss of hope and a sense of vulnerability because at any time they might be killed. So when oppression becomes unbearable people revolt. Palestinians are treated cruelly and tortured, their lands are confiscated, their heritage is destroyed, so their revolt is a legitimate resistance to an occupation.[25]

With 200–300 nuclear warheads, Israel is the fifth largest nuclear power in the world. It is in reality a regional superpower. Israel has the largest navy of any country in the world besides the US. US aid (taxpayers' money) to Israel from 1949 to 1996 totalled $62.5 billion. *Occupation 101* gave the following data:[26]

- Israeli tanks: 3,930
- Palestinian tanks: 0
- Israeli jet fighters: 362
- Palestinian jet fighters: 0

Israeli and Palestinian casualties from September 2000 to February 2007:

- Palestinians killed by Israelis: 4,009
- Israelis killed by Palestinians: 1,021
- 935 children killed (816 Palestinians and 119 Israelis)

On 27 December 2008 Israel launched air attacks on Gaza in response to rocket attacks commenced by Hamas. The conflict ended on 18 January 2009 after Hamas and Israel agreed to a ceasefire. The casualties during the 22-day Gaza war were as follows: Palestinians: 1,300 dead and 5,100 injured; Israelis: 13 dead and 80 injured.[27] Another example of Israeli heavy-handedness is that in May 2010, when a flotilla of civilian vessels (carrying humanitarian aid, food and medicine) tried to break the Israeli naval blockade of Gaza, Israeli forces killed nine Turkish activists. Turkey demanded an apology and compensation for the families of the activists. In December 2010, Israeli prime minister Benjamin Netanyahu ruled out making an apology to Turkey, stating, 'We will not apologise, but express our regrets to Turkey.'[28]

Some local young Palestinians are keen to migrate to the USA because they are not hopeful that Palestine will ever become an independent state. This was portrayed in the film *Amreeka* (2009), where a Palestinian schoolboy convinced his reluctant mother to migrate to the USA (after his mother received a US migration document) by saying, 'Do you know how many people dream of this opportunity . . . It is better than being prisoners in our own country.' Finally, when they (mother and son) migrated to the US, at the US airport they were asked which country they were from. The mother replied that they did not have a country. It had been an occupied land for forty years.

Participants' observations on the Palestinian issue

In this section I examine the views of the participants on the Palestinian issue. First, I show the key points of their responses (Table 6.1), and then elaborate on the responses in turn.

Table 6.1 Views of American Muslims of Palestinian background

Number of participants	Responses	Key points
6 m, 9 f	Being Palestinian is not easy	Differential treatment.
2 m, 1 f	Airport experience	Racial profiling.
1 m, 1 f	Use of terror techniques	It is dehumanising.
0 m, 1 f	No easy access to Jerusalem	Israel decides Palestinian identity.
0 m, 1 f	*Hijab* is the ultimate marker	They gave me a tough time because of my *hijab*.
1 m, 3 f	It was scary	It is a war zone.
2 m, 0 f	Mention of original owner of the land	Injustice still prevails.
1 m, 2 f	Feelings for fellow Palestinians	*Alhamdulillah*, we are safe, but we feel for them.
1 m, 1 f	It is a human issue	We should be allowed to raise funds for Palestine.
2 m, 0 f	Placed between a rock and a hard place	We are hated there because we are Palestinians *and* we are Americans.
0 m, 1 f	Obama under the spotlight	President Obama did not answer my question.
0 m, 3 f	Don't say they are Jews	They are Israelis.
1 m, 0 f	No hope for Palestine	The Israelis won't give up resources, e.g. water.
1 m, 1 f	Thank God we live in America	Reflection on freedom in the US.
3 m, 1 f	Some optimism	We integrated with the Jewish settlers.
2 m, 5 f	No comments	Never visited. I went there at a very young age so I don't remember much.

Total number of participants: 23 m, 30 f

The fifty-three participants spoke mostly about their firsthand experiences when visiting or living in Palestine for some time. Most participants said they enjoyed visiting their extended families in Palestine, but they were dismayed at the treatment they received from Israeli soldiers at the airport, borders and checkpoints. A few participants (e.g. Jamila and Waleed) also spoke about other issues that they felt were relevant to the discussion of the 'Palestinian question'.

Being Palestinian is not easy

Fifteen participants spoke of the Israeli authorities' differential treatment towards them and their family members when they visited Palestine. For example, Ruhee (female, over 30, overseas born, national identity: Arab American) said that when she first visited Palestine in 1997 she had a lot of negative experiences when dealing with Israelis and even some Arabs at checkpoints and at the airports. She said, 'It was a new experience for me and I guess when I went the second time with my family, with my mother and sisters, it wasn't that much of a surprise because I had received my first dose earlier.' On her next visit to Palestine in 2000 with her mother and sisters, Ruhee said that her sisters were very disturbed by the Israeli authorities' treatment of her mother:

> My two sisters and I, we were the only people riding the bus after we left the airport, you know, to go to Jerusalem. And my mother, because she was not a US citizen then, she had to go on a different bus, so for us we felt it was very unfair. You know, this is our mother, and so it was very difficult to explain to my younger sisters as well. So again this is an obstacle and a challenge that we overcame at that time, but in retrospect, just trying to think about what the people go through that live there, it's very tough . . . the hardships that they're going through day in and day out.
>
> I held [out] the blue US passport, yes I was put on a bus that was air-conditioned but they [the Israeli guards] weren't nice. I would not describe my experience as being treated with respect. But for my mother, again, this was nothing because she grew up there, she's been in that situation for quite a bit of her life. It didn't come as a shock to her, more than it came for us . . . But hopefully things are better there. To be honest with you I don't have any desire, at least at this time, to go visit, just because of that bitter experience. (Interview, Florida, March 2010)

Fawaz (male, 17, US born, national identity: Arab American), who visits Palestine almost every year, described similar experiences of differential treatment:

> It's so much fun to visit family there, but you can't leave the house. It's very complicated when we go there.
>
> Because my dad got us a Palestinian citizenship, so when you go there, it's horrible. Yeah, there are two different ways. There's the Palestinian [way, through Jordan] and there's the American way [through Tel Aviv]. It may be like three or four hours from Jordan and they [the Israeli guards] won't let us in. There's a lot of checkpoints because we have also an Israeli car and if you have a Palestinian passport, you're not allowed to drive an Israeli car . . . My cousins, they don't have Palestinian citizenship, they drive that and everything . . . It's very hard . . . the way they treat us is horrible. (Interview, Michigan, April 2010)

Aaneesah (female, 17, US born, national identity: American Muslim, Palestinian) gave a similar account of her ordeal:

> Yeah, I go to Palestine every year through Jordan. We have to go through the border, which over there is not like the borders over here. It's horrible, it takes a whole day

and it's hot. They have buses, un-air-conditioned in the heat, 100 degrees outside. Like five checkpoints and they take your luggage and they throw it in a huge area and everyone has to go find their luggage and pick it up and toss it onto another bus, and you pay and keep paying and paying and paying until they get there. It's only about 2 miles to our destination in Palestine. (Interview, Florida, March 2010)

Apart from the border ordeal, Aaneesah said that sometimes at the checkpoints they had to pay a price for being jubilant:

Sometimes if you're doing something that they [Israeli security guards] don't like or whatever, they'll just tell you 'Okay, well, ten-minute punishment, you have to sit here for ten minutes, you can't go through.' Yeah, like two years ago we were going to a wedding once and they came along and they were angry that everyone was happy and they said, 'Okay, ten-minute punishment', and they put the bus on the side.

Most participants were critical of Israeli treatment towards them at the borders, particularly at the Israeli–Jordanian border, though they loved to visit their relatives in Palestine. And a few were so frustrated with their treatment that they felt discouraged from obtaining a Palestinian ID card. For example, Rameez (male, 16, US born, national identity: Palestinian) said:

I'm from the West Bank. Yeah, Ramallah doesn't have much tension. I went there a year ago. Oh, it's changed a lot from last time. I mean like more buildings have gone up, there's more Jews all over the place and there's like borders everywhere, there's always checkpoints. You have to carry a passport everywhere. Sometimes the Israeli soldiers at the checkpoints give you problems. I have seen them treating my grandfather badly at the Jordanian border when we were trying to enter Palestine . . .
    I won't take the *hawiyya* card [Palestinian identity card]. I don't want to settle in Palestine. (Interview, New York, November 2009)

Speaking of his ordeal at the River Jordan crossing checkpoint, an American-Palestinian traveller said that in 2007, after being detained for several hours, he was denied access to Palestine and deported back to Jordan. Apparently the Israeli security guards/soldiers had discovered that the traveller had a *hawiyya* card which had not been activated. The traveller had entered Israel before with his US passport, but they refused to hear his arguments that the border was only for foreigners, and that he was a Palestinian.[29] The next day, he was held at the Allenby Bridge for not possessing the *tasreeh* that, they informed him, his mother must have had several years ago. Later he was allowed entrance to Palestine. The traveller then acquired a Palestinian *hawiyya* card and *tasreeh* when he was at the West Bank.[30]
    Palestinians are not only subjected to many hours' delay at the checkpoints. Sometimes men are ordered at gunpoint to take off their clothes.[31] In 2010, the

Tikun Olam website reported that some Israelis not only uprooted Palestinian villages and harassed Palestinians at checkpoints; they also converted the names of many places from Arabic to Hebrew, and now they are 'judaizing Palestinian East Jerusalem'. For example, Nilin, the site of protests against the West Bank Barrier, will become Kiryat HaSefer. Critics say that the Hebrew names are designed to convey to Palestinians the message that Israel is in control. It would also convey that the soldiers and border crossing personnel were not protecting a Palestinian area but Israeli territory.[32]

Airport experiences

Abdul (male, 17, US born, national identity: Palestinian American) said, 'They held my brother at the airport for six hours [in Palestine]. 'Cos you know how Israel is really close friends with America? So they [Israelis] think the same but even worse over there' (interview, Florida, March 2010). Jamila (female, 18, overseas born, national identity: Muslim Palestinian) commented:

> I have US citizenship, so I can go through Tel Aviv airport. I was interrogated for seven hours. By myself, I didn't go with my parents . . . They sent me to fifteen different supervisors; everyone said that they were sending me to their supervisor and they asked me the same ten or so questions, like 'Who's your father, who's your mother, who's your grandfather, what was his name?' Things I wouldn't even know, like 'Who's your great-great-grandfather?' I don't know who my great-great-grandfather is. (Interview, Florida, March 2010)

Waleed (male, 30, overseas born, national identity: Palestinian American) lived in Palestine for five years in the 1990s. He said:

> Sure, yeah, the US Patriotic [*sic*] Act definitely has impact on us; my last name being Mohammad, that to them stands out very clearly. As far as airport screenings, extra security [is concerned,] as a Palestinian, we're pretty much used to that because of the way Israelis inspect us at their airport. So even though it might have been something new here in the States, in general for us it was something we got used to, so it didn't bother us that much. (Interview, New York, November 2009)

In Chapter 3, I discussed how some participants in this study felt frustrated by the US authorities' racial profiling at airports (under the Patriot Act). So in the context of racial profiling by the Israeli authorities, Waleed was not upset because, as a Palestinian, he had encountered differential treatment before at Tel Aviv airport. Abdul observed that, because Israel is an ally of the US, such profiling (or even worse treatment) can be expected.

Use of terror techniques

Medina (female, 16, US born, national identity: Arab American) said that she was from Jenin in Palestine and her town was generally safe. But she felt intimidated when she went near the border where she saw jeeps full of Israeli soldiers. Medina said:

> If I want to visit my family, and they're a little far away, it's going to take us twice the time, plus we have to stop at checkpoints and there's always things like soldiers who have these big guns . . .
>
> Once I was visiting my relatives in a taxi with my mother, brothers and sisters. So on the way sometimes the Israeli soldiers, they take the paths that people usually take and they bulldoze huge rocks onto them so that they [our cars and taxis] can't pass, just like to annoy us, to cause trouble for us. So there was a long line of taxis of other people waiting; it was a main route but it was closed off. So some men had shovels in their taxis and cleared the road.
>
> But all of a sudden, maybe ten jeeps came out of nowhere and the children started running out and they [the jeeps] started stopping all the cars; some cars got away, other cars were stopped; we were at the beginning of the line so we were stuck there of course. And then they started opening the taxis to see if there were any young men in there because they wanted to see who was helping to do that [clear the road].
>
> They opened our taxi boot and my brother, he was like sixteen, he looked like he could go and help out with that so they pulled him out of the car and one of the soldiers started talking to him in Hebrew. My brother couldn't understand, and the soldier, he started pointing the gun at his head, saying 'Did you do this, did you do this?' and then the taxi driver came out of the car and tried to explain to him [the Israeli soldier] that he didn't do it, that he was too young, and then they let him go. But it was very, very scary. I thought my brother was going to die. (Interview, New York, November 2009)

Minhaj (male, 16, US born, national identity: '75 per cent Palestinian and 25 per cent Colombian') said:

> I've been there, last year actually, in the summer. I went to Palestine and Jordan. I have relatives in both . . . Checkpoints, yeah . . . While I was there, a guy, an Israeli soldier stopped our taxi for no reason and he made us come out of the car and he was talking to me in Hebrew, but I didn't really understand. He thought I was giving him attitude and he pulled out his gun; it was devastating. And I just showed him my [American] passport and he was like 'Sorry, sorry', and he let me go. (Interview, Michigan, April 2010)

Other anecdotes and photographs posted on websites reveal similar ordeals of travellers inside Palestine. The photographs are vivid and have immediate impact on the viewers. For example, a photo taken by a traveller on 1 June 2006 showed people in cars who had been waiting for several hours on their way to Ramallah.[33] The caption mentioned that the Israeli military authorities often close down roads throughout Palestine on a whim. This leads to several hours of backed-up traffic, 'an experience that is both dehumanizing and inconvenient'.[34] At Israeli checkpoints in Palestine the local Palestinians (including the children and elderly) are often subjected to harassment, sexist insults and inhumane treatment.

Further inconvenience at the checkpoints was described by a local Palestinian, Jarrar, who lived and worked in Ramallah, but he and his wife and their two-year-old son used to visit his parents in Jenin. They used to get dropped off at the Hawara checkpoint, which, he said, 'is one of the most difficult in the West Bank. It takes sometimes four to five hours to pass it, if at all. More than once people are sent back, without any reason.'[35] After Israel imposed further restrictions, Khaled Jarrar and his family visited their parents at Jenin less frequently. Jarrar took a couple of photos of the checkpoint at Hawara, which showed the barbed wire fence next to the path that those who want to cross the checkpoint from either side have to use. He commented that the soldiers did not let them go until they had looked at their checkpoint photos. 'One of the soldiers, a young woman, suddenly felt she needed to defend herself and her comrades by saying they have to protect their country and that it is legitimate to fight terrorists!'[36] Anecdotes reveal that travellers' suffering during peace-time can be exhausting but during crises it can lead to fatalities. For example, during the second intifada in 2000, sixty-eight pregnant women were unable to access hospitals and were forced subsequently to give birth at checkpoints; as a consequence, four women died and thirty-four suffered miscarriages. During 2001 and 2002, about 74 per cent of the forty-six Palestinian deaths occurred because of the denial of access to medical facilities.[37]

Access to Jerusalem

Jamila (female, 18, overseas born, national identity: Muslim Palestinian) spoke of restrictions people face when they visit Jerusalem:

> We went to Jerusalem and we wanted to go and pray, but we weren't allowed in because they said that we weren't Muslims; so we had to prove ourselves as Muslims to the Israeli soldiers and that was very disrespectful, you know, for someone who is going to their holy land to pray. It should be a thirty-minute drive, but because of the checkpoints and stuff, it's a three-hour drive and you have to switch buses continuously because taxi drivers can only drive in a certain area. So it's really hard to go through things like that and then you go to Bethlehem. Actually the day we were in Bethlehem two people, Palestinians, were killed.

Jamila continued with her grievances:

> A lot of the times when you want to go to Israel to visit the beautiful places like Kaffa and the beach and the historical places, Palestinians can't go because you have to be an Israeli to go; but we are allowed to go because we have US citizenship. So it's really hard trying to find someone to take you to go because you want to see this place that you are coming to visit for this first time. (Interview, Florida, March 2010)

On the disparate treatment of Palestinians in their everyday lives, Saree Makdisi wrote:

> It is, however, the Israelis, not the Palestinians, who decide what identity is conferred on which Palestinian, and they make the decision . . . family life, intimately personal spaces, the nature (and the very existence) of the family home, and even personal identity – who one is, where one can go, where one can live and work.[38]

Makdisi noted that all these factors are politically motivated and founded on the 'distinction between someone who happens to be Jewish and someone who does not'.[39] Makdisi further said that if a Jewish baby is born in Jerusalem (or in Israel or in the Israeli settlements in the occupied territories), he or she is automatically granted a birth certificate and a state identity number (similar to the US social security card). However, if a Palestinian baby is born in Jerusalem with one parent who is a Jerusalem resident and the other a resident of the West Bank, the baby is not automatically granted the same privilege. Moreover, Palestinian babies born in the occupied areas are not granted the same rights as Jewish babies born there. For example, a Jewish child born in the settlement areas of the West Bank is issued an Israeli identity card and a Palestinian child a West Bank one.[40]

Speaking of the suffering of Palestinian adults, Makdisi discussed the case of a Palestinian couple. In 1996, Hala, a Palestinian resident of Jerusalem, married Odeh, a Palestinian resident with Jordanian citizenship. Hala submitted an application for family reunion so that they could live together. The Israeli authorities can take several years to approve such an application. In the meantime, Odeh was caught in Jerusalem without a permit, so he was expelled to Jordan. When Hala's baby was born, according to the standard procedure the Israeli Ministry of Interior did not give her an identity number. When Hala and her baby went to visit Odeh in Jordan, the Israeli soldiers recorded her baby on an exit permit so it was only with tremendous difficulty that Hala and her baby were allowed to return to Jerusalem (through several applications and appeals), because the baby did not have an Israeli identity number.[41]

Some of the Palestinian participants in this study said that their extended families had settled in Jordan. But in Jordan (though it is an Arab country) displaced Palestinians are treated as the 'other'. For example, on 11 December 2010, there was a soccer game between the Palestinian team Wihdat and a Jordanian team, Faisali. Most of Faisali's players and fans are from native Jordanian Bedouin tribes, whereas most of Wihdat's players and fans are Palestinians who have settled in Jordan. When Faisali lost the game, their fans attacked the Palestinian team and inflicted bodily harm on some of the players. It is alleged the Jordanian police were associated with this violence. Witnesses blamed the police for preventing the Wihdat fans from leaving the stadium when angry Faisali supporters threw stones at them. Many Wihdat supporters said the police were biased against them and reacted to their victory over Faisali, a team that is 'a fertile ground for Jordanian nationalists'.[42] On 11 December 2010, Fox News reported that the clash resulted in 250 injuries among fans of both teams.[43] There is a long history of violence between supporters of the two teams, originating in decades of tension with Jordan's large Palestinian population.

Jordan's Palestinian population consists of about 1.8 million refugees, including those displaced when Israel was created in 1948 and their descendants. Although most of Jordan's Palestinians – excluding natives of the Gaza Strip – carry Jordanian passports and enjoy citizenship rights unmatched by other Arab host governments, many of them complain that they are barred from taking up security and army posts or holding top positions in the Jordanian government.[44]

The *hijab* is the ultimate marker

Sadiqah (female, 23, US born, national identity: Arab Muslim) said that before she started wearing the *hijab* it was very easy for her to get around and to enter Palestine, but once she started to wear the *hijab* Israeli soldiers detained her for five hours. She commented, 'Before, I think I [was] perceived as a threat, but this visual identifier completely changed everything, so it became a lot more difficult. They gave me a lot more problems even though I had my American passport.' (Interview, Florida, March 2010)

It is scary

Shayla (female, 16, US born, national identity: Muslim) said that when she lived in Jerusalem she did not see any fighting, but when they had to cross over to go to a different *masjid* on the other side, armies would stop them. Shayla said, 'They had their tanks and trucks, it's a little scary' (interview, Florida, March 2010). Similarly, Seerat (female, 16, US born, national identity: Arab American) said that she had lived in Beltunia, fifteen minutes away from Ramallah, which was 'pretty safe':

But when we went out to the mullah, we had to pass the border where there were the army men, the soldiers. And they did ask us questions. And we answered them politely and we just went in.

And I remember a few times, when I was sleeping, we could hear the planes fly from the Israel part to, I think it was Gaza, or some other place. I remember hearing them, and I remember going into my mom's room and just sleeping with her then. I was scared.

It's really disturbing, it's heartbreaking. Yeah, thank God, my family is fine there. (Interview, Florida, March 2010)

Lisa Haque (female, 16, US born, national identity: Pakistani Palestinian) said that she had not visited Palestine yet, but she showed some awareness of what it was like when she said, 'When I was younger I remember when my grandma came, she had a foot problem too, because they [the Israelis] shot her in the foot. So they [grandparents] had to leave. They lost all their land and everything overseas' (interview, Massachusetts, April 2010).

Mention of the original owners of the land

Aadil (male, over 30, overseas born, national identity: 'Muslim American of Palestinian heritage') said:

It's a matter of freedom, and the right for people to live peacefully. And when you see on the news the aggravation and the harsh procedure that's used by the Israelis against the Palestinians there, the original owners of the land, you're surprised that injustice is still there. (Interview, Massachusetts, October 2009)

Abdallah (male, 17, US born, national identity: Arab American) commented:

In a nutshell, I was born in New York. My roots are from Palestine. Long story short, my grandparents were kicked out of their original homeland and had to move to USA. My father came here with my grandparents when he was young. But our extended family still lives in Palestine. I've been there I'd say a good four, five, six times. It's my second home. I'm a citizen of that area. I could live there if I want to and I have my ID so . . . (Interview, New York, November 2009)

Mateen (male, 15, US born, national identity: Palestinian American) said:

I have never been to Palestine but I watch news with my mom, grandma and grandpa. I watch it with them sometimes, and when I watch what's going on in my country, Palestine, everything going on with Palestinians and the Jewish people. But they don't show much . . . I mean the news here [in America] is owned by the Jewish people, so what they do is they block out the majority of the stuff and they show you just little bits of stuff of what we're doing, but if you watch the real Arabic news they show you both sides: what the Jewish people are doing to Palestinians and what the Palestinians are doing to the Jewish people. Yeah, America, if they [Americans] don't like somebody they'll turn everybody against them. So they'll do whatever they can to make the other people look bad. (Interview, Michigan, April 2010)

Although the interviewees expressed their identities differently, they spoke passionately about Palestine. Often they used the words 'we', 'us' or 'our' when referring to Palestinians, and 'they' or 'them' for Israel and its ally the United States. The interviewees also alluded to Palestinians as the 'original owners of the land'.

Feelings for fellow Palestinians

Adiba (female, 23, US born, national identity: Arab American) said that her extended family lived in a peaceful place in Palestine called Beit Hanina. She commented:

Alhamdulillah, it's very calm, it's definitely not what I see on the news. I know what's going on there when I see the wall built and . . . and the checkpoints make it harder to get to other towns . . . I do feel it, and I've friends who live in those towns that are like war torn, but, *alhamdulillah*, it's not where I visit. (Interview, New York, November 2009)

Muznah (female, 20, US born, national identity: Arab American) said:

My parents were born in West Bank . . . Totally we're always connected every time something happens, we have satellite TV at home so we're watching it as it happens, as it unfolds. We definitely feel with them what they're going through and we sympathise with them . . . We try to do fundraisers, we go to demonstrations, we just try to voice our opinions in different ways. Because we can't be there we're kind of helpless in any other way. But we definitely feel with them. (Interview, New York, January 2010.)

Safwan (male, 16, US born, national identity: Muslim Arab) said that he and his family were from Ramallah, which was peaceful and not like the Gaza Strip:

We don't feel it [the oppression] but we know about it. Ramallah to Gaza is about two or three minutes' drive. It's not too big a country but ever since the Jews made it complicated you have to go all around the country just to get there; it takes us two to three hours now. I like Palestine, it's nice . . . When there is disturbances we all feel affected of course 'cos these are our people, they're only a few minutes away and we can't help them, we have no power to help them so . . .

When I asked Safwan if he was optimistic about President Obama, he replied:

> Well, I was pretty happy because he started focusing on being an ally of Palestine instead of an enemy. So I thought, I had hopes that maybe the war would end . . . but so far I'm not seeing much change from him. He also spoke for Palestine initially, I guess he's quiet now that he got his job . . . his presidential seat, he doesn't care much, it looks like, yeah. (Interview, New York, November 2010)

Critics observe that pro-Israel lobby groups have control of US foreign policy decision making, so the US president may not have much control over his actions. For example, the American Israel Public Affairs Committee (AIPAC) lobby group is powerful. It has millions of dollars to spend on influencing American politicians. Congressmen fear that if they oppose what Israel wants, then in the next election they might be defeated.[45]

Some participants believed that the US, being a strong ally of Israel, blindly supports Israel even though it is considered by critics to be a regime that represses Palestinians. For example, at the United Nations conference on racism in Durban, South Africa, in September 2001, the Israeli and the US delegates jointly walked out when the original draft resolution to the conference expressed a 'deep concern' at the 'increase of racist practices of Zionism and anti-Semitism' and referred to the emergence of 'movements based on racism and discriminatory ideas, in particular the Zionist movement, which is based on racial superiority'. The resolution also made direct criticisms of Israeli repression against the Palestinians in the West Bank as a 'new kind of apartheid, a crime against humanity'.[46]

It is also a human issue

Mehjabeen (female, 25, US born, national identity: Palestinian) perceived that during any natural calamities on American soil, such as Hurricane Katrina, the US government is keen to collect donations to help the victims, but not when it comes to American Muslims collecting donations for destitute people in Palestine:

> It's upsetting and lots of people have been branded as terrorists because of them raising money for Palestine and for Gaza. But when we had the hurricane and that hit, everyone is sending money over and being able to donate; text messages are set up and we can't even set up a text message donation for Gaza . . . In Gaza we have got children who are starving. We have got women who are starving, and we have got men without jobs.

Once the USA Patriot Act was passed in 2001, several Islamic charitable organisations were banned. For example, in July 2004, the Holy Land

Foundation for Relief and Development was charged with supporting the militant Palestinian group Hamas with money laundering and conspiracy.[47] Ten interviewees in this study told me that two of their Palestinian mentors had been deported for sending funds to Palestine. So raising funds for the destitute people of Gaza is regarded as a security threat to the US. On some occasions, however, Americans have been allowed to raise funds for Palestine (discussed later). Mehjabeen continued with her observations:

> America should be fair with the situation because it's bombs against rocks. Who is going to win really, honestly? We are not going to come out on top, not now at least, but the future with the grace of Allah and the will of Allah we will, but it's difficult ... we are looked at like we are the terrorist and we don't even have anything to go by, except for our little rocks and our little pebbles. (Interview, Michigan, May 2010)

Mehjabeen's Palestinian identity came to the fore when she stated, 'We [Palestinians] won't give up, but the problem is that we are already labelled as "terrorists".'

Between a rock and a hard place

Naved (male, 17, US born, national identity: American) said:

> I am from Silwad, it's a small city [in Palestine]. I have been there three times in my life ... I hated it. They [the Palestinians] thought I was a Jew ... When I went to school over there they hurt me and stuff, they threw rocks. Yeah, that's why I don't like going there any more. I took it like a man and I didn't hit them back. I went home ... I didn't cry!
>   Oh, yeah they do that 'cos you come from America, then they start going crazy, they ask you all these questions, 'Oh, enter from America', this and that ... they go crazy. If they ask in Arabic if you like Bush and if you say 'Yes', then they won't like you, they'll be cool with you but they won't like you. (Interview, Florida, March 2010)

Another participant, Ahmed (male, 19, US born, national identity: American Palestinian), who travels between USA and Palestine on a regular basis, said that, when he and his family lived in Ramallah, during wartime it was 'scary' for all of them. I asked him if there was electricity and running water in Ramallah. He replied, 'Yeah, Ramallah's good.' Regarding the checkpoints, Ahmed said, 'Yeah, too much search.' When I asked him if he felt bad about what was happening in the West Bank, he replied, 'Yeah, I feel bad, everybody must feel bad.' Regarding the economic conditions in Palestine, he said, 'There is no work.' Talking about security searches, Ahmed said that he is searched at the Palestinian checkpoints, and when he comes from Palestine he faces more searches at US airports. I asked him about the profile of Hamas in Palestine. Ahmed replied, 'Hamas is doing good work in the hospitals and other places. Good work but they are getting a bad name from the US and Israel' (interview, New York, November 2009).

Obama under the spotlight

Jamila (female, 18, US born, national identity: Muslim Palestinian) said that she attended a town hall meeting in the USA where President Obama came to give a speech:

> President Obama said he would take seven questions from the audience. So I happened to be the first person and I asked him about why America financially funds Israel and Egypt, although they have human rights violations. President Obama didn't end up answering my question, but I didn't ask the question because I wanted an answer. I know the answer. I asked the question because I wanted to create awareness of the conflict. (Interview, Florida, May 2010)

Political analyst Halim Rane has observed that, in President Obama's efforts to establish peace in the Middle East, he requested the Israeli government to stop the construction of settlements on Palestinian territory. Yet his request was not reinforced by any threat of aid reduction or sanctions against Israel. So the continuation of Israeli settlement in the Palestinian territory is detrimental to the peace process with the Muslim world.[48]

In April 2010, the *Christian Science Monitor* reported that in 2008 a Congressional Research Service study found that since 1949 the US has given Israel more than $101 billion in aid, including $53 billion in military help, $31 billion in economic aid, and $15 billion in other grants. Although Israel is a relatively rich country, it gets slightly more than the annual $2.6 billion US aid going to impoverished Afghanistan. Between 1949 and 2008 Israel received a total of $101 billion in US aid. The US is far more generous to Israel than to the next largest recipients of its aid, Egypt, Pakistan and Jordan.[49] Other reports revealed that, as part of his $3.8 trillion budget request to Congress for fiscal year 2011, President Obama has asked for $3 billion in military aid to Israel – a $225 million increase from the previous year. The foreign aid bill includes much more than US security assistance to Israel. By contrast President Obama has requested only $550.4 million in aid for the Palestinian Authority.[50]

Between 29 June and 20 July 2010, the University of Maryland and Zogby International surveyed 3,976 people from Egypt, Jordan, Lebanon, Morocco, Saudi Arabia and the United Arab Emirates. Large numbers of respondents called for a halt to US aid to Israel. The overwhelming majority would agree to a peace deal with Israel but a firm majority did not believe Israel wants peace.

A small percentage said Arabs should fight on even if Israel withdraws from territory occupied in 1967.[51]

'Don't say they are Jews, say they are Israelis'

On her identity, Fariha (female, 16, US born) said, 'I am mostly American, half Arab, and I am Muslim.' To my question 'How would Muslims contribute to harmony with the wider society?' Fariha replied:

> I have not been to Palestine yet. My dad has kept going there regularly. I don't know, besides being nice people, being fully approachable and maybe not saying things that get people, I don't know, man, sometimes people are just really horrible. Sometimes my dad will go and say common things like 'Oh, those Jews' or something. And I think that you need to sort of cut down on that. Like if you mean Israel's latest policy, then say Israel's policy, don't just label everyone. Also, Muslims need to work together more, be more cohesive . . . If we want to take part in a service project in the broader community, we should all get up and get behind it and not squabble about it . . . I think we should volunteer and get out there and do things. (Interview, Michigan, April 2010)

Maysoon (female, 16, US born, national identity: Palestinian American) passionately spoke of her humanitarian activities during the Gaza War:

> Actually, yeah, last year [December 2008] we raised about $70,000 for Gaza. We had a lot of fundraising things, we had activists come from outside and speak to us. We had a big event in a hall where we invited a lot of people and we had poetry and all that stuff. We raised a lot of money for it and we'd always like to keep everybody aware of what's going on there. Yeah, I'm very involved on the Palestinian issue.

Maysoon also spoke of the Jewish involvement in the Gaza rally:

> Well, sometimes we go to protests and during the Gaza siege we had a lot of protests in Manhattan. There was always like another protest for the Israelis. We probably had thousands of people and they probably had like ten. Actually we had some Jewish people on our side. Yeah, there were a lot of Jews that were also against [Israeli occupation of Palestine]. (Interview, New York, November 2009)

Regarding the conflict between Israel and Palestine, Maysoon clarified:

> It's Zionism we're against, not Judaism. They'll [the Israeli protestors] be holding signs saying, oh, 'Hamas are terrorists' and stuff like that. But then there'll be Jewish people that are with us, they have signs holding up, there's sometimes even Jewish speakers that come and they speak at our protests. Yeah, they are not supportive of

the Zionists. In Palestine it's not really an issue of religion, it's more of [nationalism], it's nationalistic.

The Harvard Jewish scholar Sara Roy observed that historically the dominant framework of the Israeli–Palestinian conflict and US foreign policy towards Israel is still supported by mainstream Jewish institutions, including the Jewish lobby. However, recently the US government's support for Israel has been criticised by some mainstream non-Jewish and Jewish Americans. They may have to pay a price for being critical, but the slow movement has already started. For example, former US president Jimmy Carter was criticised for publishing his book *Peace not Apartheid*, where he focused 'on the nature of the Israeli occupation and the Palestinians' consequent deprivation'.[52] Roy noted that Carter's use of the word 'apartheid' in association with Israel caused fourteen members of the Carter Center advisory board to resign in protest. His critics branded him an anti-Semite and even a Nazi sympathiser. However, his book sold around 300,000 copies and was on *The New York Times* bestseller list for some time.[53]

In 2006, the political scientists Professor John J. Mearsheimer and Professor Stephen M. Walt from the University of Chicago and Harvard University respectively wrote an article titled 'The Israel lobby' in the *London Review of Books* (after *The Atlantic* withdrew its agreement to publish it), which subsequently became a bestselling book, *The Israel Lobby and US Foreign Policy*. In their book, Mearsheimer and Walt exposed the extent of the influence that the Israel lobby group, Christian fundamentalist groups and certain individuals have on US foreign policy. The authors further asserted that the Israel lobby influenced the USA to make certain decisions, such as the Iraq war, which have proved disastrous in the long run.[54]

In the media too, overt criticism of the Israeli occupation of Palestine was considered taboo. But this trend is slowly changing. For example, in January 2009, CBS's *60 Minutes* ran a segment called 'Is peace out of reach?', which was highly critical of Israeli control and oppression of Palestinians. The reporter, Bob Simon, himself a Jew, was severely criticised by some Jewish members of his community. Similarly, the Palestinian activist Mustafa Barghouti and a Jewish American peace activist, Anna Baltzer, appeared on *The Daily Show with Jon Stewart* on 28 October 2009. Both Barghouti and Baltzer were critical of the Israeli occupation and spoke of the possibilities of peaceful co-existence in the region.[55] The documentary *Occupation 101* also included the voices of Jewish academics and human rights activists in Israel, who criticised Israel's heavy-handedness against the Palestinians, for example, Rabbi Arik Ascherman (Rabbis for Human Rights Jerusalem), Neta Golan (Israeli Peace Activists), Rabbi Rebecca Lillian (Jewish Peace Forum) and Professor Ilan Pappe (Israeli historian, Haifa University).[56]

No hope for Palestine

When I asked Kabeer (male, 16, US born, national identity: American Arab) about his visit to Palestine, he replied: 'That was three years ago. I visited with my family and it was not fun going through the border.' I then asked him, 'So do you think there's hope? One day Palestine will be an independent country?' Kabeer replied, 'No, I don't think so because I don't think there'll be any country due to the resources, like the fresh water that they have under Palestine and Israel, I don't think they're [Israel] willing to give that up' (interview, Michigan, April 2010).

'Thank God we live in America'

Two participants of Palestinian background appreciated that they lived in the United States, where there is freedom of speech and freedom of movement. For example, Murad (male, 17, US born, national identity: Muslim Palestinian American) commented:

> I have been to Palestine, many times. Just the feeling of being on lockdown that you're not used to in America because you're free, you can do whatever you want here. You have no one controlling where you go or what you do, besides your parents of course. But when you go there you've got to always have your passport on you, always checkpoints, anywhere you go, even entering the country they give you a hard time. (Interview, Florida, March 2010)

Sadiqah (female, 23, US born, national identity: Arab Muslim) said:

> Yes, I have been to Palestine many times. My father is from Hebron. Oh, it's very difficult, because I think growing up in the States, it's a very open society and you try to be politically correct all the time. When you go over there, there's just so much hatred on both sides and you feel torn because you don't like to hate anybody but when you see the injustice over there, it's really hard to keep yourself away from falling into that hating of the Israeli Zionists. It's very difficult. Very trying. (Interview, Florida, March 2010)

Murad had multiple identities but, because he appreciated living in the US, he leaned towards his American identity, whereas Sadiqah identified herself as Arab Muslim though she expressed her frustration over the identity politics of that region.[57]

Some optimism

Waleed (male, over 30, US born, national identity: Palestinian American) offered his views:

> Between the ages of ten to fifteen I lived in Palestine [in the early 1990s]. It was relatively quiet compared to these days and during that time I learned the language and the culture and the religion . . . At the age of ten I'd barely spoken any Arabic so my grandparents were upset at that so they convinced my parents to go back home, so I learned the language, the culture, the religion. I lived with my mom along with my siblings, while my dad continued working here.
>
> The village I lived in was all Palestinians; we had a couple of Jewish settlements surrounding our village and going to the actual city of Jerusalem we would pass through security checkpoints and we . . . we'd mingle with Jewish residents also. I spoke Hebrew . . . just a few phrases. English was a common language.
>
> The fact is I still relate to it and probably would even move there [Palestine] eventually in old age. (Interview, New York, November 2009)

Waleed has a positive image of Palestine from when he lived there at a much younger age. So he thinks he will to go back to Palestine in his old age. Nabil (male, 20, US born, national identity: Palestinian) also lived in Palestine in the 1990s and did not encounter much resistance from the Israelis:

> I lived right next to Nablus, a city in the West Bank. I lived there for about five years from '94 to '99. At the time I lived there it was pretty peaceful. It started picking up, like, we left when the second intifada was starting to take place. They had curfews where you can't leave the house after seven o'clock and stuff and a lot of people got into trouble because of that. Small things were like, if some trouble happens in the town people come and random people get arrested and stuff like that. And I had confrontation with Israelis where they'd push you around and stuff. Nothing ever too extreme, *alhamdulillah*. (Interview, Florida, March 2010)

Rehman (male, 15, US born, national identity: Arab American) also visited Palestine, when he was ten. He said, 'My visit was good fun. We visited Palestine, Jordan, Saudi Arabia and Iraq' (interview, Michigan, April 2010).

No comments

Seven Palestinian-background participants had no comments on the topic of Palestine. Most of them either had not visited Palestine, or had lived there at a very young age. For example, Abbas's grandparents settled in Jordan, his father was born in Jordan and Abbas was also born there. They have never been to Palestine and they moved to the USA in around 2005 (interview, New York, January 2010). Faeezah had been to Palestine only once, at the age of eight, so she did not remember much about it (interview, New York, January 2010). Haneef said, 'My father's Palestinian and my mother is Egyptian. I've never left the country [USA] actually' (interview, Florida, March 2010).

Conclusion

The Israeli–Palestinian issue is complex. Security is an issue for both Israel and Palestine. The Israelis' concern is mainly territorial security in their occupied land and the fact that they are such a minority in the region. So the Israeli authorities have toughened their border control and checkpoint scrutiny. It appears from the experiences of the interviewees that Israeli soldiers often go overboard with their security procedures, which the interviewees described as 'dehumanising'. Whereas most interviewees looked forward to visiting their extended families in Palestine, in spite of all the discomforts, a few felt discouraged about visiting Palestine or even keeping some sort of contact with Palestine (for example, some would not opt for a Palestinian ID card). Some participants were critical of the US government's blind support of Israel and Israel's continued aggression against the Palestinians. Finally, in this whole episode of Israel's aggression against Palestine, it is reassuring to see that some participants did not label all Jews as aggressors. And these participants appreciated those Jewish people who were advocating the rights of Palestinians.

Notes

1. 'Palestinian bid for statehood at UN a "distraction": U.S. President Barack Obama', Siam Daily News website, 14 September 2011, http://www.siamdaily news.com/world-breaking-news/2011/09/14/palestinian-bid-for-statehood-at-un-a-distraction-u-s-president-barack-obama/, accessed 24 May 2012.
2. Ibid.
3. 'How UNESCO countries voted on Palestinian membership', *Guardian* website, 1 November 2011, http://www.guardian.co.uk/world/2011/nov/01/unesco-coun tries-vote-palestinian-membership, accessed 29 May 2012.
4. 'Palestine recognized as the full member of UNESCO, Israel and US condemns', CNN News website, 1 November 2011, http://www.latestcnnnews.com/palestine-recognized-as-the-full-member-of-unesco-israel-and-us-condemns.html, accessed 24 May 2012.
5. Saree Makdisi, *Palestine Inside Out: An Everyday Occupation* (New York: W. W. Norton, 2008); George Bisharat, 'Israel and Palestine: a true one-state solution', *Washington Post*, 3 September 2010, p. A21; Cherien Dabis (dir.), *Amreeka* (National Geographic, 2009).

6. Kwame Anthony Appiah, 'The Politics of Identity', *Daedalus*, Fall 2006, pp. 15–22.

7. Richard Jenkins, *Social Identity*, 3rd edn (London: Routledge, 2008).

8. Edward Said, *Orientalism* (New York: Vintage, 1979).

9. Ibid., p. 335.

10. Abdallah Omeish and Sufyan Omeish (dirs), *Occupation 101: Voices of the Silent Majority* (Triple Eye Films, 2006).

11. *Occupation 101*; Makdisi, *Palestine Inside Out*.

12. Makdisi, *Palestine Inside Out*, pp. 106–7.

13. Tobias Kelly, *Law, Violence and Sovereignty among West Bank Palestinians* (Cambridge: Cambridge University Press, 2006); Leila Farkash, review of Kelly, *Law, Violence and Sovereignty among West Bank Palestinians*, *American Ethnologist* 35:3 (2008), pp. 3009–12.

14. Ibid.

15. *Occupation 101*.

16. Scott Wilson, 'Israeli court orders rerouting of barrier; decision backs Palestinian villagers', *Washington Post*, 5 September 2007, p. 16.

17. *Occupation 101*.

18. Ibid.

19. Ibid.

20. Makdisi, *Palestine Inside Out*, p. 102.

21. *Occupation 101*; Philip Weiss, 'Tutu: issue is the same in Palestine as it was in South Africa, "equality" ', Mondoweiss website, 11 April 2010, http://mondo-weiss.net/2010/04/tutu-issue-is-the-same-in-palestine-as-it-was-in-south-africa-equality.html, accessed 24 May 2012.

22. Makdisi, *Palestine Inside Out*, p. 280.

23 S. Sayyid, 'Mirror, Mirror: Western Democrats, Oriental Despots?' *Ethnicities* 5:1 (2005), pp. 30–50, see p. 39.

24. *Occupation 101*.

25. Ibid.

26 Ibid.

27 Paddy Allen, 'The Israeli attacks on Gaza', *Guardian* website, 19 January 2009, http://www.guardian.co.uk/world/interactive/2009/jan/03/israelandthepalestinians, accessed 24 May 2012.

28. 'No apology to Turkey: Netanyahu', World News Australia website, 28 December 2010, http://www.sbs.com.au/news/article/1453251/No-apology-to-Turkey:-Netanyahu, accessed 24 May 2012.

29. 'Attempted to enter at the Jordan River crossing on 12/16/07 and was turned away. Entered through the Allenby bridge on 12/17/07', Right to Enter website, http://www.righttoenter.ps/previous_cases.php?id=563, accessed 24 May 2012.

30. Ibid.

31. 'IDF kashers checkpoints, replacing Arabic with Hebrew names', Tikun Olam website, http://www.richardsilverstein.com/tikun_olam/2010/11/06/idf-kashers-checkpoints-with-hebrew-names/, accessed 24 May 2012.

32. Ibid.
33. '3 hour wait near Hawara checkpoint in Nablus, Palestine', Flickr website, 1 June 2006, http://www.flickr.com/photos/einkarem1948/3664604620/, accessed 24 May 2012.
34. Ibid.
35. Khaled Jarrar, 'At the checkpoint', *This Week in Palestine*, March 2007, p. 62.
36. Ibid.
37. UN-OCHA, *Israeli-Palestinian Fatalities since 2000: Key Trends* (New York: United Nations Office for the Coordination of Humanitarian Affairs, 2007).
38. Makdisi, *Palestine Inside Out*, p. 102.
39. Ibid.
40. Ibid. pp. 113–14.
41. Ibid. pp. 114–15.
42. 'Jordanian football violence leaves 250 hurt', SBS World News Australia website, 11 December 2011, http://www.sbs.com.au/news/article/1439581/Jordanian-football-violence-leaves-250-hurt, accessed 25 May 2012.
43. 'Jordanian, Palestinian soccer fans clash', Fox News website, 11 December 2010, http://www.foxnews.com/world/2010/12/11/jordanian-palestinian-soccer-fans-clash/, accessed 25 May 2012.
44 Ibid.
45. *Occupation 101*.
46. Chris Marsden, 'Israel and US walk out of UN Conference on Racism', World Socialist Web Site, 6 September 2001, http://www.wsws.org/articles/2001/sep2001/isr-s06.shtml, accessed 25 May 2012.
47. Abdus Sattar Ghazali, *Islam and Muslims in the post-9/11 America: A Source Book* (Modesto, CA: Eagle Enterprises, 2008), p. 36; see also Louise Cainkar, *Homeland Insecurity: The Arab American and Muslim American Experience after 9/11* (New York: Russell Sage Foundation, 2011), pp. 184–5.
48. Halim Rane, *Islam and Contemporary Civilisation: Evolving Ideas, Transforming Relations* (Melbourne: Melbourne University Publishing, 2010).
49. David R. Francis, 'US can raise the pressure on Israel without cutting aid', *Christian Science Monitor* website, 5 April 2010, http://www.csmonitor.com/Commentary/David-R.-Francis/2010/0405/US-can-raise-the-pressure-on-Israel-without-cutting-aid, accessed 25 May 2012.
50. 'Obama budget includes $3 billion in Israel aid', Near East Report website, 23 February 2010, http://www.aipac.org/NearEastReport/20100223/obama_budget_includes_three_bil_israel_aid.html, accessed 25 May 2012.
51. Michael Jansen, 'Obama's popularity plunges in Arab world,' *Irish Times*, 7 August 2010, p. 11.
52. Sara Roy, 'Reflection on the Israeli–Palestinian Conflict in U.S. Public Discourse: Legitimizing Dissent', *Journal of Palestinian Studies* 39:2 (2010), pp. 23–38.
53. Ibid. p. 27.
54. Ibid.

55. Ibid. 28–9.

56. *Occupation 101*; see also John L. Esposito, *The Future of Islam* (New York: Oxford University Press, 2010), p. 85.

57. See also Leila Farsakh, 'Exiles and Home,' *Human Architecture* 6:2 (2008), pp. 79–90. Leila Farsakh wrote about her feelings for Palestine while living in exile.

CHAPTER

7

FROM HERE TO WHERE?

In this study 379 young American Muslims from Massachusetts, New York, Virginia, Maryland, Florida and Michigan defined their identities variously, ranging from single to dual or multiple identities. The interviewees were mostly second-generation 15–30-year-old Muslims. In the process of investigating their identity/identities, I came to realise that the participants framed their identities according to several contexts, such as culture, media and politics. In my research, I was also keen to find out if they were involved in leisure activities, such as music and sport, and the extent to which they had retained their parents' culture and adopted American cultures. I begin with a brief summary of all the chapters, then I discuss the areas that needs to be discussed in both the Muslim community and the wider society. These areas also need the attention of policy makers so they can take necessary action to develop a cohesive society. Finally I discuss the topic of harmony or social cohesion, which is important for American society.

Brief summary of chapters

In Chapter 1, I noted that Muslim contact with the United States began in the eighteenth century when slaves were brought from Africa. Later, in the late nineteenth century, Muslims began to migrate to the United States in small numbers from Arab countries. Muslim numbers expanded in the twentieth and twenty-first centuries, to the point when they reached almost 1 per cent of the population in 2011. I also outlined how different developments in the Islamic world (for example, the Iranian hostage crisis) have impacted on America, culminating tragically with the 9/11 Twin Towers attacks, and the 'othering' of Muslims generally. In Chapter 1, I also introduced social identity theory and how different categories (emotions, stereotypes and so on) impact on one's identity. I also described the research method of this study.

In Chapter 2, I examined the cultural influences and expectations on young Muslims and how they shaped their identity. I also analysed the economic situation of the participants in this study. In Chapter 3, I focused on the various identities of the respondents, such as single, dual/hyphenated and multiple identities, including how identities are formed, and the reasons behind their formation. In Chapter 3, I also examined the respondents' interest in sport, and found that sport can impact on identity, and lead to social inclusion and healing. It can also help in the development of self-esteem of young Muslims. In this chapter, I introduced the concept of biculturalism and argued that it should be considered an aspect of cultural capital rather than a deficit.

Chapter 4 brought up the media debate. Most respondents (all but twenty-five) had raised this topic in their interview. I retrieved some print media data to check the validity of the participants' views. In Chapter 5, I discussed President Barack Hussein Obama. It was interesting to see how the respondents in this study regarded the president. Only about 8 per cent (about thirty-one) of the respondents were critical of him. I believe that the respondents' unsolicited views on the media and politics were important in examining the identity of young people. Finally in Chapter 6, I analysed the perceptions of the participants of Palestinian background about their country of origin. Their views on the 'Palestinian question' were unsolicited. The respondents raised the issue when they spoke about the media or President Obama's foreign policy.

Throughout this book, I have reflected on the various factors that seemed to impact on the participants' identity: upbringing, education, heritage, length of residence in the host country, emotions, acceptance and recognition, and distribution of power and resources. I now discuss some of the issues that need to be raised in both the Muslim community and the wider society to improve the condition of some Muslims. The relevant US state departments and policy makers should also pay attention to the following areas to develop a cohesive society.

Areas that need attention

Muslim women

The United States was appreciated by most participants both for its diversity and for the promotion of a 'melting pot' society, yet it appears from the interviews that there is pressure on immigrants to 'fit in' with this wider society. For example, in this study I found that several young women who wear the *hijab* had pierced their lips to become part of the youth subculture. Yet they said that the US media still targeted them as the 'other'. Perhaps their Islamic visibility (their *hijab*) contributed to them being marked as the 'other'.

Some university-educated women who wore the *hijab* speculated that they had been discriminated against in the labour market because of their Islamic visibility. Other research has found that Muslim women are frequently either ridiculed or discriminated against because of their ethnicity and religion.[1] An employee can bring a lawsuit against her employer for infringement of her First Amendment rights. There have indeed been cases in the US where Muslim women have sued their employers for religious discrimination but failed to win their cases.[2]

In the absence of US official census data on the basis of religion, it was not possible to evaluate American Muslims' labour market status, but through my research data I found that 70 per cent of the mothers of young participants (aged fifteen to thirty) were 'stay-at-home mums'. It appears some of the mothers chose to stay at home for home duties, but there is also a possibility that their educational levels were low, or their English language skills were insufficient, so they were unable to work. In this study, Aysegül, of Turkish background (female, 15, US born, national identity: 'Turkish 100 per cent'), said that she wanted to pursue a career but pointed out that in her family women's higher education was not a priority (interview, New York, February 2010).

Within the Muslim community, women also face cultural restrictions such as, for example, arranged marriages. In some cases, these marriages are successful, whereas in other cases they end up in a divorce. In any event it is very important that the Muslim community prioritises women's education. This would empower women in times of crisis – for example, when it is necessary to seek employment to support the family. Also, a mother's education is crucial for the early education and upbringing of her children. It would set a good example to her children if she pursued higher education. From my personal observations, I have found that in some parts of the world Muslim women are not encouraged by their family members to pursue higher education. The discouragement sometimes comes from women's mothers, who are keen to have their daughters married, and sometimes from a lack of interest by married women in pursuing further education. So the barrier is not always imposed by the male members of the family.

Economy

The norm in the Muslim community is that men are the breadwinners. It is likely that Muslim men also experience high levels of unemployment in the US. For example, in 2010, the overall unemployment rate in the state of Michigan was 15 per cent, and it is likely that Muslim unemployment in that state would be much higher. In August 2011, the national unemployment rate in the US was 9 per cent.[3] In the UK and Australia in 2006 the unemployment rate of Muslims was three times higher than the national average,[4] so it is likely that under the economic downturn in the US, Muslims' unemployment rate would be much higher.

The sociologist Saskia Sassen observed that since the 1980s the crisis of inequality has become acute, especially in global cities such as New York. She wrote, 'A growing share of households and firms have seen their incomes and profits rise sharply, and a growing share of others have seen their incomes and profits fall'.[5] Since 2006 the US has seen rapid home foreclosures among low- and modest-income households under certain newly introduced mortgages, and Sassen predicted that foreclosures were expected to reach their highest point from 2010 to 2011.[6] In my interviews with the participants in this study the topic of home foreclosures did not arise, yet when I visited a friend's place in Florida, I was told that many people (mostly non-Muslims) in their neighbourhood could not manage their mortgage repayments and just abandoned their homes. In my study, however, the most affected people appeared to be recent university graduates. Some of my interviewees (both male and female new university graduates) expressed their concern about the uncertain labour market.

Muslim youth

In this book, I have discussed some of the cultural constraints young people face. Within the Muslim community, there is constant pressure from their peers for young people to remain within their cultural boundaries. The urge to remain within one's culture, be it ethnic, racial or religious, was not confined only to immigrant families, as it was also prevalent among some African American Muslim families. In this study, however, I found that the practices of homeschooling and of sending children back to their 'home' countries for a few years were prevalent among immigrant Muslim communities.

The second-generation immigrant youths, particularly those who were newly arrived, were sometimes disadvantaged by the migratory move. For example, some parents with low-level English-language skills who were seeking employment relied on their children to help them as interpreters, while at the same time the children struggled to cope with language and social adjustment in their new school environment. I also found that sometimes young people were not happy with their parents' decisions about their career choice as reflected in their secondary school subjects. A few boys had received scholarships in technical institutions but their parents preferred them to study more academic subjects, or if they had been accepted in an elite-level sport programme their parents did not allow them to take up the offer because they, the parents, feared that their culture would be lost.

In some cases, men had been persuaded to get married young (for example while still teenagers) for cultural reasons, and in some cases they were expected to go back to the home country and get married because their parents were ill and required help. A few male high school students were involved in drugs and gang cultures. But most of my participants appeared to be focused on their studies and pursuing a career.

Biculturalism

Biculturalism is generally represented as 'comfort and proficiency with both one's heritage culture and the culture of the country or region in which one has settled'.[7] It is applicable to immigrants who have moved to a new country and to their children who were either born or raised in the receiving host country. Young people usually acquire bicultural skills by first living within their parents' ethnic culture, and being exposed to language, values and beliefs from their parents' culture. Then, with their exposure to the wider society's culture, young people grasp the receiving/mainstream culture, for example English-language skills.

First-generation immigrants develop bicultural skills gradually as they settle in their receiving/host country. Research in the United States has found that if schools introduce a bilingual programme, for example Spanish for Latino children, and involve the parents in classroom interaction, then their children will do better in school.[8] Educational psychologist Jim Cummins observed, '[Minority] students who are empowered by their school experiences develop ability, confidence, and motivation to succeed academically.'[9]

Seth Schwartz and Jennifer Unger observed that in some places in the United States where monoculturalism is very strong, such as in the Midwest, exhibiting one's bicultural skills may be very difficult because of the threat of perceived discrimination. Yet if immigrants decide to display their 'ethnic pride' it will 'eventually help monocultural communities to adjust to the presence of immigrants'.[10] In this context, I would argue that in a monocultural workplace there might be opposition to biculturalism. For example, firstly, a person with a minority bicultural identity (for example, a Muslim name) may not be selected into the workforce. Secondly, if they do obtain work, they may be subjected to tremendous pressure to abide by the monocultural 'rules'. In these instances, policy makers can provide incentives or should introduce a quota for the recruitment of ethnic people. On the other hand, affirmative action on the basis of gender or ethnicity is likely to meet with political contestation, especially in the private sector. Schwartz and Unger noted that in a country where there are nationally sanctioned laws, such as in France, where Muslim headscarves are banned in public schools, then 'such a hostile political climate may decrease the advantages of biculturalism and may increase the advantages of assimilating and blending in'.[11]

Overall, in my previous studies on young Australian and British Muslim people, I found that most participants had acquired bicultural skills. For example, they spoke their ethnic language, some of them practised their religion, they appreciated their parental culture in terms of food and ceremonies/ festivals, and at the same time they had adapted to the mainstream culture, such as speaking English, enjoying mainstream sports, reading books and listening to music. Of course, this varied across populations but, paradoxically, the more receptive the host society was to multicultural difference the more inclined the immigrants were to integrate and even assimilate.

In this study too, I found that young American Muslims were bicultural to a degree. As Cummins observed (and I also found), bicultural skills empower young people of immigrant backgrounds. Throughout the interviews, the participants were very aware of the current events concerning Muslims in the United States and globally, and quite confident and articulate in expressing their opinions.

Music

It is a popular misconception that music is forbidden in Islam. Ultra-orthodox groups have widely publicised this idea through incidents such as the Taliban burning instruments and audiotapes in Afghanistan in 2000, so that music has become somewhat controversial in Islamic discourse. On the other hand, Sufis believe that through music one can enhance communion with the divine. And Muslim societies have also produced great artists such as the Pakistani singer Nusrat Fateh Ali Khan and the Egyptian singer Umm Kulthum. Indeed the recitation of the Quran can be very melodic, so it is impossible to reconcile the argument that music is banned in Islam.[12]

Yet the notion remains ambiguous. The British pop singer Yusuf Islam, formerly known as Cat Stevens, stopped performing publicly shortly after his conversion to Islam in 1977. He resumed his singing career some twenty-two years later, when his son bought him a guitar. Islam said, 'A lot of my songs reflected something much more than frivolous. They contained deeper spiritual meanings.'[13] There is another group of Muslim rappers, whose songs (for example, *nasheeds*) provide a spiritual reflection to their young audiences.[14]

Richard Turner's study of African American Muslim converts showed a positive connection with hip-hop music in this group.[15] Turner observed that the hip-hop culture that began in the 1970s among African American, Latino and Caribbean youth in the Bronx in New York has also become a subculture among African American Muslim converts. Hip-hop music expresses resistance to 'post-industrial conditions' that have resulted in high unemployment and poor housing and support systems, conditions that are predominant in working-class and African American communities. Turner notes that the marginalisation of African Americans has continued in the 1980s, 1990s and into the twenty-first century.[16] With the rise of a 'new prison-industrial complex' about one-third of all African American men in their twenties were incarcerated. Under these circumstances, rap music was employed as a protest against mainstream American practices aimed at the black population such as racial profiling, a new underground economy generated by widespread drug addiction, youth deaths from police brutality and torture, AIDS and new assaults on affirmative action. Therefore, the music, poetry, style, clothing, language and life experiences of hip-hop artists have also impacted on African American Muslims. Then, with the advent of racial profiling after 9/11, African American Muslims were doubly disadvantaged because they were both 'black' and 'Muslim'. Some young African American Muslims found that rap music was more than just an 'oppositional subcultural music' of resistance and pleasure. Turner wrote, 'Hip-hop culture also serves as a powerful medium to the ultimate spiritual and political concerns in their lives and their identities are paradigms for global Muslim youth.'[17]

Media

In this study, most participants were conscious and critical of the US media representation of Islam/Muslims, and many gave examples of one-sided news reporting by some media. A few also believed that the media was motivated by profit: with more sensational news headlines, more people would buy newspapers. Many participants noted that media ownership rests with a few wealthy individuals such as News International's Rupert Murdoch. In the absence of any other competitor, the media giants know how to obtain maximum profit through their publications (through the headlines and images).

Some participants were also aware that sometimes politicians align with the media to promote their own agendas for political gain.[18] Since 9/11, news of the 'Muslim other' has become both lucrative and persuasive, with negative Muslim news reports selling more copies and swaying voters.[19] Sociologist Tahir Abbas observed that with the advent of social media such as YouTube, Facebook, Twitter and internet blogging it has become 'more difficult for Muslims to compete for effective representation on the global stage'.[20]

In the American context, Jack Shaheen observed that in the electronic media (television and cinemas) Arabs and Muslim Americans have been profiled as potential security threats and portrayed as people who lose their jobs or who are detained and rounded up. Shaheen said, 'It illustrates the power of film.' It transforms the image into a 'mythology':

> The mythology is still a part of our psychic stereotype [which will] take a long time to wither away. And for many of us, we're comfortable with our prejudices. We don't want to change. We have grown accustomed to this face [to the sight of Muslims/Arabs yelling].[21]

Sonia, a participant in this study and a film producer, of Egyptian origin (female, 25, US born, national identity: Muslim), commented:

The media is not going to change until Muslims are in the media. Until the president of, like, CNN has a Muslim who is working for them and understands and empathises with what's going on and understands what's happening, then they will show that side. But for them, you know, it is all political . . . No media is *for* the Muslims. (Interview, Florida, March 2010)

Yet Razzak, of Bangladeshi background (male, 18, overseas born, national identity: 'more Bangladeshi') was critical of Muslims' 'over-sensitiveness' on media issues. Razzak commented on the controversial *South Park* animated television show. In one of its episodes, the image of Prophet Muhammad (PBUH) appeared in disguise in a bear suit. Razzak commented:

They censored it out and they wouldn't even say his name, but I don't really feel good about that because that's our Prophet right there and if you can have Jesus or some other guy on there – well, I am not saying that Jesus [PBUH] is not our Prophet; he was a messenger in our religion – but if you can say his name and stuff, why can't you say our Prophet's name? (Interview, Michigan, May 2010)

I took Razzak's comment to mean that it is time that Muslims accepted satire just as Christians accept satire involving Prophet Jesus (PBUH). Considering the Prophet Muhammad (PBUH) cartoon controversy in Denmark, Fariha, of American-Palestinian background (female, 16, US born, national identity: 'mostly American') recommended silent protest. She said that in the first instance she thought that the cartoon of Prophet Muhammad (PBUH) 'putting a bomb on his head . . . looked like a stereotypical Arab guy'. Fariha quoted her father on how to deal with such a situation in a non-violent manner:

My dad told me . . . all the Danish items that we were [going to buy], stop buying now, and I think since then everyone has been treating it like it was the right thing to do. Not just as though it was freedom of speech, but it was the right thing to do . . . And I mean the newspaper that got them published in, it was a notorious right-wing newspaper. (Interview, Michigan, April 2010)

Harmony: can it be achieved?

When I asked Rehman, of Palestinian origin (male, 16, US born, national identity: Arab American), 'What could Muslims do to establish harmony with the wider society to show that we are good people?' he replied, 'I think we should get more involved in stuff in communities, cities and states; I mean that's pretty much it' (interview, Michigan, April 2010). Daliya, of west African origin (female, 15, US born, national identity: African Muslim), said:

I think maybe they should have open houses, get people interested, show people, show them a different side to Muslims, like not all Muslims are terrorists. That's what people just don't understand. If someone sees you, automatically they just think you're a terrorist, or they just want to get away from you.

So I think they should show people that Muslims are totally different from that, opposite from terrorists, and stuff like that. And I think they should get out in the community, have events and stuff. And then I guess they can get some people interested in Islam. (Interview, Michigan, May 2010)

Nabil, of Palestinian background (male, 20, US born, national identity: Muslim Palestinian), suggested that tension should be absorbed with humour:

I worked in my dad's gas station for, like, ever since I was young. I would go help him out and you had a lot of people, you know, when they were sober they seemed like they were cool and everything but when they get drunk their real side comes out and they start being, you know, belligerent, very rude and everything. And you'd have to get in a couple of fights every now and then just to defend your points . . .

My dad was more of being really smart about it. We had one guy come in and he was like, 'Go back to your country.' My dad said, 'If it wasn't for me, Christopher Columbus would have missed the country. I'm the one that pointed it out.' And the guy was so confused he just left, he didn't know what to say. (Interview, Florida, March 2010)

Azra, of Bangladeshi background (female, 15, overseas born, national identity: Bangladeshi American), observed that not only were Muslims marginalised, Jewish people were also viewed as the 'other':

My brother, he was watching something on YouTube and which was also on the news. This Jewish guy came and all he said to these people was 'Happy Hanukkah'. And these other people, they're not Muslim, they were something else, they got mad for some reason and they were beating that guy up . . . It was by the train station. This guy gets out from the train, he's a Muslim and he sees that guy . . . And that [Muslim] guy he came and he said, 'Stop fighting.' And then he even got beaten up for it. (Interview, Michigan, May 2010)

I also viewed this particular episode on YouTube.[22] On a Friday night in December 2007 around 11.30 Walter Adler and his friends were returning from a Hanukkah party on the New York City Subway. Adler wished the passengers on the Q train 'Happy Hanukkah'. Immediately, three people attacked him, punched him and left him and his friends with black eyes. As they hit him, they said, 'You killed him. You killed Jesus. You killed him on Hanukkah. You dirty Jew. You f***ing Jew.' Immediately, a Bangladeshi Muslim, Hassan Askari, who was travelling on the same train, came to their rescue, and fought off the attackers. He was also left with a black eye. Adler said that it was a Muslim, who is always painted in the media 'as an enemy of Israel and the

Jew', who saved the Jews. The police later arrested ten men involved in the attack. So the incident revealed the anti-Semitism that prevails in the US.

The story illustrates that there is conflict at the political level (over the Israeli–Palestinian issue) but at the local level Jews and Muslims are helping each other. Arguably, there is also a need for Muslims in the US to be more outgoing in addressing the issues impacting on them as a community. Muslim leader Zahed Omar, of African American background, commented:

> We as a community, we tend to ghettoise our issues. For example, we seem to only be concerned primarily about what goes on in Palestine or having a myopic view just on issues of discrimination about *hijab* or racial profiling. We have to learn how we can help empower ourselves and address our human and civil rights.
>
> Of the external challenges, since 9/11 many Muslims have gotten to be not only timid about donating to the Islamic charities, but even timid to donate to other major national organisations, down to even being timid donating to their own mosque. So this is an external challenge that we've been dealing with in terms of what we feel as targeting the Muslim community by the Department of Treasury as well as the Federal Bureau of Investigation. It's been a serious challenge on an institutional level. (Interview, Michigan, May 2010)

Omar emphasised civic participation and suggested that voters should engage with their local congressman or governor through email, or by attending public meetings, and make their concerns known to them. He also pointed out that some donors were concerned that they might become a target of FBI surveillance.

Isn't harmony a two-way street?

So far I have discussed the opinions of Muslims on how to live in harmony with the wider society. But there are certain issues within the wider society that need to be addressed. For example, in 2010 the anti-Muslim rhetoric of Pat Robertson, Jerry Falwell, Saxby Chambliss and Franklin Graham against the proposed Islamic centre at Park51 in New York revealed the rapid rise of the Tea Party movement in the USA.[23] And in March 2011, the incident in Gainesville, Florida where Pastor Terry Jones (not associated with the Tea Party) burned the Quran was not helpful.

Also in March 2011, Peter King, the chairman of the House Homeland Security Committee (a Republican from Long Island in his tenth term) held his first session of congressional inquiry to investigate 'self-radicalisation going on within the Muslim community'. King alleged that Muslim Americans have failed to demonstrate 'sufficient cooperation' with law enforcement bodies in uncovering terrorist plots.[24] King characterised American Muslims as one Muslim monolithic group who were not doing enough for the security of the

United States. His critics said that, in this exercise, King ignored the presence of mainstream American Muslims who were also concerned about the Islamists' acts. Critics also observed that a recent report from Duke University and the University of North Carolina found that it was fellow Muslims who had turned in 48 of the 120 Muslims suspected of plotting domestic terrorist attacks since 11 September 2001, but King appeared to ignore this datum.[25] King was also opposed to the proposed plan for the Islamic centre near Ground Zero.[26]

During the hearing, King singled out CAIR as the 'other'. Yet a representative of CAIR submitted thirty pages of written testimony revealing that they had repeatedly condemned terrorist attacks in the United States and Israel. It would seem that singling out CAIR was a political action. One of the participants in my study (also a government employee) commented that one year earlier a powerful Jewish group exerted their influence on a project he was carrying out in collaboration with CAIR:

> A group called Americans against Hate. It's actually led by a Jewish group . . . I get these callers from America against Hate trying to rustle up an argument about an assignment at work, so it's very stressful for me right now dealing with that, but you know, I'm on the basis of, it's freedom of speech in America. Until you're proven guilty you're innocent . . . but there are certain things that this group is putting out that CAIR is related to Hamas. (Interview, May 2010)

From a comment of another interviewee, who was also involved with CAIR, I gathered that there is a general consensus among some American Muslims that being critical of US foreign policy is not safe. For example Yusef said:

> I think [CAIR is] a strong organisation that talks about Palestine. That scares the hell out of people because they're telling Muslims to get engaged . . . If Iraq and Palestine matters to them, they should go to their congressperson, they should talk about it. Because any criticism we make of Jews, I think, is really, there shouldn't be any criticism of Jews and, like, 'Oh, they're [the Jewish lobby group] so effective and so powerful'. (Interview, Florida, March 2010)

As discussed earlier, there are some Jewish people who are sympathetic to the Palestinian cause. For example, the Jewish professor Noam Chomsky, who was awarded the Sydney Peace Prize in Australia in November 2011, has been a critic of American foreign policy. It is surprising that the United States has failed to recognise his contribution towards peace. On 31 October 2011, when a large majority of UNESCO delegates voted in favour of Palestine's bid for membership (107 voted for and 14 voted against while 52 abstained), the US government, which provides 22 per cent of UNESCO's budget, decided to cut off all its funding.[27] Such overt partiality by the United States does not help promote world peace.

On 5 August 2012, Wade Michael Page, age 40, a US army veteran (he served in the army for six years until 1998), shot dead six people and injured three more in a *gurdwara* (Sikh temple) in Oak Creek, Wisconsin. Officials in Wisconsin identified the shooting as a possible act of 'domestic terrorism', but many people in the Sikh community suspected that the attack was a hate crime, and the most violent crime against Muslims and Sikhs since 11 September 2001.[28] Sikhs have sometimes been mistaken for Muslims because of their appearance (turban and beard).

It was reported that Wade Michael Page was involved in neo-Nazi groups, and was well-known for the white supremacist music that he produced in a band called End Apathy. On his arm he had a tattoo of a Celtic cross marked with the number 14. The number is a code for a 14-word slogan, 'We must secure the existence of our people and [a] future of white children'.[29] Some witnesses observed that Page also had a '9/11' tattoo on his arm.[30]

Critics said that the United States should implement laws that prevent people having easy access to guns. There have been several tragedies based on the availability of guns, for example, the Virginia Tech (April 2007) and Arizona (January 2011) shooting incidents (discussed in Chapter 4). Critics also speculated that it is an election year, so President Barack Hussein Obama would not speak out about gun control in apprehension that the powerful gun lobby might retaliate against him.[31] One editorial commented:

> Once again, Americans must ask themselves: Is there something about our culture that is causing the isolation and rage behind these mass killings? We do know this: guns may not be the source of this sickness, but once again, they have magnified its lethality.[32]

I believe harmony is a two-way street. US Homeland Security officials can sometimes go overboard with racial profiling of visible minorities (discussed in Chapter 3). It is time for them to start being vigilant about the rise of white supremacists. The constant representation of the 'Muslim other' in some media has not been helpful.

To sum up

Throughout this book, and especially in Chapter 3, I have discussed the dynamics of young American Muslims' identity/identities. I tried to find the basis of their identity construction. In some cases, their identities appeared to be natural; for example, when they said they were American Muslims or just Muslims or just Americans, they felt connected to those particular groups. In some cases, their definition of identity was spontaneous, that is they said what they felt on the spur of the moment. Other times, they negotiated their identity depending on the circumstances they encountered. But in times of crisis, their identity would crystallise; for example, an Iranian American would feel very Iranian if she felt her ethnicity was under attack. Sometimes an Arab American's identity would polarise, for example, because of repercussions they faced after the 9/11 attacks.

In this chapter, I have put particular emphasis on these issues: the status of women, economy, youth, biculturalism, music, media and harmony. I have taken the position that it is important for minorities (such as Muslims) to feel connected to their host countries, and argued that this is possible only when people are economically solvent, feel accepted in society and also learn to be a part of mainstream society. Young Muslim Americans need support from their own community and the wider community and, unless they feel accepted and recognised by both sectors, their identity will be in a state of flux and they may feel insecure in American society. I believe that a policy of biculturalism needs to be adopted by all concerned. It offers young people from any background the best prospect for negotiating a viable identity in a rapidly changing American society.

This study has been an exploration of the identity of young American Muslims. The questions I prepared for the participants were semi-structured, allowing room for them to express their naturally occurring concerns, and some themes were not solicited by the questions. For example, an unexpected outcome of this study was the Palestinian question. When I asked questions about the media or President Obama, some participants, while critiquing the media or US foreign policy, raised the question of Palestine.

Overall, most young people were surprisingly vigilant and concerned about global politics, such as the Israeli–Palestinian conflict and the US involvement in Iraq and Afghanistan. They were enthusiastic about the election of the first black American president, Barack Hussein Obama, but a few were also disappointed with him and considered that he was just like any other US president who did not bring the 'change' that he had promised before he was elected.

The study also revealed an impressive degree of maturity and fair-mindedness in the participants. Conscious of the injustice of the media and American foreign policy, the young American Muslims tried hard to be even-handed in their criticism. I am not able to compare their outlook with mainstream American youths but the participants were remarkably aware of international issues, sometimes from the vantage point of the Muslim diaspora in the sense that they were 'on the edge', conscious of the stigma driven unjustifiably by the media and some politicians, and therefore of their minority status.

The participants also spoke about cultural issues, mindful of the restrictions placed upon them by both cultures. But their acquisition of bicultural skills will surely stand them in good stead in an uncertain world. In spite of eruptions of anti-Islamic sentiment from time to time, these young participants have acquired an optimistic view of America and beyond, which augurs well for them and society at large.

Notes

1. Yvonne Yazbeck Haddad, Jane I. Smith and Kathleen M. Moore, *Muslim Women in America: The Challenges of Islamic Identity Today* (New York: Oxford University Press, 2006), pp. 107–10.

2. Ibid. pp. 109–10.

3. US Bureau of Labor Statistics, 'Unemployment rate', http://www.google.com.au/publicdata/explore?ds=z1ebjpgk2654c1_&met_y=unemployment_rate&tdim=true&fdim_y=seasonality:S&dl=en&hl=en&q=unemployment+rate+in+the+us, accessed 25 May 2012.

4. Erich Kolig and Nahid A. Kabir, 'Not Friend, Not Foe: The Rocky Road of Enfranchisement of Muslims into Multicultural Nationhood in Australia and New Zealand', *Immigrants and Minorities* 26:3 (2008), pp. 266–300; Nahid Afrose Kabir, *Young British Muslims: Identity, Culture, Politics and the Media* (Edinburgh: Edinburgh University Press, 2010).

5. Saskia Sassen, 'Challenges facing global cities in the 21st century', *Asahi Shimbun*, http://www.columbia.edu/~sjs2/PDFs/Asahi.pdf, accessed 25 May 2012.

6. Saskia Sassen, 'Mortgage Capital and Its Particularities: A New Frontier for Global Finance', *Journal of International Affairs* 62:1 (2008), pp. 180–212, see p. 188.

7. Seth J. Schwartz and Jennifer B. Unger, 'Biculturalism and Context: What Is Biculturalism, and When Is It Adaptive? Commentary on Mistry and Wu', *Human Development* 53:1 (2010), pp. 26–32, see p. 26.

8. Jim Cummins, 'Empowering Minority Students: A Framework for Intervention', *Harvard Educational Review*, 71:4 (2001), pp. 656–75.

9. Ibid. p. 661.

10. Schwartz and Unger, 'Biculturalism and Context', p. 30.

11. Ibid. p. 30.

12. Katherine Butler Brown, 'The Problem with Parables', in S. Sayyid and AbdoolKarim Vakil (eds), *Thinking through Islamophobia: Global Perspectives* (New York: Columbia University Press, 2010), pp. 45–50, see pp. 46–7.

13. 'The Cat's comeback: from rock star to Muslim devotee to a melding of the two, Yusuf Islam, formerly known as Cat Stevens, assures his fans: "I didn't change, I just developed"', *Globe and Mail* (Toronto), 22 May 2000, p. R1.

14. See 'Muslim rappers reflect on Ramadan', *Patriot-News* (Harrisburg, PA), 1 November 2002, p. E05.

15. Richard Brent Turner, 'Constructing Masculinity: Interactions between Islam and African-American Youth since C. Eric Lincoln, *The Black Muslims in America*', *Souls* 8:4 (2006), pp. 31–44.

16. Ibid. pp. 33–40.

17. Ibid. p. 41.

18. See also Tahir Abbas, *Islamic Radicalism and Multicultural Politics: The British Experience* (London: Routledge, 2011), pp. 87–8.

19. Kabir, *Young British Muslims*, pp. 112–42.

20. Abbas, *Islamic Radicalism and Multicultural Politics*, p. 88.

21 Jeremy Earp and Sut Jhally (dirs), *Reel Bad Arabs: How Hollywood Vilifies a People*, DVD (Northampton, MA: Media Education Foundation, 2006).

22. 'Hero Muslim saves Jew from Christian thugs on NY subway', YouTube, 13 December 2007, https://www.youtube.com/watch?v=Xlwc0mE0lCU&feature=player_embedded, accessed 25 May 2012.

23. 'Is America Islamophobic?', *Time*, 30 August 2010.

24. Eugene Robinson, 'Aiding the jihadists', *Washington Post*, 8 March 2011, p. 15.

25. Robert Kolker, 'Peter King's Muslim problem', States News Service, 6 March 2011, http://www.highbeam.com/doc/1G1-250817157.html, accessed 25 May 2012.

26. 'Peter King', *New York Times* website, 11 March 2011, http://topics.nytimes.com/topics/reference/timestopics/people/k/peter_t_king/index.html, accessed 25 May 2012.

27. Scott Bobb, 'UNESCO grants Palestinians full membership', Voice of America website, 31 October 2011, http://www.voanews.com/english/news/UNESCO-Grants-Palestine-Full-Membership-132913673.html, accessed 25 May 2012.

28. Will Pavia, 'Sikh massacre gunman "led white power band" – United States', *Times* (London), 7 August 2012, p. 26.

29. Ravinder Kaur, 'Sharing the same difference', *Hindu* (Chennai, India), 13 August 2012.

30. Ibid.

31. Seema Sirohi, 'Easy access to guns and US paranoia since 9/11 led to the killing of Sikhs in Wisconsin', *Economic Times* (Bombay, India), 10 August 2012. See also, 'Letters to the Editor', *Hindu* (Chennai, India), 9 August 2012.

32. Editorial, 'Definite hate', *San Francisco Chronicle* (CA), 7 August 2012, p. A 9.

SELECT BIBLIOGRAPHY

Abbas, Tahir, *Islamic Radicalism and Multicultural Politics: The British Experience* (London: Routledge, 2011).

Ahmad, Fauzia, 'The Scandal of "Arranged Marriages" and the Pathologisation of BrAsian Families', in N. Ali, V. S. Karla and S. Sayyid (eds), *A Postcolonial People: South Asians in Britain* (New York: Columbia University Press, 2008), pp. 272–90.

Appiah, Kwame Anthony, *The Ethics of Identity* (Princeton, NJ: Princeton University Press, 2005).

Bagby, Ishan, Paul M. Perl and Bryan T. Froehle, *The Mosque in America: A National Portrait – A Report from the Mosque Study Project* (Washington, DC: Council on American–Islamic Relations, 2001).

Baha, Abu-Laban, 'The Canadian Muslim Community: The Need for a New Survival Strategy', in Earle H. Waugh, Baha Abu-Laban and Regula B. Qureishi (eds), *The Muslim Community in North America* (Edmonton: University of Alberta Press, 1983), pp. 75–92.

Bhabha, Homi, *The Location of Culture* (London: Routledge, 1994).

Brah, Avtar, 'Non-binarized Identities of Similarity and Difference', in Margaret Wetherell, Michelynn Laflèche and Robert Berkeley (eds), *Identity, Ethnic Diversity and Community Cohesion* (London: Sage, 2007), pp. 136–45.

Burke, Peter J. and Jan E. Stets, *Identity Theory* (Oxford: Oxford University Press, 2009).

Cainkar, Louise, *Homeland Insecurity: The Arab American and Muslim American Experience after 9/11* (New York: Russell Sage Foundation, 2011).

Esposito, John L., *The Future of Islam* (New York: Oxford University Press, 2010).

Falk, Gerhard, *Football and American Identity* (New York: Haworth Press, 2005).

Farooq, Samaya and Andrew Parker, 'Sport, Religion and Social Identity: Physical Education and Muslim Independent Schooling', in John Harris and Andrew Parker (eds), *Sport and Social Identities* (Basingstoke: Palgrave Macmillan, 2009), pp. 109–31.

Gaskew, Tony, *Policing American Muslim Communities: A Compendium of Post 9/11 Interviews* (Lewiston, NY: Edwin Mellen Press, 2008).

Germain, Elsa R., 'Culture or Race? Phenotype and Cultural Identity Development in Minority Australian Adolescents', *Australian Psychologist* 39:2 (2004), pp. 134–42.

Haddad, Yvonne Yazbeck, 'American Foreign Policy in the Middle East and Its Impact on the Identity of Arab Muslims in the United States', in Yvonne Yazbeck Haddad (ed.), *The Muslims of America* (New York: Oxford University Press, 1991), pp. 217–35.

Haddad, Yvonne Yazbeck, Jane I. Smith and Kathleen M. Moore, *Muslim Women in America: The Challenges of Islamic Identity Today* (New York: Oxford University Press, 2006).

Hall, Stuart, 'Introduction: Who Needs "Identity"?', in Stuart Hall and Paul du Gay (eds), *Questions of Cultural Identity* (London: Sage, 1996), pp. 1–17.

Ismael, Jacqueline S. and Tareq Y. Ismael, 'The Arab Americans and the Middle East', *Middle East Journal* 30:3 (1976), pp. 390–405.

Jenkins, Richard, *Social Identity*, 3rd edn (London: Routledge, 2008).

Kabir, Nahid Afrose, 'Are Young Muslims Adopting Australian Values?', *Australian Journal of Education* 52:3 (2008), pp. 229–41.

Kabir, Nahid Afrose, *Muslims in Australia: Immigration, Race Relations and Cultural History* (London: Routledge, 2005).

Kabir, Nahid, 'Representation of Islam and Muslims in the Australian Media, 2001–2005', *Journal of Muslim Minority Affairs* 26:3 (2006), pp. 313–28.

Kabir, Nahid Afrose, 'To Be or Not to Be an Australian: Focus on Australian Muslim Youth', *National Identities*, 10:4 (2008), pp. 399–419.

Kabir, Nahid, 'What Does It Mean to Be Un-Australian? Views of Australian Muslim Students in 2006', *People and Place* 15:1 (2007), pp. 51–68.

Kabir, Nahid Afrose, *Young British Muslims: Identity, Culture, Politics and the Media* (Edinburgh: Edinburgh University Press, 2010).

Karim, Jamillah A., 'To Be Black, Female, and Muslim: A Candid Conversation about Race in the American *Ummah*', *Journal of Muslim Minority Affairs* 26:2 (2006), pp. 225–33.

Kausar, Zeenath, 'Communal Riots in India: Hindu–Muslim Conflict and Resolution', *Journal of Muslim Minority Affairs* 26:3 (2006), pp. 353–70.

Kibria, Nazli, *Muslims in Motion: Islam and National Identity in the Bangladeshi Diaspora* (New Brunswick, NJ: Rutgers University Press, 2011).

Lake, Obiagele, *Blue Veins and Kinky Hair: Naming and Color Consciousness in African America* (Westport, CT: Praeger, 2003).

Lake, Obiagele, 'Towards a Pan-African Identity: Diaspora of African Repatriates in Ghana', *Anthropological Quarterly* 68:1 (1995), pp. 21–36.

MacClancy, Jeremy (ed.), *Sport, Identity and Ethnicity* (Oxford: Berg, 1996).

Marshall, Susan E. and Jen'nan Ghazal Read, 'Identity Politics among Arab American Women', *Social Science Quarterly* 84:4 (2003), pp. 875–91.

Moll, Yasmin, 'Screening Faith, Making Muslims: Islamic Media for Muslim American Children and Politics of Identity', in Yvonne Yazbeck Haddad, Farid Senzai and Jane I. Smith (eds), *Educating the Muslims of America* (Oxford: Oxford University Press, 2009), pp. 155–77.

Naber, Nadine, 'Ambiguous Insiders: An Investigation of Arab American Invisibility', *Ethnic and Racial Studies* 23:1 (2000), pp. 37–61.

Nagel, Caroline R. and Lynn A. Staeheli, 'Citizenship, Identity and Transnational Migration: Arab Immigrants to the United States', *Space and Polity* 8:1 (2004), pp. 2–23.

Ogden, David C. and Michael L. Hilt, 'Collective Identity and Basketball: An Explanation for the Decreasing Number of African-Americans on America's Baseball Diamonds', *Journal of Leisure Research* 35:2 (2003), pp. 213–27.

Parker, Andrew and John Harris, 'Introduction: Sport and Social Identities', in John Harris and Andrew Parker (eds), *Sport and Social Identities* (Basingstoke: Palgrave Macmillan, 2009), pp. 1–14.

The Polity Reader in Cultural Theory (Cambridge: Polity Press, 1994).

Polletta, Francesca and James M. Jasper, 'Collective Identity and Social Movements', *Annual Review of Sociology* 27 (2001), pp. 283–305.

Roskin, Michael, *Countries and Concepts: Politics, Geography, Culture*, 11th edn (Boston: Pearson Longman, 2011).

Rutherford, Jonathan, 'The Third Space: Interview with Homi Bhabha', in Jonathan Rutherford (ed.), *Identity: Community, Culture, Difference* (London: Lawrence and Wishart, 1990), pp. 207–21.

Said, Edward, *Covering Islam: How the Media and the Experts Determine How We See the Rest of the World*, rev. edn (New York: Vintage, 1997).

Salaita, Steven George, 'Ethnic Identity and Imperative Patriotism: Arab Americans before and after 9/11', *College Literature*, 32:2 (2005), pp. 146–68.

Sayyid, S. and AbdoolKarim Vakil (eds), *Thinking through Islamophobia: Global Perspectives* (London: Hurst, 2010).

Schirato, Tony, *Understanding Sports Culture* (Los Angeles: Sage, 2007).

Sen, Amartya, *Identity and Violence: The Illusion of Destiny* (London: Allen Lane, 2006).

Shryock, Andrew, 'The Moral Analogies of Race', in Amaney Jamal and Nadine Naber (eds), *Race and Arab Americans before and after 9/11: From Invisible Citizens to Visible Subjects* (Syracuse, NY: Syracuse University Press, 2008), pp. 81–113.

Sirin, Selcuk R. and Michelle Fine, 'Hyphenated Selves: Muslim American Youth Negotiating Identities on the Fault Lines of Global Conflict', *Applied Development Science* 11:3 (2007), pp. 151–63.

Sirin, Selcuk R. and Michelle Fine, *Muslim American Youth: Understanding Hyphenated Identities through Multiple Methods* (New York: New York University Press, 2008).

Smith, Anthony D., *National Identity* (London: Penguin, 1991).

Smith, Jane I., *Islam in America*, 2nd edn (New York: Columbia University Press, 2010).

Tajfel, Henri (ed.), *Human Groups and Social Categories: Studies in Social Psychology* (Cambridge: Cambridge University Press, 1981).

Tajfel, Henri and John C. Turner, 'The Social Identity Theory of Intergroup Behaviour', in Stephen Worchel and William G. Austin (eds), *Psychology of Intergroup Relations*, 2nd edn (Chicago: Nelson-Hall, 1986), pp. 7–24.

Takim, Liyakat Nathani, *Shi'ism in America* (New York: New York University Press, 2009).

Thomas, Anita Jones and Sara E. Schwarzbaum, *Culture and Identity: Life Stories for Counselors and Therapists* (Thousand Oaks, CA: Sage, 2006).

Turner, Richard Brent, 'Constructing Masculinity: Interactions between Islam and African-American Youth since C. Eric Lincoln, *The Black Muslims in America*', *Souls*, 8:4 (2006), pp. 31–44.

Weller, Susie, 'Young People's Social Capital: Complex Identities, Dynamic Networks', *Ethnic and Racial Studies* 33:5 (2009), pp. 872–88.

Yates, Joshua J., 'Making Sense of Cosmopolitanism: A Conversation with Kwame Anthony Appiah', *Hedgehog Review*, Fall 2009, pp. 42–50.

INDEX